SUPERFAST

SOPHIE DEVONSHIRE

SUPERFAST
LEAD AT
SPEED

Also available as an ebook

To everyone who made this book possible but most especially to my husband, Tom, and my daughters, Rosie and George, for their unstinting love and endless patience during the research and writing.

Contents

Introduction

I am an acceleration addict.

I have written this book because I have seen the thrill of making businesses grow fast. Having worked in and with different businesses for over 20 years, I have always been obsessed with the strategic breakthroughs that unlock pace – the creative approach which leads to hyper-scaling; the leadership courage which delivers fast growth. Good leaders are pace-setters.

Speed in business, however, is far from being automatic. Some people want it, some are scared of it; some organizations block it by their very structure or the nature of their leadership. Setting the right pace in business is a labyrinthine leadership challenge, mainly because it involves *humans* (fallible, emotional, complex beasts) – humans who buy or buy into your business offer; humans who work for you; and you, yourself, a wonderfully complex human. The pace of acceleration that people are focusing on is being driven by technology (and will continue to feature artificial intelligence as a key component) but the ability to steer through with *anthropoid* intelligence remains fundamental.

I lead a business where we work with 'impatient leaders', and I see the frustration of those who realize that shouting more loudly doesn't lead inexorably to progress. I also have seen the overwhelming nature of the need for leaders to navigate this 'changing and ambiguous' world, where previous experience is no longer protection against nervousness around decision-making.

Witnessing the pain of many clients and friends who want to move faster and yet not being able to, I was curious about what tools and techniques leaders have discovered as ways to speed up their success. I also wanted to understand how people at the helm of what I call here 'Superfast' organizations have managed their own personal uncertainties, and how they have coped with the pace and pressure placed on them.

This book is based on candid interviews with over 100 pace-setters from organizations around the globe, those leading diverse businesses from start-ups to multibillion-dollar businesses, in categories from the civil service to retail to consumer-goods companies to law companies to hyperscaling tech companies. Some of those leaders are well known or from companies that are internationally famous. Others have less of a well-known name but are highly regarded in their field. It was particularly interesting to seek out those who don't normally agree to interviews and those who haven't shared much of their story before. All interviewees had gone through a personal process to understand how best to manage the velocity of business change and how to steer the best course.

Speed and pace

Leaders today need to be able to ride the fast waves of change and to be able to navigate the white-water rapids of this volatile and high-velocity world. However, it is essential to understand speed in more than just a one-dimensional way. We need to look at the complex question of *pace*.

How do you, as a leader, set the right pace? This includes managing your own pace personally in addition to inspiring and supporting an appropriate pace within your team and company.

The balance of when you and the business need to go more slowly and when you must accelerate becomes key. Leaders are sometimes nervous of, or prone to, moving so fast that they can alienate their teams. But if they move too slowly, they can lose their relevance in a constantly shifting world and they can frustrate the ambitious in their teams and among their investors and customers. In today's highly competitive global environment caution is safer in the short term but can be highly dangerous in the long term.

Finding ways to keep our pace competitive to meet the demands of the short-term and protect against the challenges of the long-term is essential.

A perspective on pace

Companies are growing at phenomenal rates and they are disappearing fast as well.

In 1965 the average tenure of companies on the S&P 500 in the USA was 33 years. By 1990, it was 20 years. It is forecast to shrink to 14 years by 2026. In the UK, it's a similar story. Of the 100 companies in the FTSE 100 in 1984, only 24 were still breathing in 2012. Bigger companies can still fail.

Newer companies are taking power faster than ever. The high-flying start-ups known as 'unicorns' can win their billion-dollar valuations within a year or two of coming into being and can decimate industries that took many decades to build. With some other start-ups it's a tougher tale – 50 per cent of SMEs in the UK fail to celebrate their fifth birthday. Meanwhile, we all see the 'start-ups' who scale at a lickety-split pace (that's the technical term). Uber, at the time of writing, is a company with questions about its leadership and its ability for ongoing category dominance. But it showed what could be done. It drove true disruption and went from scratch to a $58-billion valuation within only five years. And, in the same timeframe, the Dollar Shave Club was created, built and sold for $1 billion to Unilever.

Facebook's continued growth is a staggering example of scale and speed. Now the world's sixth largest company, it catapulted to success from birth in a university dorm – from 1 million users in 2004 to 608 million six years later. Today there are more Facebook users than there were people alive on the entire planet 100 years ago.

In 2015 there was much celebration as Marriott Hotels opened its millionth hotel room, only 88 years after launching. The same year, Airbnb celebrated its millionth room – a paltry seven years after launch. The rapid growth of Airbnb highlights a salient fact about today's virtual economy: the masters of scale are often selling things they don't need to buy first. Uber, the world's largest taxi company, owns no vehicles. Facebook the world's most popular media owner, creates no content. Airbnb, the world's largest accommodation provider, owns no real estate.

In a world where the Internet of no-things creates businesses that grow at warp speed, investors and impatient leaders want to find ways to speed up their success. Legislation struggles to keep up (inventions take two to three years; patents often five to seven). Consumers, too, expect more. People's patience is shrinking. In 1999 websites would lose a third of their traffic if they took 8 seconds to load. By 2006 that had shrunk to 4 seconds. Now Google puts them on notice if it takes more than two.

'Always in motion is the future'

Will the acceleration of business continue? The small, wise and very powerful Jedi Master Yoda points out the obvious: 'Always in motion is the future.' The fast pace of technological change has driven customer expectations, the responsiveness of businesses and their ability to scale. Most forecasters believe that innovation and improvements in business will continue at a vertiginous tempo. The only certainty is that change will continue to be fast.

Many are nervous about this rate of change. The Pulitzer prize-winning journalist Thomas Friedman says that we have found our world divided politically into 'web' people and 'wall' people. Those who embrace the onset of constant change that the Internet has accelerated and those who want to put up a wall to stop it. This is being played out in politics; in business, there are similar backlashes against the speedy evolution of the business environment. Friedman, however, is positive about 'the age of accelerations', and so am I.

Responsive and responsible leadership

The increased velocity of our world has led to vulnerabilities both political and economic, but I am also encouraged by the equally rapid growth in business leaders who are interested in being not just responsive but also responsible – those looking to create purpose and a positive world.

In 2014 after a career which included working for big multinationals, advising clients on their brands, setting up, running and selling my own e-commerce business and working across the globe, I joined the Caffeine Partnership as CEO. Caffeine is a strategic leadership consultancy which specializes in accelerating growth. I joined because I believe in their mission – to stimulate business for the greatest good for the greatest number of people; because I believe in the transformative power of business for economic, social and personal good. It creates wealth, purpose and dignity. It's a privilege as part of that work and the research for this book to be able to explore how to help 'impatient leaders' deliver good growth at speed.

This book is not for the fearful or those who are meanderers in life. It's deliberately designed for those who enjoy the satisfaction of progress, of creating momentum, and who want to make the most of the time they have available. It's for those who want to do the right thing, and who want to do it at the right time.

This book is a celebration of how to ride the waves and enjoy doing it.

Learning from others is a smart short cut

If you are reading this, you will be someone who is ambitious to achieve, fast. Think of this book as a well of inspiration and stimulation from which you can draw to help you lead at speed. *Superfast*, however, is not a recipe book; you won't find an exact formula to follow to help you achieve velocity. The only real thing you'll find that all successful people have in common is that they are all successful.

But insights from those who have managed to learn – from their mistakes and their successes – can help provoke your thinking and guide how you test out approaches for yourself. As Eleanor Roosevelt said: 'Learn from the mistakes of others. You cannot live long enough to make them all yourself.' This was a woman who was not just the wife of an American president; she was a ground-breaking reformer in her own right. Her career included overseeing the drafting of the Universal Declaration of Human Rights and being the first chair of the UN Commission on Human Rights.

Like those I interviewed when researching this book, Roosevelt had an avid 'learning mindset', a belief in the power of curiosity and constant development. Her philosophy perfectly articulates one of the key tenets of this book:

> Anyone who'd rather go fast loves a short cut.

The speed smorgasbord – dip in

The interviewees for this book and the inspiration in it should be seen as a speed smorgasbord; choose the ideas that help thinking for you, your personality, your personal situation. Use them to stimulate your own map for navigating the pace of a Superfast world.

The research for this book and writing this book have been particularly satisfying for me, as there are plenty of insights in here which have already helped provide short cuts for clients I've worked with and for what I do myself.

Some things are just better when they can be done faster, notable exceptions being seduction and casseroles. So this book is designed to be read at a swift pace.

I have written this to keep the content light simple and stimulating, clear and pacey. So please don't expect an encyclopaedia or a full thesis here; this book has been deliberately designed to be easily digestible and dip-in-able. There is rigour in how it's put together but it's created to incite vigour not torpor, to encourage you to ask questions and to tickle your desire to think smarter and act faster. And, above all, to work out how to judge the right pace. Great leaders do not always rush; they go slowly when they can and fast when they must. Judging how to get that cadence right is a delicate balance.

Superfast shares ways to make it easy to make that call and how to pare down your approach to be genuinely more agile, nimble and responsive – in a responsible way. Throughout the chapters you'll find cases studies and examples that highlight the ideas I discuss (in the grey-tinted boxes) as well as brief nuggets that might almost serve as mantras for the Superfast leader (in the plain ruled boxes). At the end of each chapter, too, you'll find 'Espresso takeaways', which do exactly what 'it says on the tin': provide a useful, digestible summary of the chapter's main points for you to 'carry out'. Finally, at the end of the book you'll find the 'Pace-setter profiles' – potted biographies of the interviewees whose words of advice and wisdom pepper the content – as well as a list of my main sources (books, journal articles and so on) that also serves as 'further reading'.

I hope you enjoy reading this as much as I've enjoyed researching it. If you want more, there is more: at www.superfast-thebook.com/ you can find more from some of the interviews of the most interesting leaders I met as well as downloadable nuggets to use and explore.

But, for now, please dip into this wellspring of ideas and experiences and enjoy discovering how to lead at speed.

The hummingbird – Superfast icon

You'll have noticed on the cover of this book and else-where the hummingbird motif. Why? Well, for me the hummingbird - agile, aerodynamic and energy-smart - is the iconic creature of our time. It's the perfect symbol for the whole Superfast philosophy. One of the world's fastest creatures relative to its size, the hummingbird is beautiful to watch and exquisitely efficient in the way it is structured.

At first glance, you might think the hummingbird is struggling with the pace of its life, with its wings flapping furiously – so fast they make the hum that gives it its name. But the hummingbird is a creature perfectly designed for performance. The Trochilidae are great listeners with highly acute hearing and they also have sensational vision; they can see every colour that we humans can and, since their eyes can process ultraviolet light, probably many more.

No other bird on earth has such brain capacity. Their smart brain and memory allow them to plan out precise feeding routes with maximum efficiency. Not only do they remember every flower they've ever visited but they have a great sense of timing; they figure out how long to wait between visits so that flowers have time to regenerate nectar.

They live a high-energy lifestyle but are hyper-efficient with their energy conservation and use. Their ability to move is phenomenal – they perform the most impressive stunts of any bird. They can fly forwards, backwards and sideways, hover, and even fly upside-down. They do all of this often so fast we can't even see their wings, beating between 70 and 200 times per second.

Hummingbirds are fast. Superfast.

Their power, precision and ability to move quickly allow them to reach speeds of up to about 54 kilometres per hour (34 mph) while flying and 79 kilometres per hour (49 mph) while diving. Researchers at Stanford University, USA, compared 12 hummingbird species with one of the smallest drones in the world, the Black Hornet Nano, which is used by the military for reconnaissance. A helicopter should be much more efficient than either a bird or a man at hovering but most of the species performed similarly to the tiny drone.

Hummingbirds are also highly sensitive to visual stimuli; they respond to even tiny motions in any direction by quickly reorienting themselves mid-flight. They move fast when they need to; they pivot, they re-plan, they respond. They are also expertly attuned to fast-pattern velocities, which means that they can adopt perfect collision avoidance during forward flight.

Thanks to the precision of their decisions and their sensitivity to their surroundings, hummingbirds are able to hover in place while in complex, dynamic natural environments – they can control themselves perfectly to enable them to pause in the moment in the right place at the right time for them.

In a world where we need to move at speed, the hummingbird is a metaphor for how leaders need to maximize their ability to use their energy and senses effectively. This magnificent bird serves as a symbol for leaders' agility and ability to course-correct and respond to changes fast, their power to pause and hover, and their impeccable sense of timing.

The pace race

Why repeated pace-setting is an essential leadership practice

'Now, here, you see, it takes all the running you can do, to keep in the same place. If you want to get somewhere else, you must run at least twice as fast as that!'

The Red Queen, in Lewis Carroll,
Alice's Adventures in Wonderland

How do you as a leader build the momentum you need in your team and your organization, and how do you maintain it over time? To address the idea of how to lead at speed, we must start with the slippery, complex concept of 'pace'. Conscious pace-planning is an essential responsibility of a leader for one very simple reason: some things should be done fast while others need to have more time made for them. Understanding the difference between these things can give you a significant competitive advantage.

We are facing another decade of change and acceleration. Eric Ries, the writer behind the iconic bible of agile thinking, *The Lean Startup,* predicts that the world is going to continue to accelerate: 'We will look back and think this was a slow decade – it's going to get so much faster and weirder.' If we feel that we are moving in a world which is moving faster, where tech layers on tech, pressure builds on pressure, must we all rush? Is speed an addictive drug and an essential management practice always? Does it make a difference what type of organization you operate in? Is it really about moving faster, shouting louder, doing more? Or is it about understanding the need for us to sustain a varied pace?

In this chapter, we explore *what* you can do to vary the intensity of the pace and *why* you should consider that when you want to accelerate better, smarter, faster. We'll look at how that varies according to the type of organization, the type of challenge your business is facing, and the stage that you're at with planning solutions. We'll look at rational thinking and at the importance of understanding the emotional response your people face in varying their pace and comprehending a leader's desire for speed.

In his seminal book *Great by Choice*, Jim Collins conducted research on ten companies that dramatically outperformed their competitors by ten times or more. One of the findings was that the leaders of the organizations that succeeded were those who 'knew when to slow down and when to move fast'. Collins's advice based on his findings was simple: 'Move fast when you must, slow when you can.' Pace does need to be varied. Smart people know that an unrelenting, unstopping Superfast pace is unsustainable and … unsmart.

So, how do we think about leading in a way which is smarter?

- By planning how we will manage the pace
- By pausing to plan
- By understanding the context of the world's velocity
- By appreciating the pace of the people we work with
- By knowing when to act at speed and when we need to slow down to go faster.

> To go fast, to win the race … you must regularly pause and plan your pace.

Why 'pace perspective' helps

A responsive and responsible leader plans an organization which operates at varied velocities:

1 It believes in cosmic velocity – aiming high.
2 It runs pace-setting on two parallel time frames – now and next – to deliver today and build tomorrow.

Aiming for cosmic velocity

There's a very good reason why rocket ships and the space race are frequently used as an attractive, exciting metaphor for fast-growing, bold, ambitious businesses. Rockets move fast. Very, very, very Superfast. In fact, they have to move at something called cosmic velocity. For a rocket to get into orbit around the Earth, it needs to reach a velocity of about 8 kilometres (5 miles) per second; to leave Earth's orbit, a velocity of 11 kilometres (7 miles) per second. These are the first and second cosmic velocities.

Sheryl Sandberg eloquently outlined the potential of 'leaning in' by sharing a great piece of advice that Google co-founder Eric Schmidt gave her: 'If someone offers you a seat on a rocket ship, you don't ask which seat.' She chose to join Google and then the next rocket ship in her life – Facebook. After only a decade of moving beyond campus-only users, Facebook is the world's largest social network, connecting over 2 billion people worldwide at the time of writing and with five new profiles being created every second.

Moonshots

Google famously use the 'Moonshots' name for their most exploratory and ground-breaking projects. Matt Brittin, EMEA President of Google, describes the philosophy behind it thus:

Look at it this way. If you try and make something 10 per cent better, you're likely to take an incremental approach – start from what you've got, and refine it.

If you try and make something ten times better, though, you've got to start from scratch – first principles – find a new way. To compete in the age of the Internet, that's what you need to do, because the rate of change in the digital world is faster than it's ever been. *Good ideas can come from everywhere and everyone.* So, to innovate first, and only then to think about how you can monetize your invention, is the right sequence of things.

So we make sure that we innovate all across the world – here in the UK, over half of our 2,000 or so staff are engineers. We also set up X, an experimental facility near our HQ in California, dedicated entirely to 'moonshots': ambitious, speculative research projects from which we may never make a profit – but which all have the ambition of making a huge leap forward.

A strong pace-setter believes in what can be achieved and shares the belief that we can shoot for the moon, that we can achieve cosmic velocity.

There is a danger in unceasing speed, though, known in aeronautics as Max Q. This is the point you reach when the increasing speed and decreasing air density are at their maximum, which means all aircraft (whether rockets, missiles or aircraft) can last for only a limited time without damage. In aeronautical engineering, much work has been done to identify an exact point at which this will happen; in business, it is, of course, harder to identify. So, a word of caution on getting the fast pace you want and need: as a smart sense-check, set up the right people in your organization to monitor individuals' moments of Max Q – not the point of no return but the point at which you hit diminishing returns. This is the time to pause, refresh and repair.

> To be a responsive but also a responsible leader, watch out for Max Q.

The two-pace race: now and next

The vast majority of leaders are working to build the profits of the short term alongside the foundations of the future. It's about thriving today and about surviving tomorrow – and keeping up the momentum on both. Here is how GE's long-term CEO Jack Welch – who presided over a 4,000 per cent rise in value for the company – describes it:

> You've got to eat while you dream. You've got to deliver on short-range commitments, while you develop a long-range strategy and vision and implement it. The success of doing both. Walking and chewing gum if you will. Getting it done in the short-range, and delivering a long-range plan, and executing on that.

It's one of the biggest challenges today's leaders face. The hot breath of the shareholder, the obsessive focus on delivering against targets, means that today takes precedence and your organization is left exposed in the long term. If you're building a legacy, you must set up processes for long-term focus.

Simon Devonshire was appointed the UK government's Entrepreneur in Residence in 2014, and he speaks and consults on business. He supports the notion that 'time, chronology, place, and speed are fundamental to business success' and talks to people about the concept of 'TQ':

> TQ is time intelligence. It's all about an innate, intrinsic subconscious, almost fanatical addiction to the monitoring of time and its commercial practice and commercial performance results over time.

It's clear that there should be multiple levels of pace-setting going on within organizations, but not all leaders pause to take time to assess this. We have to deal with two different timeframes which sometimes require a variety of pace – and invariably these are frequently managed by the same people. Sometimes the pace is too intense for the short term and not intense enough for the long term.

We are all aware of how this happens to all of us personally (the daily battle of the urgent versus the important), but it's not just about us. As leaders, we need to make sure that the business keeps up the pace as we work to ensure that this year's targets are met, at the same time as making sure that when we come to hand over our leadership baton we deliver a strong business which will continue to develop and prosper.

Pace-setting is about working out the variety that's needed in your velocity in order to achieve sustainable success.

How to approach being a go-getter pace-setter

A successful accelerator assesses and understands other people's pace. Smart pace-setting is about planning when to go fast and preparing so that you can.

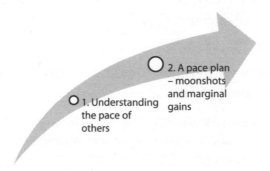

FIGURE 1.1 The pace-setter's strategy

Here's another example of someone who looks at the world through the lens of a broader universe, the US astrophysicist and cosmologist Neil deGrasse Tyson:

> Humans aren't as good as we should be in our capacity to empathize with feelings and thoughts of others, be they humans or other animals on Earth. So maybe part of our formal education should be training in empathy. Imagine how different the world would be if, in fact, that were 'reading, writing, arithmetic, empathy'.

This brings us to an important point about the ability to be a strong pace-setter – the priceless skill that is empathy, the rare value that is the ability to observe and understand the pace of those around you (people in other companies and people in yours).

A successful accelerator assesses and understands other people's pace

Think about comparative pace. Other people (other companies) may be moving faster than you – and other people (internally) are likely to be thinking, moving and acting more slowly than you. Being aware of other people's pace therefore covers two different areas:

1 Contextual intelligence and an awareness of the broader competitive environment outside the organization
2 Emotional intelligence and a smart understanding that any organization can't survive with just one type of person.

A sensitivity to people's pace also must include your consumer radar

Some of the smartest people we've met in organizations fall down on this point. They know their market inside out and their position relative to that of other brands in the same category, but they do not remember that consumers judge brands and business against one another, regardless of what the category is. I wish everything I could buy gave me the convenience of Amazon Prime. I love the customer service of Octopus Energy and therefore find the inhuman corporate-speak of buying from Habitat disturbing. I do not compare within one category; I compare across my full world of consumer experience.

Tim Leberecht, TED speaker and award-winning author of *The Business Romantic*, works with leaders to help them become more customer-centric. He reminds them of this by referring to the company's 'category competitors' and 'experiential competitors', those whose customer experience is a point of reference whatever service you provide. Customers compare their experience of a banking service to their experience of buying books, say, or of drinking coffee in a café. Online and offline experiences are not separate and categories are irrelevant. Pace expectations are set by customers with very broad experiences in our fast-moving world.

Our clients or our consumers or our customers – they all now know what an incredible pace can be achieved by some companies. That has ratcheted up expectations. We must march to a tempo that has been set by companies very different from our own.

Acquisition is a speed tool – because younger companies will get there before you

How could EE move so fast and create a revolutionary network that was then sold for £12.5 billion – and create it in less than a year? Partly, as the founder Olaf Swantee recognizes, 'because they were led by an extremely powerful purpose: to turn the UK from a laggard to a leader in terms of its digital infrastructure'. And partly, by creating a new company and brand from scratch, they were able to act more like a start-up. So, although the 4G network was built on two mobile networks coming together (Orange and T-Mobile), it was a fresh new company that could move at the speed it needed to bring the technology to people fast.

Hyper-focused start-ups can make things happen at almost 'cosmic velocity'; unencumbered by history and distractions, they can get to the future fast because they have no past. There are fewer people with minds to be changed; there is no risk to brand equity with consumers; there are probably fewer share-holders/investors to convince and ultimately much less risk in moving fast. All of this makes it harder for existing bigger companies to compete with the start-ups in that context.

That's why big companies buy start-ups. It's harder for major innovation to come from within big organizations – their infra-structure costs around development are large and their pace is slower. So now the trend is that they don't bother. They let the world burn through start-ups (some fail, some survive) and then they buy the successes. Imagine the comparative invest-ment for the big companies – they'd have to fund and back several different innovation experiments, many of which would ultimately fail. There's a natural selection that goes into the marketplace which means that the big companies don't take that risk. Yes, they then pay significant amounts for the start-ups but in general the risk is smaller than if they'd tried to develop the innovation in-house. And, of course, it's faster.

GE is a great example of this. It has made a significant number of tech start-up acquisitions, and this fits in with its plan to move away from being a group with a disparate number of financial and manufacturing businesses to being a more streamlined company focused on digital solutions.

As companies recognize the cost of in-house development, acquisition is a good way to get what you want fast.

Sometimes bigger is better

The person moving at a faster pace than you may not be the newest, nimblest start-up. It may be a big supertanker of a corporate but one with the resources to invest more and risk more. They may have the audacity and the legal firepower to steal the ideas you worked on, to use your hard-won tools as 'inspiration' for theirs.

An awareness of the competitive and comparative pace of those around you can give a sense of urgency internally as well. If you stumble, if you go too slowly, there will be those who will help your impatient customers get what they need.

Knowledge of competitors' pace can be a tactical tool. Simon Devonshire headed the business division of O2 for five years, doubling the number of customers it had in that time before he became the UK government's Entrepreneur in Residence. One of the most effective tactics he used was a knowledge of competitor timing. Watching a key competitor, he and his team noticed that there was a regular timing of announcements and initiatives. They therefore made sure that they timed theirs to hit before or at the same time. It was simple and highly effective.

Pace perspective is not about being mindlessly reactive to the competition

Nothing in this book should encourage you to think that smart leadership is just about mindless competitive response. This is not about copying others and responding to every idea out there. The co-founders of Innocent share openly the relative failure of their initial orange juice launch: they 'rushed' to beat the competition rather than focusing on consumer need; only when they had taken time to get it right did they achieve success. Our Caffeine advice to the impatient leaders we work with is to 'be in a hurry not in a rush'.

Some leaders deliberately accept that speed will be slightly compromised by principles. Unilever CEO Paul Polman's belief in the purpose of the organization 'sometimes means we grow more slowly than we might otherwise', and Giles Andrews of Zopa says 'without question we could've grown faster but doing it responsibly was so important to us'. It's an attitude that attracts great talent to their principled organizations, which in turn helps them grow at the right pace over a more sustained period.

Fast doesn't always mean being first

Understanding comparative pace is *not* about obsessing with being first to market. History shows us that businesses do not need to be pioneers to be the pace-setters for the category. A case in point is the story of the early social networks. We think of Facebook as a pioneer but in fact Facebook was not the first; Friendster got there way before them. The story of Friendster is a salutary tale of the Superfast rise and Superfast fall of a great idea, well funded yet ineffectively implemented and with a disunited leadership team. Friendster was Silicon Valley's first social network, initially growing fast with 2 million users in the first seven months and backed over time by significant investment. Launched in 2003, it turned down a $30 million buyout offer from Google the following year. It was a disastrous decision – Friendster was dead in the United States just three years later.

First to market is not a 'win': it's just the start. Jim Collins in *From Good to Great* shares more compelling examples:

Gillette didn't pioneer the safety razor, Star did. Polaroid didn't pioneer the instant camera, Dubroni did. Microsoft didn't pioneer the personal computer spreadsheet, VisiCorp did. Amazon didn't pioneer online bookselling.

Be aware of the 'second mover advantage' in many categories; let the competition do the work and spend the money in establishing a category or changing people's behaviour.

INNOCENT — PAUSING TO PLAN

Adam Balon, the co-founder of Innocent, admits that 'when we rushed we got things wrong'. Conversely, they paused to plan before the original launch of Innocent. The three founders famously asked their customers for a vote of confidence on their first iteration of the smoothies:

> At a music festival, we put up a big sign asking people if they thought we should give up our jobs to make smoothies, and put a bin saying 'Yes' and a bin saying 'No' in front of the stall. Then we got people to vote with their empties. At the end of the weekend, the 'Yes' bin was full, so we resigned from our jobs the next day and got cracking.

The detail of the story is interesting, as it's an example of pausing to plan. Balon recalls:

> We resigned in August and initially we were like 'We've made smoothies, we can get them on the market for the very end of summer, for September', but one of the best decisions we made was not to rush at that point. We unpicked everything: we completely made it in a different way, raised money which we had not raised. Those nine months were the best nine months we have ever invested because, by the time we launched it in April the following year, we had a completely different product – made in a different way, funded in a different way, with a different brand – everything was completely different, and it turned out to be the right way of doing it rather than the wrong way of doing it. It is not always about being the first, because, actually, being a fast follower and doing it three times better is a much better position to be in.

Equally, it's unlikely to be your idea which is truly, world-shatteringly original; it is very often your *persistence* that will be more unique. Or the thought you've put into the brand (Innocent was not the first smoothie to the market but it was a bold, distinctive brand with personality). Or the obsessive attention to detail.

APPLE – PRESSING PAUSE

Steve Jobs, one of business's all-time fast thinkers and fast actors, knew when to press pause.

It was spring 2001 and Apple was prepping to open its first retail store. Ron Johnson, Apple's retail chief, and Jobs were on their way to a weekly planning meeting when Johnson spoke up about something that had been bothering him. Apple had been setting up its store like any other – organized around the different *products* that it would be selling. 'But if Apple's going to organize around activities like music and movies, well, the store should be organized around music and movies and things you do,' he told Jobs. 'Do you know how big a change that is?' he recalls Jobs saying. 'I don't have time to redesign the store.'

It seemed like that was that, but ten minutes later when the pair walked into the meeting, Jobs immediately spoke up. 'Well, Ron thinks our store is all wrong,' Jobs said. 'And he's right, so I'm going to leave now. And, Ron, you work with the team and design the store.' Even though it would take longer to open the store because of the redesign, Jobs knew that it was worth taking the extra time to get it right. 'It's not about speed to market,' Johnson says. 'It's really about doing your level best.'

So don't panic about being a pioneer. You don't have to be the first one to get there … though you do have to move at pace. Jonathan Abrams, founder of Friendster, also shares openly the ideas he'd had about setting up a college network and setting up a news feed on Friendster – ideas Facebook got out to the consumer before him. That must have hurt.

You must be aware of the way the world is moving to help keep your business moving at the right pace

Complacency is dangerous. In Jim Collins's research, he clearly identified the 'constructive paranoia' of the leaders involved as a characteristic that strongly correlated with success. This paranoia led to them working on preparing for the worst. Interestingly, his study shows clearly that it wasn't those who innovated more who succeeded but rather those who were able to *take innovations and scale them quickly*. So, again, it's not about being first; it's about what you then do with the innovation, how you get it to reach people, and how you optimize the experience to make it really work.

It's not just about the market but being aware of the natural pace of those around you

To be successful in leading at speed, it's not just about understanding the relative pace of the market but also about understanding the pace at which those around you work. As well as being aware of the pace of the market and the pace your customer is experiencing elsewhere (cross-categories, cross-platform, cross-continents), as a leader you must pause and take stock of the need to work with people who are fundamentally different from you.

There's not a right and a wrong, but there will be people who are Superfast by nature and those who are more analytical, more contemplative and who want to understand things more thoroughly than you or spend more time reviewing and getting comfortable with concepts and ideas before they adopt them personally themselves. (There is more on this in Chapter 6: Human understanding.)

A majority of the interviewees for this book have shared openly that this was an important discovery for them on their leadership journey. They are quick people – they are agitators, accelerators and drivers. They are also smart enough to realize that not everyone is like that. This is not a competitive judgement of other people but a sage appreciation of the differences in people.

A new CEO joined a celebrated company I know recently, one with huge ambition and huge budgets but which had been stalled by an over-controlling ex-chief. The new leader came in keen to turn the business around, and he is a firecracker when it comes to ideas. As a result, his executive team is experiencing the 'popcorn effect' – a plethora of emails and ideas being fired out. They're hot and they are delivered fast and often. It's exciting and refreshing for them and they respect it … but it's sometimes hard for them to process the speed of their leader, and as a consequence they come across as less enthusiastic than they really are.

One of the most important times to get this understanding of people right is at the start of a role. To be a 'Hundred-Day Hero' and get it right within the first three months, you probably do need to go more slowly than you'd normally want to. It's not just about overwhelm but also about not underestimating the power of belief. Some people believe quickly; others need more time to absorb; still others need to trust first, listen second. Some will struggle to believe that you are able to make smart decisions so early on in your time in a role or a company, so it's important to weigh up carefully the risks of too much action too soon.

So an emotionally intelligent approach to winning friends and influencing people is a fantastically effective way of moving things faster, but it does require your delivery be slower at times than seems natural and for you to invest time in building the understanding and belief.

> As a pace-setter, you need to understand the personal pace of others first.

However, it's not just about the people; it's also about your planning.

Planning when to go fast – and preparing so you can

Like comedy, business leadership is all about timing. The ancient Greeks had two words for time:

- *Chronos* (time as we understand it, calendar time)
- *Kairos* (that moment when everything comes together).

In business, timing is critical – when a few things come together at the right time success is yours.

Often, of course, it is serendipity – happy chance and circumstance, fortune and coincidence, right places, right time. Timing success also comes from leaders who understand the broader world, the macro-trends and the people involved, and who are able to judge the right moment to move. It's about being ready and spotting when you are ready.

Being right isn't enough; you have to be right at the right time. The early twentieth-century newspaper editor William Peter Hamilton pointed out that 'Wall Street's graveyards are filled with men who were right too soon.' Anna Wintour, Editor-in-Chief of American *Vogue* and doyenne of the world of fashion, also points to the importance of *kairos*: 'It's always about timing. If it's too soon, no one understands. If it's too late, everyone's forgotten.'

The analysis of the companies that outperformed their rivals by more than ten times, covered in Jim Collins's *Good to Great* books and studies, also looked at timing. It wasn't just about speed but about getting the timing right. Collins explained that the leaders of the '10x companies' were able to

recognize changes and threats early ... but then take the time available – whether that be short or long – to make rigorous decisions and take disciplined action. The key question is not 'should we go fast or slow? but 'How much time do we have before the risk profile changes?'

They go slow when they can, fast when they must. If they have time, they're comfortable letting events unfold, while preparing to act decisively when the time comes.' Be aware of macro timing issues, and when something unexpected or unwanted happens you should be conscious of the question 'How much time do we have?'

On top of this there is the need for tenacious, conscious, considered patience as well. Understand that transformations take time (changing people's minds particularly is a slower process than people want). Have the patience to persist and grasp that, to get real change, you need to repeat, repeat, repeat – what you are communicating, what you are testing, what you are doing.

Timing is particularly challenging for business leaders in today's rapidly accelerating world. Many focus internally and on the numbers rather than taking the broader view. You need to plan for the short term and for the long term, the now and the next. Both of these involve planning your pace.

The lessons from sport

Many of the people I meet who are ambitious leaders have also competed, or continue to participate, in highly competitive sports. EMEA Google President Matt Brittin's 'relaxation' is rowing. He competed at a high level when younger and still does it as part of his life. Rowing is a sport which requires great commitment and drive. Louisa Clarke – a partner at Caffeine and an expert coach in influential selling and presentation – rowed for Great Britain, showing yet again that the desire to win in sports and business runs together frequently (she's an amazing pub quiz queen, too). Cresta Norris, who owns Premium Publishing, a B2B audio and written content company, says she is always biased in favour of those who row as she sees it as a sport where you have to show an incredible amount of stoicism, personal discipline and an unrelenting commitment to the team. (As Louisa says, 'It is often early, often cold, but if you don't turn up the team can't do it without you.')

There is much to be learned from sport, and, of course, the most useful executive coaching approaches were born from an appreciation of the impact coaches have on the physical and mental strength training needed by athletes. Jenny Ashmore, President of the Chartered Institute of Marketing in the UK, has used her extensive sporting experience to help manage her business planning. She and I talked at length about the pattern of training in sport and its parallels in business:

> A great sports coach looks at your training plan over a period of time. They work out with you where your A games and your B games fit within that. Some matches or competitions or games are more critical than others, and your effort, training and planning should reflect that. It is an energy and a focus prioritization tool that allows you to build sustained stamina. Applying that to business allows you to pace what is needed.

In other words, you pace the preparation and the planning over a period of time.

In a later chapter in this book (Chapter 5: Editing is expediting), we talk about the responsibility of the leader being to 'take things away from the team'. Working out together where the team needs to put in maximum effort and focus and where they can operate at a 'B game' level shows a recognition of the need for people and organizations to pace themselves. The need to say 'no' to certain pitches or accept that some may be a 'give it a go' rather than a 'must-win' is a leadership imperative.

This takes us back to Simon Devonshire's 'TQ' approach: 'For me, pace is not as simple as how fast do I run – it's about how, intelligently I can plan things out.'

The back-up: two is one and one is none

Success is not only planning the variety of pace but placing an obsessive, disciplined focus on the preparation. The Navy Seals (the US Special Ops on Sea, Air and Land) have an expression 'Two is one and one is none'. What this adage quite simply means: always have a back-up. If you have two of something, you may well lose one, but having one is a game-changer if someone else has none.

Studying Robert Scott's versus Roald Amundsen's relative trips to the South Pole reveals a powerful metaphor for the successful leader. Both were experienced and ambitious, but one (Amundsen) led his team to glory, the other (Scott) to tragedy. Amundsen had prepared personally with great physical discipline but had also put together a plan to travel with enough supplies to cover his team if they could not make it to the supply bases. The plan also included killing weaker animals to feed other animals and the men having 'agreed to shrink from nothing in order to achieve our goal', including eating their dogs.

There has rarely been a more dramatic or moving story to illustrate that to go fast on your journey (and to win and to survive), you need to put time into the practice and the preparation and develop a 'paranoia' about what will happen if things go wrong.

The A games and the B games idea shows that pace-setting is often about taking things away from your teams, to streamline and focus their energy and their mental to-do lists. It's also about giving them the focus and the time to practise, prepare and work out what to be paranoid about. However, to be a pace-setter you need to show progress. Your role is to share and give a sense of moving forwards, to provide the stories of success and evidence that things are progressing. Fear of failure and paranoia about the things that can go wrong are drivers and motivators but so is the sense of progress happening.

The power of incrementalism

Sometimes, the right pace can be measured at '1 per cent'. Highlighting progress is a visible, tangible reassurance that things can be done. But it's also a tried-and-tested way of maintaining momentum and pace.

Take the concept of marginal gains as an example – a concept made famous by Sir Dave Brailsford, the Head of British Cycling (and a man with an MBA). When he took over the British team in 2002 he inherited 76 years of cycling history, during which time only one Olympic gold medal had been won. In 2008 at the Beijing Olympics his team won seven out of the ten gold medals available and achieved a similar result four years later at the London Olympics. He also led Britain's first ever professional cycling team to win three out of four Tour de France events. It was smart, sustained success, over time. He talks in depth about the power of marginal gains, of breaking down absolutely everything that goes into competing on a bike, and improving it incrementally, all adding up to powerful performance gains.

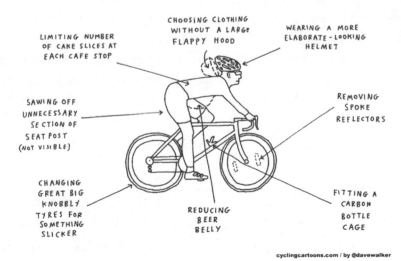

FIGURE 1.2 Marginal gains: how the professionals make small changes to improve their performance

Record breaking in other areas often comes from a similar approach; breakthroughs aren't achieved in big overnight leaps but in sustained, incremental efforts. In 1954 there had been a nine-year period where the record for running a mile stood at a tantalizing 4.01 minutes. Roger Bannister worked to beat this by making incremental improvements over several years and this included looking at every single detail, from lighter shoes to innovative approaches such as interval training. It's also worth noting that within nine weeks Bannister's new record had been broken. Nine years to hit it and then only nine weeks to break it again. Pace sets pace.

Clive Woodward, who led the English rugby team to their first World Cup success, also had a similarly persistent approach to progression at an incremental pace: 'Greatness is achieved through the discipline of attending to detail. We had a simple catchphrase that we used that said, "If we can do 100 things 1 per cent better then we can become world champions."' This '1 per cent' or '100 things' approach has many benefits, not least the way in which it feels achievable to people. It is bite-sized progress.

Many business leaders have adopted this approach. Oliver Tress, founder of retailer Oliver Bonas, with his business partner Tim Hollidge, used the rugby saying to focus his team to weather the financial crisis and tough times of 2008–9 to get the business to grow:

> Everyone got behind the saying and thought about what they could do if they wasted less paper, or renegotiated a contract and so on. Everyone felt that they could do something. It was tough, but we weathered the storm and managed to grow our way out of it.

A marginal gains approach feels logical and feels achievable. Incidentally, Oliver Bonas was the first high-street retailer in the UK to pay its staff a living wage (in a year when 5,839 shops in the UK closed and in a challenging retail environment), and the founder's personal motto is an inspiration to many, myself included. It's simply 'Work hard, play hard, be kind.' One per cent at a time, tweak, test and explore, and you will get where you need to faster than you think.

Google runs 12,000 data-driven experiments annually in order to discover vulnerabilities and opportunities to improve. One such experiment found that by tweaking the shade of the Google toolbar from a darker to a lighter blue, it increased the number of click-throughs. This marginal change increased revenue dramatically.

The power of incrementalism: compound or exponential impact

We do live in a world where everyone is looking for moon-shots, and we could continue to find ways to explore what we can do that are audacious and exciting. But there is a place, even for Superfast companies (*especially* for Superfast companies), to systematically drive an incrementalist approach.

It's no surprise that those who have a strong grasp of maths and financials will be keen to explore this approach. Invest-ment of time and effort in the financial world has a benefit, thanks to the fun and glory of 'compound interest'. Legend has it that Albert Einstein, when asked what the world's greatest invention was, replied 'compound interest'. This is highly likely to be apocryphal, which is a shame as it made me chuckle. However, many a money manager has enjoyed the benefits of this – investments in the financial world don't lead to lin-ear results thanks to this concept (you earn interest on your interest). They don't in the business world either. Choose right where you invest your time and the pace you'll achieve won't be marginal and incremental for ever; it will either build in a compound manner and/or it will lead to exponential gains.

Greg Jackson, serial investor, entrepreneur and now CEO of Octopus Energy (which went from £0 to £20 million per month within two years), drew me the following graph to help illustrate the discovery a number of tech start-ups have made:

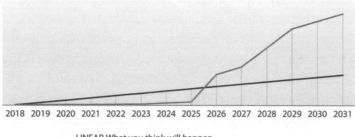

2018 2019 2020 2021 2022 2023 2024 2025 2026 2027 2028 2029 2030 2031

—— LINEAR What you think will happen

—— EXPONENTIAL What is more likely to happen (done right)

FIGURE 1.3 Growth can, and should be, exponential in start-ups.

He explains:

> People always plan a linear growth line like this. In start-up and scale-ups it is more likely to be lower than you think and then higher than you think. You connect with the right people, you lay the foundations and suddenly – boom, it explodes.

> Think about the potential of the exponential. Build incremental gains to lead to exponential results. Aim for cosmic velocity while being fully conscious of knowing the preparation and patience that's needed.

Elephants and getting there faster

For many businesses, the big, innovative, sparkly new ideas are not what delivers growth; it is that continued, manageable pace, moving onwards and upwards. It is, of course, less exciting for business leaders; it's not the big win of a lottery ticket, a major acquisition or the new product of the decade.

Incrementalism and marginal gains do feel as though they require some patience; the Superfast leader must patiently ensure that they are being implemented in order to lead successfully. Giving ownership of that 1 per cent to the team will also allow you to focus on other areas (partnerships, overall strategy), while knowing that the organization is empowered to improve everything it can.

It is also a way to learn, if done well. Matthew Syed in *Black Box Thinking* highlights the value of creating A/B testing equivalents to really understand the power of marginal gains. It shouldn't be seen as a question of 'Let's go slowly', though, but more a 'test and learn' approach.

In a previous team I worked with we talked often about the big challenges we had and discussed 'elephanting' them, by which we meant how to break down a big challenge into manageable chunks: 'How do you eat an elephant? One bite at a time.' It's a disciplined approach which works for some, but sometimes it seems too logical and linear. I would argue that there may be ways to speed up the elephant eating. (Can you get other people to help? Can you practise obsessively to eat faster?)

A great example of this is José Neves, founder of one of the UK's only 'unicorns', the luxury boutique aggregator Farfetch. Now over ten years old, it is one of the fastest-growing and most revolutionary companies around. Its success partly comes from José's decision at the start to move fast and learn fast. Rather than take one test market and test and learn, he knew that he wanted a global experience for his customers from day one. So, if he'd been 'eating the elephant' in this instance he would have cooked all the different parts at the same time ready to eat.

> If we'd just started with the UK first we would not have learned enough – it's not our largest market – we would have failed. We started from day one with boutiques in five countries – with a small team and no money. I really wanted to give the consumer this experience of travelling the world of fashion, of discovering new boutiques in new places.

Marginal gains and the power of incrementalism are inextricably linked to discipline and progress. They are about a smart, sustained and continued pace. Even they can benefit from creative thinking, measurement and identification, so you can conclude which are providing the most breakthrough and which can kick-start a more exponential growth opportunity.

How can you tell what's working? When do you work out which should be given an injection of pace? It's about measurement of course, but it's also about building in the time to observe, reflect and decide on the next A games to focus on.

As a leader, you should be thinking about what type of progress you need; this is part of the pace-setting process. Sometimes that progress will be leaps, bounds and moon-landing tales. However, that might not be what you want to aim for.

A final point on the question of pace. To achieve a successful pace in any race, stamina and determination will help you most. Dyson, one of the most celebrated inventors of our times, points out that every invention he's ever looked at has not been the first one. Patents were taken before him. What he did that worked was to show incredible persistence in testing, testing, testing till the products really worked ('I made 5,127 prototypes of my vacuum before I got it right. There were 5,126 failures.') and selling, selling, sharing until others believed and bought. Creating a culture that wins takes persistence.

This is how it is with nurturing a healthy pace in your organization. You have to plan and plant ideas, and you have to constantly review and persist. Look out for the gaps where you can incrementally improve and look out for the vision that you can aim for. You need the best team around you to help manage the pace smartly. And sometimes it's how they all work together that provides the speed, not just how fast they all run. It's also about finding the energy to keep the pace up. Energy is the topic of our next chapter.

> Plan your pace to win the race.

Espresso takeaways

The ten pace-race commandments: why repeated pace-setting is an essential leadership practice

A responsive and responsible leadership plans an organization which operates at varied velocities. Some things should be done fast. Some need to have more time made for them. To go fast, to win the race … you must regularly pause and plan your pace.

1 Believe in cosmic velocity. A strong pace-setter believes in what can be achieved and shares the belief that we can shoot for the moon, that we can achieve cosmic velocity.
2 To be a responsive but also a responsible leader, watch out for Max Q-. Push the pace as fast as you can without irreparable damage to your team. It is rocket science.
3 Build a business and build a legacy; eat while you dream. Pace-setting should be run on two parallel time frames to deliver today and build tomorrow.
4 Be sensitive to others' pace. A leader should recognize comparative pace (your competition and you – your past could slow down your pace; bigger and older organizations are more likely to be slower) and be aware of other people's pace (your teams, your customers). Empathy and a sensitivity to the right tempo will win friends and customers.

5 Look ahead, not around. Pace perspective is not about being mindlessly reactive to the competition and being first is not always what will make you fast in the long run. Businesses do not need to be pioneers to be the pace-setters for the category.

6 Be aware of the way the world is moving to help keep your business moving at the right pace; watch out for the next company that could come and eat your lunch. Be 'constructively paranoid', and that includes moving fast.

7 Plan your pace. Work out the A games and the B games, when you need to be full on and when you can de-prioritize. Plan, plan, plan and prepare. The preparation makes sure that you can keep up the pace.

8 If you're aiming for a big goal, break it down. Eat the elephant one bite at a time. Obsess over the exponential potential from incremental marginal gains. Pace it. Make it feel manageable.

9 Be prepared for persistence. The most successful leaders make things happen … and they keep going.

10 The secret of timing; watch out for *kairos* (the opportune moment) rather than just obsessing about *chronos* (clock time). Judge when it's right and be ready for it …

2

Time is finite – energy isn't

The secret to delivering with stamina and speed

'I firmly believe that time management is not important; energy management is.'

Paul Polman, Global CEO, Unilever

Inertia. Stasis. Without energy, nothing moves – nothing changes. To make things happen, to revolutionize or reinvent a business, you need energy. To navigate a fast-moving world or to move at pace, you need to be smart about your energy – like the hummingbird which has evolved highly effective 'just in time' ways of refuelling and smart ways of conserving energy. You need significant reservoirs of personal energy to persuade people and persevere with plans. You need energy to keep your eye on the fast-moving ball, to cope with the speed of change and to cope with the patience needed in creating change.

When you are full of energy you get things done faster, make decisions at the right pace, and think more clearly. That clarity can then help you work out how to do less and achieve more. You can react faster and more precisely. In the words of the nineteenth-century dynamic pioneer, undercover journalist, businesswoman, inventor and explorer Nellie Bly: 'Energy rightly applied and directed will accomplish anything.'

Energy and business

Effective energy management is not something that comes automatically in today's busy world of business. The majority of senior roles are beset with frequent tiring travel. Stress and pressure are standard. Sedentary meetings in airless rooms. Long hours. These are all reasons why energy maintenance and support need thought, focus and sustained attention.

To really drive breakthrough business results, it's arguably as important for senior leaders to work out how to manage their energy as it is to manage their people. All the most successful interviewees for this book consistently, obsessively thought about ways to maximize their personal energy. This is not just about the clichéd ideal of 'productivity' (more, harder, squeeze every drop). It's about self-knowledge and having a more skilled understanding of personal strengths and the ability to understand how to deliver purpose-led pace. Sometimes that comes with age – but age, of course, brings its own energy challenges. The earlier you realize the respect your body needs in order to feed its desire to achieve, the better.

> Creativity, change, boldness – anything that's needed to lead requires energy.

Baroness Gail Rebuck looks back on 22 years leading Random House (now Penguin Random House) through several business revolutions (from independent bookstores to the rise of Waterstones, from the high street to Amazon, through the digital challenges facing publishing) and reflects on what she did to help the organization cope with the challenges of change: 'I sometimes think my main job as leader was to spot the teams or departments who were lacking energy and to help give them that energy.' While I was interviewing her, she pointed to the ten light bulbs in the ceiling above her and explained:

> Think about it as me being the one to sort the light bulbs in an organization. This room would still be lit if one or two of them were not working, but less powerfully. You probably notice in the same way that someone from the outside wouldn't notice if an organization was not performing to its full potential until all the lights went out. My role was to spot and sort.

> You need energy yourself as a leader, and you need that energy to help energize others. Energy is the secret to delivering with stamina and speed.

Energy is the ultimate coping tool. Leading in our complicated and fast-moving world brings 'stress'. Stress can be great; it shouldn't always be seen as a negative word and something undesirable. Small doses of stress can deliver adrenaline, urgency and action. But the pace and pressure for leaders is consistently tough. At a senior level on an average day you may face press intrusion, social media trolling, board revolutions, constant criticisms of decisions and potentially the 'loneliness' of a senior role, coupled with the physical challenges of constant travel and long hours ... and that's all without your own worst critic: you, your ambition and impatience. You need to make sure that you have the energy to survive and thrive, to give you the strength of body and clarity of mind to maintain perspective.

The science bit

Energy and power are related although they are totally different concepts. Power is energy produced per unit of time:

$$\text{power} = \frac{\text{energy}}{\text{time}}$$

So, for example, a tank of fuel contains a certain amount of energy. This can be combusted and the process can be fast or slow; faster combustion = more power (although obviously the tank will be empty sooner in the case of high-power production – at speed – than in the case of low-power production).

So, speed leads to power, but the faster and more powerful the speed the greater is the need to 'refuel' more quickly. Conversely, the more energy you have the more you can achieve – you have power and for a longer period of time.

Energy is critical for speed and for resilience – for you and for your organization. Here are some approaches to help you work out how to get it, keep it and spread it to everyone else.

Renewable energy: your personal energy must be a priority

Some of the advice or perspectives here are ones you might like to consider and ones that may or may not prove useful for your personal and professional challenges. This was the piece of advice most consistently given by my interviewees and the most important one for you to believe:

> Your personal energy must always be a priority for you.

The advice given to parents on planes applies to leaders. Put your oxygen mask on first. If you are not able to function, others will suffer. It's not selfish, it's self-care; but it's also selfless – you will help others when you have the energy to do so.

The UK MD of Alibaba, Amee Chande, insists on the importance of taking personal responsibility for this:

> Managing your energy is essential. You have to realize that the only person responsible for your career is you and you need to know your own boundaries … A company will keep asking until you say no, not necessarily because they are evil or complex but they don't know what your boundaries are.

The route to managing your energy can be broken down into three simple areas:

- Exercise
- Scheduling around your energy levels
- Powering off to power on (work and rest).

Exercise

Exercise can't be ignored as a tried-and-tested energy creator. The vast majority of calm senior leaders seem to have worked out a way to squeeze exercise smartly into their day. Barack Obama incorporated at least 45 minutes of physical activity in to his daily schedule when President. If Obama could exercise every day, you can. He knew that the investment of time is worth it: 'The rest of my time will be more productive if you give me my workout time.'

Most of us know this but not everyone does it; it's hard to justify when life is so busy, when it may not be enjoyable, and when it feels like an indulgence. It's not an indulgence: it gives a powerful personal competitive edge at work (which is also likely to make you enjoy work more) and it's a way to cope with stress. Obama used to hold a regular basketball game with a handful of Washington friends, each with serious basketball experience — fun and fitness together. 'You have to exercise or at some point you'll just break down,' Obama commented.

Exercise is energy. Focus on the immediate benefit. Studies show that people are more motivated to change behaviour when they see a short-term benefit, not a long-term one. So, with exercise, it's helpful to remind yourself that the energy impact on your working week will be felt immediately (and logically, of course, the long-term 'live longer, feel better' side of things should reinforce that). I focus on reminding myself of the upsurge in energy I get from exercise and consciously note the impact it has on my mood and clarity of my thinking that day. As Sophie Amoros, the dynamic founder of e-commerce site NastyGirl, puts it: 'A good day is a day that starts with exercise.' Exercise gives you immediate benefits and helps your workday.

Solving your blockers to energy is about finding out what suits you. José Neves, the entrepreneur founder of Farfetch, learned yoga so he could easily do it on hotel-room balconies as he travelled so often. It's one of his top tips for entrepreneurs: 'Take your trainers with you everywhere. Work out every day – whether it's running, yoga, the gym, meditation … it doesn't really matter. You just need something to start every day focused.' Matt Brittin, Google's European President, is a former competitive rower and still rows because it's given him the incentive to stay fit. Then there's the legal legend Wim Dejonghe, who manages a massive, fast-growing global business and makes sure that he cycles to work every time he's in London because he knows the critical importance of exercise for energy … and for coping calmly. He says:

> The way to avoid that feeling of being overwhelmed? Start by doing a bit of exercise. I'm a cyclist so I bike into work – it doesn't lose much time as the Underground takes the same time. When I'm travelling I run. I discover cities at six in the morning – no traffic or people. Exercise clears my head and allows me to think.'

Sarah Wood, the entrepreneur founder of fast-growth media company Unruly, uses her commute in the same way: 'For me, the 30-minute walk to work every morning creates the headspace I need to start the day with a clear focus. It also doubles as my exercise fix.'

It's about physical energy and it's about mental strength, too. Simon Hay, the erstwhile CEO of data giant dunnhumby and now CEO of Outra, puts it simply: 'The gym is my sanity.'

> Get moving.

Scheduling around your energy levels

Make your workday fit around your energy levels. Many smart leaders know the time of the day they work best. Plan meetings and thinking time accordingly. Tackling the hardest task first works well for a rested and energized mind. A much-quoted aphorism which is often attributed to Mark Twain is: 'If it's your job to eat a frog, it's best to do it first thing in the morning. And if it's your job to eat two frogs, it's best to eat the biggest one first.' When you're feeling focused and energetic, you're going to get more work done in a shorter period of time. Work out when you're best at high-concentration work and, if you can, block your day in such a way that the first thing you work on is the thing that will have the most impact.

This works well if you're a lark, but maybe you're an owl. How you top up your energy levels is a very personal thing. Knowing yourself is critical.

Ruthless diary planning helps. Guy North, the Managing Director of Freeview, schedules time to think — and time to listen to music. On the more introverted side of the Myers-Briggs personality scale, he knows that he needs time alone to recharge, so he schedules small breaks between intense meetings. Others, like me, find networking and meeting new people stimulating and energizing, so scheduling that in doesn't deplete my energy reserves and, in fact, keeps me moving fast.

Energy + meetings – how to make it work

Meetings are a time-zapper for many, so influencing how they are run can dramatically improve energy levels. Depending on your role, you may be able to influence which ones you attend, but where you can influence how they are run you can make a significant difference to your week. Here are some questions to consider:

Can the meeting be shorter? Most meetings are too long. Fact. You lose people's attention and you lose the momentum. Preparation and a timing deadline are essential.

What kind of a meeting is it? Is it a sitting or a standing meeting? Sarah Wood, founder of Unruly, advises 'Do as few meetings sitting down as you can. Emphasize brevity and maintain momentum by doing status meetings on your feet.' Is it a phone call or a Google hangout? Is there a reason you have to travel somewhere to be with someone face to face? Absolutely if you need to build a deep relationship; absolutely not if it's about getting things done.

Tip: Improve your tech to make video calls easier. Unruly built a beautiful bespoke table in the boardroom which was tapered so that remote participants could see everyone in the room (which made them feel more included and massively increased their active participation in discussion and decision-making). For the same reason, Octopus Energy uses a Double Robotic moving video screen for people when they dial in.

What's the point? Is it a decision-making meeting or a creative ideas meeting? Is it to inform people or to get input? What are the objectives? (No clarity, no agenda should equal 'no meeting'.) Sheryl Sandberg credits Mark Zuckerberg for improving the meeting management within Facebook via a simple question: 'We try to be clear about our goal when we sit down for a meeting – are we in the room to make a decision or to have a discussion?"

How can we keep the energy levels up? By keeping people standing. Or by turning it into a 'walk and talk' and moving around together. This is particularly good for one-on-ones. You could also create drama and interest as part of the meeting.

Working out what suits you in terms of energy management across the week is worth taking time over. The same applies to working out what meetings can be optimized for which teams. It is a highly individual recipe and definitely worth it. Developing a regular, conscious 'energy check' will help you maximize the moments with momentum. Where and when are your energy levels highest? What are your energy triggers – physical, mental, social? Keep a journal across a week to help identify your energy sources.

Energy is essential for creativity. Jeremiah Dillon, head of product marketing at Google, reflected on the different rhythms of the working week and when to be most creative. The best way is to recognize that the week follows a particular rhythm, and plan accordingly. Inspired by research by psychologist Debbie Moskowitz at McGill University, Dillon outlined how the working week looks for him:

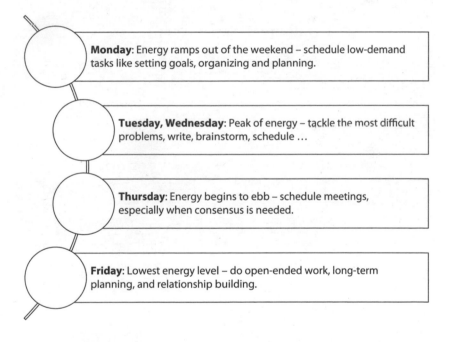

Monday: Energy ramps out of the weekend – schedule low-demand tasks like setting goals, organizing and planning.

Tuesday, Wednesday: Peak of energy – tackle the most difficult problems, write, brainstorm, schedule …

Thursday: Energy begins to ebb – schedule meetings, especially when consensus is needed.

Friday: Lowest energy level – do open-ended work, long-term planning, and relationship building.

FIGURE 2.1 The rhythm of the working week

Our Caffeine team discussed this approach and instituted a practice of 'low-fi' Fridays. Wherever possible, we save Fridays for internal conversations and administration (expenses, emails) rather than important new business meetings or running senior leadership summits which require intense energy. This isn't always possible as we have to be flexible to help our busy clients and partners, but as a general guideline it has helped us navigate the cadence of our week. People's energy is usually lower on a Friday and it's a great day to do administration or writing rather than intense face-to-face sessions.

There's also a different rhythm to consider as well. Leo Widrich, the co-founder and COO of Buffer (the social media management platform), splits his day into 90-minute windows. This is based on the chronobiological idea that our human minds can focus on any given task for 90–120 minutes, with a 20-to 30-minute break needed to achieve high performance on the next task. Widrich outlines the structure and his planning thus:

> Instead of looking at a six, eight or ten-hour workday, split it down and say you've got four, five or however many 90-minute windows. That way you will be able to have four tasks that you can get done every day much more easily.

Whether you're looking at your days, your week or at 90-minute chunks in a day, being aware of your energy levels and finding ways to optimize them isn't just about when you are focusing on work but also about when you do take a break.

Work and rest

Your diary has to reflect more than just work. A significant number of interviewees reflected on the 'work/life balance' and how to cope with a rapidly accelerating world. Most people find doing all they want to do a challenge. Much as I'd like to believe we can, we can't have it all, all the time (whether you are female or male is irrelevant to this fact). The entrepreneur Randi Zuckerberg – sister to a tech founder who has had a modicum of success, too – posted a tweet which ignited a furious debate:

FIGURE 2.2 The tweet posted by Randi Zuckerberg

She later countered the kerfuffle her statement caused by insisting it was a choice across time: 'You get three of those today, you can pick a different three tomorrow. The goal is for it to balance out over the long run, not to try to do all those five things every day.'

One of my interviewees put it like this: 'To really function at the highest level as a CEO, you have to have balance in your life.'

You have to recognize that just working more and more hours doesn't necessarily bring a better result. You have to ensure that you're mentally, physically and emotionally fit. Relationships outside work are key. You need to make sure that everything is in equilibrium. That's key to resilience.

The debate continues, though. Many of the leaders I spoke to explained that there are choices. Knowing what helps the other part of your life is smart, though. Exercise gives you energy to build a great company. Friendships give you perspectives and confidence. Family is important to everyone, no matter how driven they are to succeed.

But we can't ask God for an extension on our day. So we have to make our lives fit the time we have available. We have to choose and prioritize, and we have to be creative with time – to find ways to be smart with how we plan and what we do. To make it all possible, though, we need energy – the energy to be caring about, patient with and fun to be around our friends and family and the energy to build a great company.

It's the last of Randi Zuckerberg's 'big five' that has gained significant airtime recently. The brilliant Arianna Huffington, author and ex-CEO of *The Huffington Post*, has led a 'sleep revolution' encouraging us all to 'thrive' by being smart about sleep. She uses some compelling arguments. In her book *The Sleep Revolution*, she warns that, for one thing, not sleeping enough is not good for the vain among us:

> We wear our lack of sleep on our faces, too. A Swedish study found that sleep-deprived people were seen as 'less healthy, more tired, and less attractive', and a British study found that lack of sleep increased lines, wrinkles and blemishes on our faces. A lack of sleep also has a major impact on our ability to regulate our weight. In fact, a Mayo Clinic study found that sleep-deprived individuals ate 559 calories more a day than their well-rested counterparts.

It's not just about how you look but how long you last. Huffington says:

> Sleep deprivation is linked to increased risk of heart attack, stroke, diabetes, obesity, infertility, and more. Sleep deprivation weakens our immune system, making us more susceptible to garden-variety illnesses, like the common cold, and sets the stage for the development of more serious diseases.

Sleep is also a mood tool: it has mental benefits as well as physical ones. You're more likely to be sad without sleep: 'The Great British Sleep Survey found that sleep-deprived people were seven times more likely to experience feelings of helplessness and five times more likely to feel lonely.'

Oh, and sleeplessness isn't great for your thinking power either. Staying up for 24 hours is the cognitive equivalent of having a 0.1 per cent blood alcohol content — that's legally drunk. McKinsey published a 2016 report supporting the business case for sleep awareness programmes in which it highlighted clearly that 'sleep deficiencies impair the performance of corporate executives, notably by undermining important forms of leadership behavior, and can thereby hurt financial performance'.

Many of the people I spoke to slept well naturally. Others are more conscious of managing their sleep, like Google EMEA President Matt Brittin, who systematically works to make sure that he gets to bed and gets enough sleep. Some people are great at catnapping. Although I bemoan the fact that I'm short, it does help me nap well on planes which is handy for keeping energy levels up. Huffington approves: 'I am passionately pro power nap! It's like pushing a reset button for the day if you didn't get enough sleep the night before.' According to David Randall, the author of *Dreamland*, even a short nap 'primes our brains to function at a higher level, letting us come up with better ideas, find solutions to puzzles more quickly, identify patterns faster and recall information more accurately'.

There's a reason why high-performance football teams like Chelsea and Manchester United have brought in sleep coaches to help their players. You have to snooze better so you don't lose so often. Sleep coach Nick Littlehales assesses the temperature of players' rooms (a natural trigger for sleep is a cool room and a cool bed). 'Many clubs make massive investments of millions of pounds in their players but don't consider their sleep,' he says. 'Often footballers are young men who leave home before they know how to manage their routines or the physical and mental demands of their sport — from fatigue and pressure to hotels, travel and flights. These things all add up.'

Sleeping well feels like a small measure but the impact can be monumental for you — as Littlehales sharply summarizes: 'Sleep can affect performance, energy, mental focus and concentration. And quality sleep can bring more consistent performances, faster recovery times, higher motivation levels and better decision-making.'

Lying fallow: taking a holiday

From time to time we all need more than a good night's sleep; we need to 'lie fallow'.

A step beyond the sleep revolution is a full recharge – commonly known as a holiday. It is smart and it is sensible to consciously put yourself into energy-saving mode from time to time. Refresh, renew and come back reinvigorated.

Holidays can be terrifying for the ambitious leader, and those of us who love our work are less willing to take them. Work out a way to make them work, though, and consciously notice the impact they have on you. I asked Anthony Wreford, the former CEO of Omnicom's marketing services division, what advice he'd give his younger self. After a pause for thought he said: 'Take more holidays and find time to think.' When I laughed, he said, 'I'm totally serious. My best ideas often came when I was away, driving the car or playing golf. I always managed to achieve effective results immediately post holiday.' He admitted that 'It took me years to realize this, and that sitting in an office for long hours didn't necessarily lead to effective decision making.'

Burt Lorang, co-founder and CEO of tech company Full-Contact Inc. (cloud-based management solutions), generated some great publicity for his two-year-old organization when he introduced 'Paid Paid Vacation'. The company gives employees a $7,500 bonus if they follow two rules:

1 They have to actually go on vacation or they don't get the money.
2 They must disconnect, and hence can't work, while on vacation.

Not only was this to help individuals function better, so that the company saw people, on their return from holiday, 'shining brighter, working harder and more excited to get back into the swing of things', but also to help build a culture that couldn't depend too heavily on one person for any particular thing. 'Here's the thing,' Lorang says. 'If people know they will be disconnecting and going off the grid for an extended period of time, they might actually keep that in mind as they help build the company.'

For those of us who love our work and who are impatient to get things done, holidays can sometimes feel like an interruption. It's tempting to take only a half-break. Write a list before you go on holiday about what you want to achieve when you're back and then switch off business-as-usual (thinking time is allowed). Or find a way to smartly manage time when on holiday. Baroness Gail Rebuck, when CEO of Random House, would always take three weeks off every summer to be with her family but would work for a couple of hours every morning. It suited her. The key is in finding *your* style and *your* version of what works — by being aware, understanding and consciously observing the changes in your energy as a result of a little 'lying fallow' or a little sunshine and laughter.

I don't want to underestimate how hard this advice is for many people, especially those leading their own businesses or with a burning impatience to achieve. The new trend for the limitless holiday allowance where it's up to you to choose holiday time can be problematic for some; it requires courage and conviction when you have the ability to choose. I spoke to a private investor in a start-up who was completely horrified when the CEO took two weeks' holiday; in fact, he was furious about it. Watch the results when it's done well, though. Always judge on *results*, not on time spent on something. A break can make you work faster; the week after a holiday, those people who are dedicated can return motivated, inspired and ready to move at 150 miles per hour. You're refuelling, so you can go faster again.

Holidays help. Just as sleep refreshes your brain every night, a break gives it even more of a spa treatment. Where holidays are managed well, you will find you can focus better on the long-term needs of the business without being so distracted by the short-term niggles.

Power from the people: the role of the energizers

'The world will belong to passionate, driven leaders – people who not only have enormous amounts of energy, but who can energize those whom they lead.' Jack Welch (GE's CEO 1981–2001), who said this, identified four essential areas for successful leadership. Half of these were energy related: 'Energy' and 'Energize'. 'Edge' is the ability to take tough decisions and 'Execute' is the ability to deliver – both helped by energy as well.

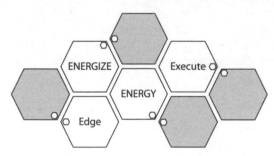

FIGURE 2.3 Four essential areas for successful leadership

Energy is about personal energy. Energizing is about the ability to stimulate that energy in others.

Energy is often just about who you work with. Take time to observe the impact people have on those they work with; do they help deliver more motivation and momentum as a result of their presence? If you want to increase your speed and that of your organization, make a conscious decision to zap the 'energy vampires' in your business – avoid working with them if you can.

And hire the right people to help. Simon Rogerson, the CEO and founder of the Octopus Group, is very clear that the right hires are critical for leaders and talks about that being energy related. He values those people who are real energizers but acknowledges that they are difficult to find: 'Every once in a blue moon, I'll interview somebody and they just bleed electricity.' It's worth considering what questions you can ask in interviews to understand how energizing people have been in the past. Can you assess their ability to do that (without being dazzled by an effective interviewee who is dynamic in presentation but not necessarily in delivery)? Group exercises or time-limited tests may be able to help.

Microsoft's CEO Satya Nadella uses this simple, brilliant assessment criterion for new hires. He asks two questions only: 'Do they create clarity and do they create energy?'

> Positive energy comes from the right people.

You may well have heard the expression 'drains and radiators'. People can be radiators. They warm you up when you are around them. They make you feel comfortable and good. Other people can be drains – people who make you feel flat and deplete your battery as they take from you – 'mood-hoovers' who vacuum up your positivity or leech your optimism.

Negative energy is a real threat to your day. It's a real threat to organization speed, too, as it slows down the desire to move.

To help your energy, think about spending more time with the people you know who act as a 'tonic' (friends, mentors, coaches, colleagues). Many leaders cite the business philosopher Jim Rohn, who asserts: 'You are the average of the five people you spend most time with.' If you believe in the law of averages, then you believe in the theory that the result of any given situation will be the average of all outcomes. Tim Ferriss, entrepreneur, author of *The 4-Hour Work Week* and angel investor/advisor to Facebook, Twitter and Uber, was given this advice at the age of 15 and says: 'It has impacted a lot of my decisions ever since – and every year I think it's more and more important.' It's certainly worth reflecting on how you can make sure that you spend time with those who stimulate and pep you up. The law of averages means that the more energy there is around you the more you will have for yourself.

Energy allows you to unblock as well as to accelerate. Liv Garfield, the FTSE 100 CEO of Severn Trent, has a very deliberate hiring policy. She prioritizes finding people with the ability and energy to 'unblock, to remove the speedbumps that slow down progress'. The role of good people is often to take things away as well as to add things in; taking away hurdles, speedbumps and blockers allows energy to flow more freely and things to accelerate.

Energy is contagious; it helps inspire, motivate and attract. We are not talking here about the idea of a charismatic, larger-than-life leader who evangelizes loudly; it's about energy, not personality. 'Energy is 100 per cent of the job. If you haven't got it, be nice.' Wise words from Paul Arden, legendary creative director and author of the iconic bestseller *It's Not How Good You Are, It's How Good You Want to Be*. Energy in a creative world is essential; the ability to keep trying new and different approaches requires cognitive power and the mental resilience to keep going.

It's possible that energy in leaders is sometimes misappropriated or mis-categorized by some as 'passion'. This is an overused word in contemporary business and some are more comfortable than others about saying they are passionate about their work. However, someone with energy is capable of being a passionate speechmaker and will, in the words of Jack Welch, 'unleash his or her inner fire in front of an audience'. Those with energy can drive a disruptive start-up or they can reorganize a small-parts manufacturer with verve and zeal. Energy makes enthusiasm easier and persistence more possible.

If you really want to accelerate change fast, it's worth remembering your physics primer. Isaac Newton's second law of motion says that an object at rest stays at rest, and an object in motion stays in motion with the same speed and in the same direction unless acted upon by an 'unbalanced force'.

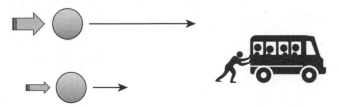

FIGURE 2.4 The more force … the more acceleration

An energized, passionate person is a force for good. Consider how you can have an energizing impact on those around you. How can you be an 'unbalanced force' for good to change direction or speed? Think about where the energy comes from and how it's communicated. Can you influence a set-up and a structure that maximizes energy? Can you motivate, inspire, take away blockers, ignite ideas? The fundamental law of energy in physics (the first law of thermodynamics) is that energy is never destroyed; in business, we repeatedly see that energy is contagious.

Find it, nurture it, sustain it.

Energy and the environment: supporting and sustaining 'the force'

Organizations are becoming more aware of the high cost of fatigue on employee focus, creativity and performance. A recent American study claimed that only 56 per cent of employees felt physically energized at work. How could you measure and treasure energy for people in your workplace?

The challenge for a leader growing at speed or moving roles is often to remember that the bigger the team you manage or the larger your organization, the more it's important that you think about structure and processes rather than principles and ideas. This means that, when it comes to energy, you can't just tell people how to behave, you have to help set up a stimulating structure so that energy is sustained and supported. This includes assessing how people work, what fuel they get (ideas, breaks, environment and food) and what happens in the culture to manage energy rather than time.

Work that works: energy-saving choices

'MARTINI' WORKING

A recent study showed that in a poll of 2,500 global business leaders 63 per cent believed that working flexibly helps staff feel more energized and motivated. Like anything else you look at in your business, it's important to question the way things have always been done and to look at the evidence around the effectiveness of how things have been done. More innovative working patterns can provide an interesting energy within an organization.

> Innovative working patterns can create new energies.

Innovative working practices have worked for Caffeine, which has spent ten years running a business with a 'Martini' way of working (a term inspired by the retro-classic ad for Martini, meaning we are set up to work 'any time, any place, anywhere'). We actively encourage our team to be consciously aware of their energy against pace. Because we work at speed and need to be sharp in sessions with clients (often facilitating complicated client sessions, which require intense energy), it's important that we allow time to reflect and recover and review. We work hard to avoid scheduling important meetings the day after facilitating a conference or one of our senior leader strategy sessions. We give people 'time sovereignty', which gives them the autonomy to plan their work against the time available using their energy wisely and well.

Food for energy

The rise of Silicon Valley's 'all you can eat' options have been seen as a fantastic perk for people joining companies like Google (which employs incredible chefs and has on-site gardens and beehives) or Facebook (which provides three meals a day, five days a week, for free). Yahoo was criticized by investor Eric Jackson for spending $450 million annually on employee food in 2015 (Marissa Mayer claimed in response that it was more like $150 million). Providing food has also been criticized as coddling millennials or controlling people by not letting them leave the office.

Whether food options provided are free or not, considering what food is provided is a simple, smart way to look at energy for your team. Consider how you feel at conferences and meetings when the snacks are biscuits, pizzas and heavy sandwiches. Often, we are in an airless room all day being fed with sleep-inducing snacks; people then being asked to 'think disruptively' or be more efficient will naturally struggle.

So you want a team which is happier, more engaged and more creative? A recent *British Journal of Health Psychology* study by Tamlin S. Conner et al. of people's consumption over a 13-day period concluded that the more fruits and vegetables people consumed (up to seven portions), the happier, more engaged and more creative they tended to be. This report looks to be correlational, so more work is needed on it, but fruits and vegetables do contain essential nutrients that stimulate the production of dopamine. Dopamine is a neurotransmitter that helps control the reward and pleasure centres of the brain; it enables us to see rewards and to move towards them. Fostering dopamine development therefore helps with engagement and motivation. It may be worth trying the carrot and celery stick approach.

Facebook have gone one step further than thinking about food and are looking at 'fuel' in a broader sense to explore the greater wellbeing of employees, including looking at Ariana Huffington's work on energy nurtured through sleep. Farfetch focus on wellness as a critical component in how they support their people.

PLAY, ENVIRONMENT AND DESIGN

Google doesn't just look at the basics of food as fuel but also considers how to stimulate and support a very important energy tool – that of 'play'. As Matt Brittin, the EMEA President of Google, explains:

> We train our people more and more on how to be playful in work situations because we tend to have a default load in work of writing and slides and a narrow set of ways in which people interact. But actually, people are kinaesthetic, people are visual, and people are oral. And if you combine all of these attributes together, then people are more engaged and you get better ideas. You get better collaboration.
>
> But you'll often see rooms with sticky notes everywhere, with props in the room, with people dressed up in weird clothes and it seems like, 'What are you doing, you childish people?' But actually, what you're doing is you're engaging people on a human level and engaging all their creativity and playfulness in coming up with ideas.

The smartest employers are able to consider the overall environment and design for energy.

To keep a structure which innovates and iterates, you need to make sure that it's not just set up to move fast but that it's set up in a way that creates 'sparks' with ideas and debate. Sparks invite fire; fire creates energy and speed. If you are designing your perfect structure, consider how to keep sparks flowing – how to encourage the cross-fertilization of ideas and avoid the dreaded 'silos' which will deliver more of the same.

Why the location of bathrooms bothered Steve Jobs

Steve Jobs led the design of a new headquarters for Pixar and obsessed over the bathrooms. His idea was that there would be only one set of bathrooms in the office's central atrium. This was purely and simply because he wanted 'serendipitous personal encounters' to occur. Walter Isaacson, his biographer, explains this in the context of the history of innovation:

Even though the Internet provided a tool for virtual and distant collaborations, another lesson of digital-age innovation is that, now as in the past, physical proximity is beneficial. The most productive teams were those that brought together people with a wide array of specialties. Bell Labs was a classic example. In its long corridors in suburban New Jersey, there were theoretical physicists, experimentalists, material scientists, engineers, a few businessmen, and even some telephone-pole climbers with grease under their fingernails. Walter Brattain, an experimentalist, and John Bardeen, a theorist, shared a workspace, like a librettist and a composer sharing a piano bench, so they could perform a call-and-response all day about how to manipulate silicon to make what became the first transistor.

There are plenty of other ways to create a hybrid set-up that allows for both the efficiency of remote working and the sparks and debate of collaboration, but the point is that

> when considering your optimal structure it's worth considering how to stimulate serendipitous encounters and to make sure that cross-silo thinking and discussion are supported and encouraged.

Karen Bowes, head of International HR at Capital One, talks about the importance of providing a stimulating environment for their people:

> Games rooms, music rooms, vast open spaces are all designed to stimulate and bring camaraderie. There is also a great focus on people's wellbeing, with courses in mindfulness and education on nutrition.

Simon Hay was CEO of dunnhumby, the data giant bought by Tesco. He was part of a growing number of businesses that moved their headquarters to the borough of Hammersmith and Fulham, a highly connected and creative part of London which is home to Yoox Net-a-Porter, BBC Worldwide and L'Oréal, among others. He knew he needed to move offices and wanted to use the move to design a workplace environment that would support the creation of energy. The resulting architect-designed office is a stunning homage to the history of the building (it's an old car factory) as well as to the energy-creating potential of space.

Around the corner from dunnhumby's creatively designed offices in Hammersmith, UKTV also has buildings designed for energy. CEO Darren Childs is fiercely proud of the egalitarian approach of their seating set-up. Every three months they randomly move everyone in the building to a different desk. 'When we first did it, people weren't sure and they grumbled but now they love it.' This significantly improves relationships, reduces 'silo' thinking and a sense of hierarchy (no one permanently has a 'better desk'), and leads to serendipitous creative thinking. Childs and his team make it a celebratory occasion, which has helped make it a hallmark of their culture.

One of my interviewees, who leads a company which has incredibly stimulating offices, expressed his frustration at how other organizations set up their workplace:

> I was at another company on Monday last week. I walked to one of their floors and immediately it just drained the energy out of you. Because it had got just desks in, there was nothing personalized anywhere, and it just looked like it could be any company anywhere. This is a consumer products company. Where are all the consumer products? Where's all the stuff about consumers? Where's anything that tells me what they do or what people enjoy? I just can't understand why you'd want to [work like that]. It doesn't cost you anything.

Finding ways to energize and stimulate your team's environment doesn't have to cost a lot or be overcomplicated. The 'beanbag' workplace is occasionally mocked, but finding places for different people to work in different ways, together or alone, is a key energy tool, as is the opportunity to link back to the consumer or the purpose of the organization. Octopus Energy, which is set up to deliver the best customer service in the energy category and is one of the UK's fastest-growing start-ups, as a result has screens on display to keep customer feedback at the forefront of everyone's mind; a highly effective focusing tool.

Flexible working, food, wellbeing, environment, design — these should be considered as important not just because you might be interested in creating a 'happy' culture but because it's about supporting and sustaining people's energy smartly.

Breaks not brakes: an energy tip for workshops

Are you bringing people together to do something particular? Do you want quality results? Always obsess over the timing and location of breaks and the nourishment provided. Hungry people are harsher (or more likely to take the easy option), as a study in the *Proceedings of the National Academy of Sciences* looking at the sentencing of judges shows. At the beginning of a session, a prisoner had a 65 per cent chance of being paroled. This fell to almost zero before a break. It rose back to 65 per cent after a break. This result was independent of any other factors.

Caroline Webb, consultant and positive psychology author, explains the importance of breaks clearly:

Decision-making quality drops the longer people go without a break. Classic cognitive biases like groupthink and confirmation bias take firmer hold, and we're more prone to sloppy thinking in general. In one study, where hospital leaders were trying to encourage the use of hand sanitizers, they found that compliance rates fell when people worked long hours without a break.

If you're planning an important meeting, 'summit' or workshop, make sure that you remember that helping people to be well fed and rested will improve your people's ability to think. Hungry and tired people are more likely to take the 'too-easy, too-lazy' decision.

Espresso takeaways

The energy grid

Time is finite. Energy isn't. It's simple. Manage your energy not just your time, and action and faster progress will be yours. Use the grid below to help.

Renewable energy	**Power to the people**	**Sustainable energy**
Prioritize your personal energy.	*Look for energy in your employees.*	*Create support systems and an environment that is energy-smart.*
Dynamic leadership requires your batteries being topped up.	*Hire for it, nurture it, reward it.*	
• Exercise: for sanity, for clarity. • Schedule and work around your energy – know what lifts you and what drains you, when and how to deal with it. • Rest and reset. Work on sleep awareness and breaks.	• Make energy a hiring criteria and a performance assessment. • Treasure it and measure it. Do people have energy and do they energize? • Surround yourself with radiators. • Energy is infectious.	• Constantly review the fuel you give people – ideas stimulation, wellness support and nutrition. • Educate your employees on energy – meetings, exercise, and inspiration.

RENEWABLE ENERGY	*POWER TO THE PEOPLE*	*SUSTAINABLE ENERGY*
Prioritise your personal energy.	*Look for energy in your employees.*	*Create support systems and an environment that is energy-smart.*
Dynamic leadership requires your batteries being topped up.	*Hire for it, nurture it, reward it.*	*Focus on the long-term health of the culture*
● Exercise: for sanity, for clarity.	● Make energy a hiring criteria and a performance assessment.	● Constantly review the fuel you give people – ideas stimulation, wellness support and nutrition.
● Schedule and work around your energy – know what lifts you and what drains you, when and how to deal with it.	● Treasure it and measure it. Do people have energy & do they energise?	● Educate your employees on energy – meetings, exercise, and inspiration.
● Rest and reset. Work on sleep awareness and breaks.	● Surround yourself with radiators.	● Watch out for 'Max Q' on your rocket ship – the moment when pressure creates damage

3

Purpose drives pace

The accelerating power of a
true mission

'Purpose can establish true momentum, passion and
motivation around transformation.'

*Olaf Swantee, CEO of Sunrise Telecoms and
founder and former CEO of EE*

Leadership today involves operating in our volatile, uncertain, complex and ambiguous world. The challenge for leaders is about being able to respond and react fast without losing your sense of direction. Your company needs a central organizing principle to help unify, clarify and focus everyone to help them continue to move in the right direction, whatever winds of change are buffeting them.

Paul Polman, Global CEO of Unilever, has some advice here:

> At this point in history, whether we like it or not, we have to deal with an economic system that produces slow growth and many companies are challenged by that. In Europe there is deflation, and generally there is a geopolitical environment which is seeing more conflicts than we have had in a long time; the Middle East is unfortunately one example, but there are many others too. Then we have the effects of climate change which are coming through at an increased rate. All of that causes a social dissatisfaction that we also have to deal with, and all these forces don't make it easy.

> If you think of that at a high level, of what you can do if you are in my position, the first thing is to be sure that your organization is driven by a strong purpose because the stronger your purpose is, and the more people are aligned with it, the more it will permeate these short-term volatilities.

If you want an organization that moves and grows, you need *motivation*. The word 'motivation' has its roots in the Latin *movere*, meaning 'to move'. Setting a purpose for the organization helps provide corporations with a coherent identity, which insulates and supports people against uncertainty and change. A sense of purpose helps protect for the long term and it helps accelerate your organization in the short term.

Understanding your purpose, then (and your organization brand – what it stands for, how it differentiates itself and what it is set up to do), has clear benefits for setting the pace.

Purpose perspectives: why bother with 'the why'?

There are two key questions to explore here:

- What is our purpose?
- What can a clear, credible and consistently delivered purpose do to help our organization move and grow?

And, based on the benefits of purpose, it's also worth asking a third question:

- Why aren't more organizations purpose-led?

What do we mean by 'purpose'?

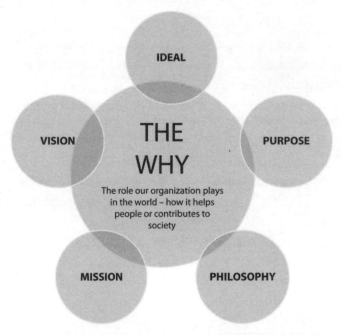

FIGURE 3.1 The why – what gives a company purpose?

Language can often be imprecise here, and descriptors are sometimes interchangeable. Purpose-driven organizations are also referred to as 'mission-driven' or 'ideal-driven'. Sometimes the purpose itself is the 'brand' for the company, or it's described as its 'philosophy'. The simplest way of thinking about it is that a company's purpose is the 'why' – why it exists, what role it plays in society, the world and in customers' lives. That's the company's mission – a goal which is not (just) about profit. EY, which carried out an extensive piece of research on the idea of purpose in business, defines it as 'an aspirational reason for being which inspires and provides a call to action for an organization'.

Businesses don't operate in a strict commercial vacuum with no consideration of the society in which they operate, and this includes considering economic, social, environmental and ethical issues. Increasingly, consumers are looking for organizations not only doing good things for them but also contributing positively to some of the wider societal issues we face.

Dave Packard, founder of Hewlett-Packard, shared his definition of 'purpose' back in the 1960s:

> Purpose (which should last at least 100 years) should not be confused with specific goals or business strategies (which should change many times in 100 years). Whereas you might achieve a goal or complete a strategy, you cannot fulfil a purpose; it's like a guiding star on the horizon – forever pursued but never reached.
>
> Yet, although purpose itself does not change, it does inspire change.
>
> The very fact that purpose can never be fully realized means that an organization can never stop stimulating change and progress.

This is a topical articulation for our times and a clear definition. For Packard, purpose was what a company strived for and something that stimulated progress, supporting a quest to keep moving.

The idea of organizations with a purpose is not just a novel contemporary phenomenon. Moving further back than Dave Packard, history shows that business leaders of the past – like Joseph Rowntree, William Kellogg and John Lewis – all knew that brands should have a business beyond profit. The commercial world has changed greatly since then but the reality is that leaders need purpose in their organizations more than ever before.

Why bother with 'purpose'?

In this multi-channel world, where consumers can buy anything, anywhere, at any time, a point of difference can be created in the minds (and hearts) of consumers who respect and admire organizations not just because of what they sell but because of who they are and what they stand for. Purpose gives employees and customers something beyond a product and an opportunity to consume or work for money; it's about being part of something larger. Simon Sinek, author of *Start with Why*, summarizes this idea well when he says: 'Great companies don't offer us something to buy, they offer us something to buy into.'

This is not something that can be artificially added to an organization's communications and brands; it has to be something that is credible and delivered in everything the organization does, inside and out. Organizations must not be opaque or secretive. Glassdoor, social media, a culture of exposing hypocrisy, and a more demanding press and public make things extremely challenging for leaders of organizations (but better for the world overall). In a world where organization brands are 'transparent', what the organization believes in and how they operate influence the decisions people make about whether to buy into their offer, to buy their offer or to become part of the organization.

Fundamentally, you could justify having a 'purpose' as a smart commercial decision. The 2017 Havas Media 'Meaningful Brands' study found that purposeful brands have outperformed the stock market by 206 per cent in the last ten years, gain nine times more share of wallet, and achieve marketing results that are double those of lower-rated brands.

Purpose drives profits. But does it also drive speed and business growth? Procter & Gamble stalwart Jim Stengal carried out global analysis on this question with a ten-year growth study involving 50,000 brands. His work shows a cause-and-effect relationship between financial performance and the company's ability to connect with fundamental human emotions, hopes, values and a sense of a greater purpose. He reported that:

> The businesses that grow faster and grow longer have something special driving them and something attracting people – attracting customers, attracting employees. And that is what I call an ideal. Some people call it a mission, some call it a purpose. I like the 'ideal' word because it has idea in it.

Why aren't more organizations purpose-led?

In 2014 a study was carried out by EY (whose own purpose is articulated as 'Building a better working world'). In their 'The Busi-ness Case for Purpose', they interviewed 474 business executives in order to understand their approach. The research base was driven primarily from the *Harvard Business Review* sub-scriber base and was a global study, in which it was found that:

- 90 per cent of questioned leaders believed in the importance of a purpose in an organization but only 46 per cent said it informed their strategic and operational decision-making
- 89 per cent of those surveyed said a strong sense of collective purpose drove employee satisfaction; 84 per cent said it could affect an organization's ability to transform, and 80 per cent said it helped to increase customer loyalty.

While the vast majority of respondents believed that 'purpose' could help their organization, only a minority said that their company was run in a purpose-driven way. Whereas 46 per cent said that their company had a strong sense of purpose, another 44 per cent said that their company was trying to develop one.

The belief in the power of purpose is probably not surprising, given the increased discussion around this question in leadership and business circles in the last few years. It seems surprising, then, that there is such a discernible gap between understanding and action. Andy Milligan is the co-author of *On Purpose* with Shaun Smith, a guide to how to put the idea of purpose into effective business practice. He believes there are that three main blockers holding companies back in this area:

- They don't understand what is meant by purpose – confusing it either with corporate social responsibility or with high-level generic brand slogans.
- They have a purpose but they don't put it into practice – they don't make the difficult decisions necessary to earn employee loyalty and customer trust.
- They don't know how to measure the impact of being purpose-led, and if they can't measure it they won't get it done.

'Purpose' is a concept which has generated huge business coverage in the last few years, as more and more leaders appreciate its appeal in principle. However, it has frequently been talked about and mainly used as a marketing tool, helping brand communications move to a more emotional positioning (famous examples include Unilever's Persil 'Dirt is Good', Dove's 'Real Beauty' and Procter & Gamble's ground-breaking work on Always and Pampers).

Product brands which have a connection to human needs are defined as purpose driven and this emotional connection to 'why' can be incredibly powerful. However, where purpose is particularly relevant for those leaders wanting to move faster is in defining your organization brand – what your company stands for. This may sometimes include standing for something that plays a wider corporate or social role, though not necessarily. 'Purpose' could be playing a role that makes people's lives more fun, more efficient, easier or better:

- Lego's purpose is 'to inspire and develop children to think creatively, reason systematically and release their potential to shape their own future – experiencing the endless human possibility' – summarized as 'to inspire and develop the builders of tomorrow'.
- The unusual cult brand Patagonia was founded in 1973 and has a 'triple mission', which is to 'build the best products, do no unnecessary harm and to use business to inspire solutions to the environmental crisis'.
- The budget hotel Premier Inn's purpose is beautifully simple, defined as 'making our guests feel brilliant through a great night's sleep'.
- Nintendo aspires to 'put smiles on the faces of everyone we touch'.
- Walgreen Boots Alliance aims to 'help people across the world lead healthier and happier lives'.

It's not just about the words on a wall, though. Defining your organization brand in this way moves far beyond communication. It is about much more than what you say. It is about what you do and about how you behave; it is about how you attract, retain and motivate, how you make high-velocity decisions and how you unify silos, individuals, projects and the business behind a purpose beyond just making a profit …

The founder of Oliver Bonas defines his shops as a 'lifestyle brand', by which he means one which 'inspires, guides and motivates people, contributing to the definition of their way of life'. The work he's done to define the purpose of the company makes it clear that the way the brand contributes to life could be through the shopping experience, the service, the communication, or a combination of these elements. This reinforces the point that the way in which an organization delivers on its purpose is not solely about a marketing approach. A great purpose informs everything.

To use purpose properly you do need to understand what it is, to put it into practice and – critically – to measure its impact. The measurement is essential. People treasure what is measured. Proof is needed that action leads to results.

Working out your purpose and getting it embedded in the organization can take some time. However, it will then save time, accelerating decision-making and motivating and directing people in a unified way. Purpose – put into practice in an intentional and consistent way within an organization – then becomes a powerful speed tool.

Lego: a successful case study in purpose building

Our ultimate purpose is to inspire and develop children to think creatively, reason systematically and release their potential to shape their own future – experiencing the endless human possibility.

Today it's seen as the world's most powerful brand, but in 2004 Lego teetered close to bankruptcy, posting a loss of $217 million and with sales declining at 35 per cent year on year. The CEO of the company, Jørgen Vig Knudstorp, was tasked with turning around a company that had moved away from the core of what had made it great.

Knudstorp went back to the 'why' to find an insight about the brand which would unite and motivate the organization and its customers. Inspiration struck when the founders of Google revealed in a cover story in *Time* that it was Lego that had shaped their young minds. At the same time Knudstorp talked to old MIT colleagues who explained that Lego is the ideal way for a child to learn how to think systematically and creatively.

Taking this insight about how playing with Lego has a formative role in people's lives, and how what it does has an impact on people and on the world, Lego articulated its purpose (or its mission) succinctly as 'to inspire and develop the builders of tomorrow'. Knudstorp undertook a fundamental reorganization of the company to make sure that everything lined up with this purpose and moved away from any ideas and initiatives that didn't support this mission.

The latter aspect is important to note. Sometimes it's easy to say no to things if they aren't making money but being true to your purpose means making difficult choices which sometimes challenge you. Bill Bernbech, creative director and co-founder of American ad agency DDB, is the person first credited with saying: 'A principle isn't a principle until it costs you something.' If you want to stand up for something (a purpose), you have to say no to things which don't support it; you have to make choices even when it's tempting to agree to everything. Purposeful brands are clear and consistent.

The clarity of Lego's definition of its purpose (an emotional and credible 'why') led to a business turnaround that has gone down in history. The near-bankruptcy of 2004 seems bewildering in the present-day context of a business that has attained the top spot as the world's biggest toymaker with seven Lego sets sold every second.

In business, what gets measured is what matters. Lego's purpose means that what it measures is ultimate consumer satisfaction. Here's Knudstrop on how that purpose translates into the way Lego recognizes and rewards success:

Our owners, being a family-controlled company, have always emphasized that we're here to serve the children. We're here to develop children. We're here to give children the very best. We want to be an irreplaceable but also irresistible brand for children. We want to be on top of their wish list and something they talk passionately about. We measure that by a Net Promoter score. Then we measure how we create value for our customers and suppliers. We really want to be sure that it's value creating for our customers and suppliers to work with us. Then we measure our employees' engagement, and that is actually the foundation of our reward system. We also reward financial value creation, but we view financial value creation as the result of being highly recommended by children, highly value creating for our business partners, and having creative and engaged employees. If we have those three things, we can't help but actually make a profit at the end of the day.

Lego has now been crowned 'the world's most powerful brand' in Brand Finance's global study, scoring highly on the Brand Strength Index in factors including familiarity, loyalty, promotion, staff satisfaction and corporate reputation. For Lego, a renewed sense and clarity of purpose have driven profit and progress.

For more on Lego's Superfast turnaround, read David Robertson's *Brick by Brick*.

The power of purpose

The leaders interviewed for this book regularly cited 'purpose' as a powerful speed generator for how they and their teams decided what to do and what not to do, and how it inspired and united people (and their customers) behind a clear goal. Some told stories of how a newly articulated purpose helped turn around stagnant performance in a big organization; others of how it drove clarity for those creating a new company; yet others of how it combined logic with emotion to connect better with everyone involved.

Sarah Wood, founder of Unruly, says:

> Companies with purpose are 400 per cent more profitable than their peers. In the team you lead, you need a purpose that is bigger than a bottom line, one that allows your people to be their bravest selves, do work that challenges the status quo and deliver meaningful impact. Purpose allows you to shape a future and an industry that you and your people want to be a part of. You can't have a successful culture without a defining purpose, so that's where you need to start.

Purpose-driven companies outperform stock market indices. They gain high levels of customer loyalty as well as market share. They have high-performing employees and enjoy superior advocacy and referral rates. They act quickly in the short term and are consistent performers in the long term.

> A clear sense of purpose can help you drive pace in your organization: purpose gives you the people (who will give you the pace); purpose attracts, inspires and motivates people.

'Want to change the world? Upset the status quo? This takes more than run-of-the-mill relationships. You need to make people dream the same dream that you do,' says Guy Kawasaki, Silicon Valley VC, ex-Apple 'chief evangelist' and founder of Google Technology Ventures.

Strong, purpose-driven organizations have a significant competitive advantage in today's world: people want to work there. I've lost count of the number of senior leaders I've met in the advertising, communication or business world who are deeply frustrated by not being able to attract the best people either at a senior or graduate level 'because everyone wants to go to Google or Facebook'.

Tech-based companies are appealing to people at the moment, partly because of the excitement of being with a fast-growth company but also because many people are keen to work in organizations which show they care about people and that are associated with a meaningful output (beyond just making more money for shareholders). Mark Zuckerberg talks eloquently and frequently about Facebook's purpose (their 'mission'):

> Facebook was not originally created to be a company. It was built to accomplish a social mission – to make the world more open and connected …
>
> Simply put: we don't build services to make money; we make money to build better services.
>
> By focusing on our mission and building great services, we believe we will create the most value for our shareholders and partners over the long term – and this in turn will enable us to keep attracting the best people and building more great services. We don't wake up in the morning with the primary goal of making money, but we understand that the best way to achieve our mission is to build a strong and valuable company.

Making money for shareholders is an important part of business, but Google, Facebook, Airbnb and Unilever are just a few organizations that talk openly about their missions, values and purpose beyond that – and as a result are winning the recruitment war.

Focusing on people and purpose will appeal to great talent. Millennials are not an amorphous blob, but in general they are a generation who are interested in the idea of a purpose-driven employer. Barry Salzberg, CEO of Deloitte Global, says: 'The message is clear: when looking at their career goals, today's millennials are just as interested in how a business develops its people and how it contributes to society as they are in its products and profits.' For six out of ten millennials, a 'sense of purpose' is part of the reason they chose to work for their current employers. A recent study by PWC agrees, pointing out that millennials are keen 'to contribute something to the world and … want to be proud of their employer'.

It's easy to generalize about this being something that inspires the younger generation, but this is an opportunity for all ages. As Daniel Pink writes in *The Surprising Truth about What Motivates*

Us: 'Humans, by their nature, seek purpose – to make a con-tribution and to be part of a cause greater and more enduring than themselves.'

Unilever offers the clearest example of the power of purpose in attracting employees. People's early career goals are unlikely to be articulated as 'when I grow up I want to work for a household goods company', but Unilever's high-profile sense of purpose has made it a sensationally popular employer in attracting millennial tal-ent across the globe. It is ranked at number 11 in the *Sunday Times* UK Top 100 Graduate Employers, number 2 in the most popular employers in the UAE after Emirates, the number 1 employer in Kenya, and number 3 in the LinkedIn analysis of the most popular employers – with only Google and Facebook ahead of it.

Global CEO Paul Polman has no doubt about the primary reason Unilever has become such a magnet for recruiting and retaining talent: putting their purpose ('making sustainable liv-ing commonplace') at the centre of everything the corporation does is 'incredibly motivating for our employees'.

Having a clear purpose is a hugely powerful way to attract the best employees (thereby helping you grow and thrive). A good purpose should be distinctive and uniquely ownable; that should then also save you time by acting as a filter for people. It makes sure that you don't attract the wrong people or people who won't fit with what you want.

Robert Stephens, founder of The Geek Squad (the com-puter company now part of Best Buy), explains how purpose acted as a people filter for them:

> For me, purpose acts like a lighthouse, but the light shines at a certain wavelength that only attracts a certain kind of person. The kind of people you want; it helps keep the others out. The purpose of The Geek Squad is to help ordinary people do extraordinary things with technology; a squad of people who combine their individual talents within a team to provide a service for the public. What they fix, whether it's PCs or tablets or phones, will change as technology changes, but how they serve customers will never change …

Recruiting the best talent helps you perform better and faster; a strong, clear, compelling organization purpose supports this. And once you have that talent, purpose 'drives' motivation. Sarah Wood, founder of Unruly, reflects on the importance of creating an engaged team for leaders:

> While many might argue that the single most important responsibility of a leader is to grow and protect profit margins or 'shareholder value', this approach ignores the fundamental reality that there are no profits without people, and there is no business of any scale without an engaged, committed and motivated team to sustain it.

Dan Pink's seminal work *Drive* argues convincingly that human motivation is largely intrinsic. He summarizes the entire book's premise simply, in a Twitter-style headline: 'Carrots & Sticks are so last century. *Drive* says for 21st-century work, we need to upgrade to autonomy, mastery and purpose.' And Pink's definition of purpose? 'The desire to do something that has meaning and is important.' He goes on to starkly express his view of why it is essential to organizations: 'Businesses that only focus on profits without valuing purpose will end up with poor customer service and unhappy employees.'

Other research indicates that there are missed opportunities for many organizations in not exploring this route. A 2016 study among American companies found that only 34 per cent of employees feel a strong connection to their company's mission. The research concluded: 'The result is low energy, inattention to detail and quality, lack of commitment, and high turnover.'

A number of interviewees in the book cite Dan Pink's work as seminal for their understanding of employee motivation. Nic Brisbourne, Managing Partner of Forward Partners (a venture capital firm that 'supercharges start-ups'), says he initially struggled to reject the seemingly logical 'carrot and stick approach'. He now believes firmly that 'the best performing teams will come to the managers who reject carrots and sticks and embrace the more complicated and tricky notion of motivating by giving their people autonomy, mastery, and purpose.'

When Antony Jenkins was CEO of Barclays, he looked at how the organization went back to its seventeenth-century roots as a financier of ambitions and opportunities. As CEO, he wanted his teams to think about the role of their bank in their community, funding opportunity and providing skills and education:

> The aim was for staff to believe in something bigger than themselves, and look beyond measuring their 'self-worth' only by their net worth. Understanding how your organization can contribute to a wider social benefit helps teams see the positive aspects of their role.

The creation of a 'purpose statement' often benefits from someone with eloquence or the ability to craft words with power. The precise choice of words can convey nuance or specificity, emotions and distinctiveness. However, purpose is not, and should not ever be seen as, a tagline. It is not a selling statement but rather a pivotal point of truth for the organization to unite behind.

Truth is the key word here, as with many elements of smart leadership and the choices you make in business. When you articulate your purpose, it should be done in a way which is truly credible. You are asking people to believe in it; it is your philosophy, it is your organization's role in life. Oversell and you lose people. The process of defining your purpose is simply a discovery process, an uncovering of what your business can deliver.

Start with the truth. Look at what is true about you and what positive role your organization or brand plays in the lives of people. Then think about what is true about what appeals to your employees and customers. Lastly, question what will remain relevant over time (a strong purpose must endure as your business evolves). Then find the right words to capture what your purpose is in a way which is both memorable for all involved and meaningful to those who matter.

The Oliver Bonas story: a promise and a philosophy designed for the people

Oliver Tress, a man who loves words, ideas and great design, is the founder of the successful retail emporiums you see on many high streets, Oliver Bonas. He went through a long period of contemplation and reflection before his organization found a way to define its purpose in a distinctive and interesting way.

Oliver Bonas is a chain of stores that has brightened up the British high street for over 25 years with well-designed products and a positive approach. The business has been run with the founder's succinct motto at the heart of it. Tress has always believed that everyone should always 'Work hard, play hard and be kind'. This includes treating his employees smartly and kindly, and part of that is helping them understand how to navigate their decisions when it comes to product choice or design, store environment decisions and brand communications.

In a terrifyingly competitive retail environment, Oliver Bonas's owners wanted to articulate more clearly what Oliver Bonas was like when it was at its best. They were looking for a definition of this to help provide more consistency across its communications, buying and approach to employees. They wanted to capture their philosophy to help provide focus as their staff numbers grew and their business spread across more locations.

The inspiration for the company's 'philosophy' came from an interesting combination of the words of one of the world's best storytellers, the musings of an ancient philosopher, a seminal classification of a social anthropologist – and from a realistic, pragmatic understanding of what role a gifts and accessories store could play in society.

Oliver Tress has always loved the words of the master storyteller Hans Christian Andersen who said: 'Just living is not enough. One must have sunshine, freedom … and a little flower.' This quotation sparked a thought behind the definition of the company's purpose. The enjoyment of a gorgeous velvet chair or a well-designed necklace is the equivalent of 'sunshine'.

Allowing different ideas to 'percolate' in his brain, Tress also reflected on the concept of *eudaimonia*, which is an ancient Greek way of defining happiness, human welfare or 'human flourishing'. Aristotle's version of this acknowledges that, although this type of happiness is largely driven by virtue, it can also be delivered through external factors. So Tress focused the organization around delivering a 'eudaimonic promise'. They aim to be 'a little flower' in people's lives. Employees and the company were able to 'do our bit to make living a joyful experience and give cause for optimism'.

This definition of their purpose has helped Oliver Bonas staff as it acts as a decision-making tool, speeding up the velocity of their choices for products, activities and communications. It also acts as a foundation for ideas, inspiring and stimulating innovative approaches. (Tress cites specific examples of cynical, cool products which the team agree are good and would sell but aren't right for this optimistic approach.)

Above all, Tress wants his staff to feel proud of what they achieve – they do all work hard and the sense that they are providing 'flowers' to other hard-working people is motivating – and based in reality. It is not an over-claim; it is a way of sharing the positivity of what the company does with a distinctive dash of creativity and style, in keeping with the brand itself and the experience it offers to its customers and its people. And the only KPI he focuses on personally? The percentage of his employees who feel proud to be part of this experience.

> The clear definition of a company's purpose can provide a decision-making tool for staff.

A clarity of purpose is a unifying tool; it's a way to articulate what people can achieve together, a goal and an objective which means something to people. Let's return to Dave Packard, the prescient founder of Hewlett-Packard, outlining his point of view back in the 1960s:

> Many people assume wrongly that a company exists simply to make money. While this is an important result of a company's existence, we have to go deeper and find the real reason for our being. As we investigate this, we inevitably come to the conclusion that a group of people get together and exist as an institution that we call a company so that they are able to accomplish something collectively that they could not accomplish separately. They make a contribution to society, a phrase which sounds trite but is fundamental.

Being clear on how your role contributes to the organization's overall purpose helps motivate individuals and it also operates at a team level, helping drive high-performance teams. We all know the evidence that shows that a more diverse team leads to a more innovative culture, but the reality of hiring for that diversity means that you will inevitably have people with different perspectives, backgrounds and skills. Purpose has a unifying role to play, providing a shared goal for everyone. Rick Goings, the long-term CEO of Tupperware Brands (in charge for over two decades), describes it simply: 'Purpose is the glue that holds people together.'

> Purpose has a unifying role to play, providing a shared goal for everyone.

Purpose gives people meaning in their work. Dr Amy Wrzesniewski, Associate Professor of Organizational Behavior at Yale University's School of Management, has been researching ways to help people find job satisfaction for the last two decades. Her research estimates that only a third of people naturally find meaning in their work. The Google re:Work study 'Project Aristotle' looked extensively at what factors contributed to the success of high-performance teams. The conclusion to the report cited five factors that helped ensure team success. Fourth on the list was 'Meaning of work' (Am I doing something that is personally important to me?) and 'Impact of work' (Do I fundamentally believe that the work we're doing matters?). Both of these are united through a sense of purpose. Motivating employees is about having a sense of purpose and showing them clearly the effect of their role against that greater purpose.

Dan Pink looks at this by separating out two types of purpose. Purpose with a capital *P* is about 'making a difference' in the world, while purpose with a lowercase *p* is about 'making a contribution'. Both types of purpose can be motivating. As Pink says:

> People want to either make a difference, or contribution, or both. And so when you're looking to motivate yourself or looking to motivate other people, you need to be able to answer this question on their behalf: am I making a difference, but also am I making a contribution?

What does this mean? It means moving beyond just looking at numbers and measurements and showing employees how what they do has an impact on the world – on consumers or society – with stories, experiences and visuals rather than just graphs and numbers. As a leader, giving your employees a story about what a difference they make to the company and what a difference the company makes to people and the world has been clearly shown to be more motivating than money.

So if you want to help your people to go faster, give them a sense of *purpose* and show what their *purpose* is in achieving that.

Move fast in the right direction: purpose drives smart decision-making at speed

When Kerry Glazer, the Chief Executive of AAR, the search and selection consultancy, took over the reins of WACL, the communications and marketing networking group bringing together the most senior female leaders in the business, she knew that there was a choice facing her and the organization. The organization was much loved by its members as a support-ive, fundraising network that people enjoyed being part of. But the organization, which has been going since 1923, was facing criticism for its 'elitist' approach, and members were genuinely frustrated by the stagnation of the change in the industry. In a world where there are more CEOs named Dave in the FTSE 100 than female CEOs, the advertising and communications industry was very aware there was a role to play in supporting real change. Within three months of taking over as president, Glazer had called an extraordinary general meeting to persuade the members of WACL to vote to adopt a new purpose:

> There are some nettles that you just have to grasp, even if you know that finding solutions won't be quick or easy. This thought occurred to me when I started working with a number of my WACL colleagues, thinking about the shape we were in as we approached the club's centenary. Are we a networking and events organization with a charity fundraising focus … or a transformative voice around leadership issues in our industry? Are we there for all women in the industry or just the women in the club? This led to the members of WACL voting to adopt a new purpose. We have agreed that our purpose is to accelerate gender equality in communications and marketing via ample doses of inspiration, support and campaigning.

Glazer quickly identified that the way to get to solutions faster in this tricky situation was to get agreement and alignment behind a strong purpose for the organization. 'When your pur-pose is clear, every future decision becomes much easier.' Pur-pose gives your organization the key to business velocity. The definition of velocity is speed, in the right direction.

Purpose sets the direction, meaning decisions are quicker, faster and easier. Angela Ahrendts, former CEO of Burberry and now SVP of Apple Retail, agrees: 'There is always this balance between hard and soft strategies, investment and intuition, but if you have a greater purpose, it becomes relatively easy to make those calls.'

Many of the leaders I interviewed cited slow decision-making as the number-one speed-killer in organizations. The ability to make decisions quickly is particularly critical when we are faced with a crisis. However, organizations are faced with the need to make decisions at speed on an everyday, regular basis. It allows you to move fast. Brand expert Andy Milligan shared a very clear example of how decisions are quicker and better when you follow your purpose:

> In 2017, within hours of President Trump's executive order banning all visitors to the USA from seven mainly Muslim nations as well as all refugees from anywhere, Airbnb offered to house immigrants in its properties. Explaining its decision, it cited its purpose to give people a sense of belonging, not just a sense of place. 'Anyone can belong anywhere.'
>
> The New York Taxi Drivers' Alliance organized a strike at JFK Airport, citing their purpose to welcome all visitors. 'We go to work to welcome people to a land that once welcomed us.' Uber, on the other hand, faced fierce criticism for not joining the strike and also for lifting its surge pricing policy at the airport, a move interpreted as an attempt to gain commercial advantage from the situation. Travis Kalanick, Uber's CEO, was stung by the criticism but by the time he had clarified his opposition to the ban, #deleteuber was already trending and a reported 200,000 Uber accounts were deleted.

Paul Polman, Unilever's CEO, cites purpose as one of the key ways in which a global organization like Unilever sails confidently through an uncertain and constantly changing world: for him, 'The most important thing in an uncertain world is to have a strong sense of purpose', because 'a very strong sense of purpose helps people to react very fast; it creates clear alignment on what needs to be done.'

Polman points out that there are many things that can't be exactly planned for: 'for example the terrible floods we had in Latin America a while back or even the shock of floods that hit the North of England – or the conflicts that beset the Middle East'. He shared a story of how this type of unpredictable event challenged leaders when the political disruption flared up in Egypt:

> All of a sudden the Egyptian general manager calls me and says, 'The people are on the street. The prisoners are out of prison. They are attacking our factories. They are attacking my home at the same time. They're trying to get to materials from our company that might be inflammable. What do I do?' He has to be very fast. We don't have a procedure or a guideline for that. But because he has a strong purpose, he knows what the philosophy of the company is. He has no conflict. He knows that it's not about protecting the profits for that quarter. He knows it's the safety of our people first. He knows it's the interest of the communities. He operates under a purpose so the decision-making is very simple to see.

Purpose provides a North Star to guide an organization when things are dark, unclear or uncertain. However, as Polman points out:

> It's not a strategy – purpose isn't a strategy and it needs to be accompanied by clear strategies that are consistent, and by a clear understanding of people's roles and responsibilities – these things help give people the guidance and they are then fully empowered to make the right decisions, on the ground and fast.

Clarity of purpose also helps companies make better investment decisions for products and customer experiences, including what kind of innovations to bring to market. For example, Unilever's purpose influenced its decision to develop a groundbreaking 'Superfast' soap that cleans hands in ten seconds and not the usual 30 seconds – reducing the water needed to wash hands and improving the chances of children in developing countries to live beyond six years old by encouraging them to wash their hands.

Premier Inn identified a compelling insight about what would attract people to its hotels rather than to others – getting a great night's sleep. So its purpose was identified as 'We exist to make our guests feel brilliant through a great night's sleep.' This informed its strategy and everything it then decided to do. It became its promise and it became the framework for communications and commercial decisions. Once it had clarified its purpose, all its investments went into supporting that, including buying the best beds, silent air conditioning, removing phones from rooms, and providing a check-in person specifically focused on working with their guests to ensure that nothing prevented them from having a good night's sleep. The payoff? An amazing customer experience that helped fuel Premier Inn to the number-one spot for value hotel brands in the UK.

Authors John O'Brien and Andrew Cave, in their book *The Power of Purpose*, conclude:

> Purposeful business leaders … have found that one of the most sought-after skill sets in today's complicated world is, quite simply, the ability to focus on what is most important and make whatever is desired happen. This is clarity of purpose.

Responsive and responsible leadership: purpose allows an empowered, lean and agile leadership approach

Business leaders have to be both highly responsive to change and acutely aware that their actions contribute to a broader societal, community and political situation. Klaus Schwab, founder and Executive Chair of the World Economic Forum, opened Davos 2017 with a call for 'responsive and responsible leadership':

Leaders have to be responsive and responsible; they must understand that we are living in a world marked by uncertainty, volatility and deep transformational changes. Many people are living in precarious situations and searching for identity and meaning in a fast-changing world. They want to regain their sense of purpose. More than ever, leadership means taking responsibility. It requires courage and commitment to listen and honestly explain the breadth and complexity of issues, to proactively generate solutions and to take action based on core values.

Schwab sets the challenge in the context of our Superfast world:

We are living in a world no longer driven by linear change, but rather exponential change occurring simultaneously in all fields. This is creating extreme volatility, uncertainty and, as a consequence, an understandable nostalgia to 'turn back the clock'. The traditionally slow and reactive response mechanisms and structures for dealing with problems have contributed to the present situation.

The rate of change in the world highlights the need for businesses, politicians and all world citizens to understand that they need to work together and to work at speed. A sense of purpose and a sense of responsibility as well as a sense of awareness of change remain the critical combination:

Leaders need sensitivity and empathy to serve as their radar system, and values and vision as their compass. Without a radar system, leaders can't be responsive; and without a compass, they can't exercise leadership responsibly.

So, if setting a sense of purpose helps deliver responsible leadership, how do we make sure that we are also responsive to change in this hyper-fast world?

If you want to follow the principles of lean agility and empower those 'closest to the knowledge' to be the ones who make the (right) decision fast, then an aligned purpose allows you to feel confident that people will know what to do.

The British Royal Navy is one of the most successful organizations in the world. Neil Morrissetti, a retired rear admiral who has advised government and educational institutions on leadership, talks about the importance in the Navy of leaders practising what he calls 'extreme delegation'. The Royal Navy practises extreme delegation because, in the chaos of combat, it has to trust the moment-by-moment decision-making of its people. It can do that because it's made sure that everyone knows the common purpose. Its people are missionaries, not mercenaries; they believe in what they are doing and what needs to be done.

Sometimes organizations are naturally closer to their customers; that helps the link between the greater purpose and the purpose of what people do. Justine Roberts, founder of Mumsnet, the online parenting forum, says, 'Our purpose always came from the user base – we were driven by them.'

Purpose is a clear North Star; it provides consistent guidance in fast-moving times to allow greater autonomous decision-making. 'It's important to create a business which is anchored in very strong foundations – clarity and leadership and consistency,' says Unilever's Polman.

Purpose actually frees employees. Rather than restricting them, it liberates them to achieve greater things, providing a framework for innovation and creativity that drive a business forward. With clarity of purpose, you are more able to run the business 'tight and loose'. It is a framework, a foundation and a filter which then means that your teams and your people can act in an agile, lean way, fully empowered to make decisions fast.

> Having a clear sense of purpose provides a great foundation for ideas and a fantastic filter for success.

Making it happen: putting purpose into practice

Here is a perfect example of where you need to slow down to speed up. Articulating your purpose and getting the culture to move behind it is not something that can be done instantly. Unilever's Paul Polman admits that: 'We spent a long time creating a sense of purpose.' It's key to defining your organization's 'brand', so you need to find ways to articulate it which is true and credible, based on past associations, current reality and future aspirations. It needs to be credible, it needs to be appealing to employees, customers and potential partners, but it also needs to be clear and differentiated. (Wishy-washy words are dangerous and forgettable, and you don't want to express your brand in the same way as other people.)

What does your organization do to help people? What is the difference you're seeking to make in the lives of customers and consumers? Why is it good to be part of what you do? How do you define this in a memorable and compelling way?

Your response needs to be authentic and based on the truth about what you do and why it matters to your audiences. Developing the definition of this should be done with care and insight. To be credible, a purpose statement needs to be based on the truth. To make it distinctive, differentiated and ownable, it's useful to understand the organization and what's happened in the past.

Sara Bennison gives a valuable insight into this, learned from her work repositioning the Nationwide via a beautifully simple statement that captured in shorthand the desire for the organization to go back to its roots as a 'building society', a trustworthy, community-based alternative to banks that helps support people and society at every level everywhere. The CMO of Nationwide Building Society loves words. Highly articulate, Bennison is (like so many of the interviewees in this book) a prodigious reader and a sharp, smart communicator. She is also an extremely fast thinker: throw a difficult question at her and she parries it with ease; send a financial document over and she'll devour it at speed. She recognizes, however, that getting to the point of really understanding an organization's brand and defining its purpose is a slower process:

> The interesting bit is the bit that you put into the recipe which is not the same as other 'cooks'. Everyone else has got a futurologist telling them what the big trends are that are on the horizon. Everyone else has got the same regulatory pressure, the same digital transformation agenda, the same cost/income issues in the area that we're operating in. The important thing is to ask what's different. So, why were you founded, what was your original purpose, what's the nature of individuals who run it and shape the culture? All of these things are unique and precious.

> Nationwide's mission statement is simply 'Building Society, Nationwide', which is intended to 'pull together our past, our present, and our future'.

If your company's purpose is complicated, convoluted or packed with corporate speak, you can't expect your employees to be able to embody it. It needs to be understandable and it needs to be tangible and real, inspiring your people to build the business's reputation and drive the customer experiences that build brand loyalty and growth.

Airbnb: uncovering a mission statement

Airbnb, the hyper-growth business, started work on redefining their brand purpose 'to better articulate the elements that made using its platform so unique'. The company's new global head of community, Douglas Atkin, posed some probing questions about Airbnb, such as 'Why does Airbnb exist?' and 'What's its role in the world?' The company started out by listening, getting closer to understanding its audience. Interviews conducted internally and externally with employees, guests and hosts around the world found a consistent insight: 'The last thing guests want to be is tourists.' Instead of being visitors and tourists, Airbnb customers want to be 'insiders' who are engaged with the people and cultures of the places they are visiting. This human need is matched with a real truth about the brand offer – it offers 'hosts' who open up their homes, rather than just physical houses or apartments to rent.

The idea of 'belonging' began to emerge, and within a few months a new mission statement was finalized: 'To make people around the world feel like they could "belong anywhere".' This 'belonging' positioning has informed communications (of course) but also acts as a filter for product development, leading to the ground-breaking 'Trips' offer for Airbnb.

It was a process which was informed by Airbnb listening to its customers, and this then informed its decisions about what to share with its customers and filtered and focused the new product developments.

How do you articulate your purpose and align people behind it?

If you want to create an organization which is purpose-driven at every level, a 'mission statement' on a wall won't cut it. You need to put something in place that sticks. These are the six crucial steps to turning purpose into practice which the Caffeine Partnership follow in helping organizations to define their purpose and align the organization behind it:

- **Establish clear governance at a senior level.** This is critical. Purpose is not a marketing add-on or a sticking plaster. It should be hard-wired into leadership thinking and everything that the leaders in the organization do.

- **Follow an insight-in, inside-out approach.** Leaders need to find the best of a company's culture and the truths which come from inside-out. They also need to look at bringing insights in, bringing in the understanding of what the future opportunity is for consumer or customer growth.
- **Know your purpose.** Focus on 'what matters most' to the customer and define a purpose that transforms positively the customer's experience and the world in which they live.
- **Focus ruthlessly on the key strategic priorities.** These are the ones that drive the greatest return for both the customer and company in line with the purpose. Focus on doing the things that matter most to the customer and excelling at those, rather than trying to be good at everything. (See Chapter 5: Editing is expediting.)
- **Engage everyone emotionally.** Everyone inside the organization feels pride and a sense of common purpose, and feels empowered to act in accordance with it, making daily decisions based on it.
- **Track success.** Measure understanding, engagement and impact, and link these to the most important business metrics.

Here's Unruly's CEO, Sarah Wood, on what to actually do with your purpose:

There's no point having a guiding purpose if you don't stick to it. Everything you do should be in some way contributing to both your personal leadership mission and the mission of the business you run. Use mission as a benchmark for the decisions you make and the actions you prioritize. The purpose you set for yourself and your team should be the lens through which you view:

- which clients to take on

- which products to build and

- how you work together as a team.

Keep asking yourself: 'Does this feed into the mission? Does this help take us closer to where we want to be?' And if the answers are no, you probably need to start reconsidering.

> Take a stand, today and for the long term.

Andy Milligan and Shaun Smith in *On Purpose* articulate the three defining features of successful organizations that are bold, purpose-driven brands:

- **Stand up:** Purposeful brands have a clear sense of who they are and *why* they exist. They stand for something beyond making a profit.
- **Stand out:** They are different from competitors in some meaningful way that creates value for customers. They are intentional in delivering their purpose via their customer experience across multiple channels.
- **Stand firm:** They create cultures that sustain them and continually innovate to stay ahead.

And it's the last point that is about creating something that will endure over time. Getting the culture right, the habits and rituals which support your purpose, that's what will allow you to move faster over time. But, as Nicola Mendelsohn, EMEA Facebook VP, says: 'Culture is like a garden. You can't just plant something and hope for the best. You need to nurture it, feed it, take out weeds, water it – and then you will see it grow and flourish.'

This is where leaders need patience – building a business for the long term requires commitment to making sure that your purpose isn't just a poster on a wall but is authentic and real, and to building a culture that makes it happen. As Antony Jenkins puts it: 'Purpose is not an add-on, it's not an initiative. It is a culture change and it never finishes.'

Espresso takeaways

Define it. Love it. Live it.

'Purpose' is your long-term vision for your business: what it does to make a difference. It connects to individual employees to help them understand 'why' and how they contribute.

A sense of purpose helps protect for the long term, and it helps accelerate your organization in the short term. It acts as both the foundation for the future and the 'filter' and focus for the immediate prioritization challenges you face.

Purpose gives employees and customers something beyond a product and an opportunity to consume or work for money. It's about being part of something larger. It will attract, motivate and energize your people, simplify decision-making at speed, and allow an empowered, lean and agile leadership approach.

If you want to drive pace consistently and positively across the organization, start with this:

DEFINE

IT: Get a team together to define a credible articulation of where you are going and your role in the world. Make it true, relevant and clear. Give people the destination to aim for.

LOVE

IT: Articulate it as clearly and compellingly as possible. You may turn it into a 'story' that engages – it may drive your internal communications (and your external ones) – but do it in a way which is crystal clear using human and direct language and which builds on the truth about the people you want to believe in this … your people and your customers.

LIVE

IT: Understand and define your purpose. Communicate it relentlessly, consistently and authentically – it should be part of everything you do and should help you decide what you don't do. Make sure that your senior leaders buy into this and can share and live it too.

Make sure this moves far beyond communication. It is about much more than what you *say*. It is about what you *do* and about how you *behave*; it is about how you attract, retain and motivate; how you make high-velocity decisions, and how you unify silos, individuals, projects and the business behind a purpose beyond just making profit.

4

Structure for speed

Fast frameworks

'You need to be good at quickly recognizing and correcting bad decisions. If you're good at course correcting, being wrong may be less costly than you think, whereas being slow is going to be expensive for sure.'

Jeff Bezos, founder, Chair and
Chief Executive Officer of Amazon

If you want to go fast, you must fashion the right vehicle.

Structure, framework, layers, organizational design, team design … your speed will be helped or hindered by the shape and way in which your company, squad or team is set up. There are many different ways to look at making it faster – from formal delayering in the overall structure to overcoming silos, from squads to 'jet skis'. Questioning, reviewing and being decisive about what the right structure is for your needs can be one of the most influential acts you take as a leader.

In business, sometimes working with 'the default settings' is the easy and smart option. Not here. The structure you choose for your team or your company should always be sharply questioned. Speed is contextual and choosing the right vehicle depends on the length of your journey, your ultimate destination and what kind of bumps and accidents you are prepared to tolerate getting to there. Getting one which is right for you and for your situation requires analysis, clever thinking and (frequently) a dose of courage.

Why does the structure matter?

A smart structure drives precision of roles and responsibilities. It allows debate and analysis, input and support, without too much discussion and insufficient decision-making. Here are three considerations when setting up the optimal structures for speed and success:

1 Reducing the chain of command will increase your pace. An excessive number of decision-makers and other people who have to be consulted and have an input will be a highly effective speed-killer. If you were appointed as an undercover saboteur in an organization, working to destroy it from within, then one of your best moves would be to increase the number of sign-off

levels. (Making the chain of decision-makers slightly unclear would be another method.)

2 Great ideas are completely worthless without the ability to make them happen. When talking about making an organization more innovative, many people fixate on the creation of ideas, but it is as important to make sure that you can make them happen. You need a structure that brings intentions to life, that makes your great theories something your customers, clients or consumers will actually see.

3 If you need to move in a different direction, you do it by creating a different vehicle. Finding structural ways to think differently to stimulate and promote speed is key for change and acceleration.

And one last point: these types of vehicle are not 'autonomous drive'.

> The right structure requires the right people in the right environment to deliver.

Consider how you will structure to deliver a) serendipity, b) sharing and c) stimulation:

- The serendipity of different people, different mindsets sparking off each other
- The ability to communicate and work together by sharing easily
- The stimulation of ideas, learning, different perspectives.

If you want to move at a good speed, you need enough opportunities for different thinking and the right diversity of input to increase the number and quality of ideas ...

A smart vehicle also allows great communication, fast. Bigger organizations risk the 'silo effect' where parts of the organization work in isolated or independent ways from each other, reducing the opportunities for efficiency and cross-fertilization of ideas.

They don't communicate or communicate slowly, so you find examples of different people in different parts of the organization realizing that they are either working on the same projects at the same time or missing opportunities for the connectivity of ideas. The slow-moving nature of a big siloed organization makes it highly vulnerable to the energy of leaner, faster start-ups that work more collaboratively. Sam Altman, the founder of Y Combinator, the tech accelerator, advises entrepreneurs: 'Move fast. Speed is one of your main advantages over large competitors.'

The chief designer of Tesla, Franz von Holzhausen, cites good communication as essential to its competitive advantage. 'Our communication allows us to move incredibly fast. That is an element that isn't happening in the rest of the automotive world. They are siloed organizations that take a long time to communicate.' Fewer people means faster interaction. The tendency of a fast-moving, fast-growing organization is to keep adding more people.

Gary Coombe from Procter & Gamble is cautious about the big organization's tendency to add more people. 'Traditionally when a problem needed to be solved, we hired someone or moved someone into a role. Now I always check first – is there an algorithm for that?' The rise in tech companies also allows more organizations to scale with smaller teams. WhatsApp was acquired by Facebook (with its 420 million monthly users) for $19 billion. At the time, the organization had only 35 engineers and 50 employees.

The danger with not having enough people on a project team? Burn-out or not enough resource to achieve the goals.
The danger of having too many? Never forget that 'social loafing' is an entirely human phenomenon.

Social loafing is the concept (or human reality) of how people are often likely to put less effort in if they are in a group versus when they work alone. Working in groups is so often seen as a way to improve the accomplishment of a task by pooling the skills and talents of the individuals in that group. But, in some groups, there is a tendency on the part of participants to contribute less to the group's goal than if they were doing the same task themselves.

This type of 'idle loafing' (conscious or subconscious) is more likely if you have:

- a large group – it's easier to hide lack of performance when there are ten of you
- a lack of motivation
- people with a reduced sense of the importance of their role.

A great example of the last is voting – people believing that their contribution doesn't make any impact and so they don't vote ...

You can reduce social loafing with smart high-performance team actions, but it's worth being aware of it as a danger in a 'fatter' (less lean) structure. It's also dependent on you choosing the right people. The advent of AI will change the shape of companies but, for most leaders reading this, the majority of the vehicles within your company aren't self-driving: people matter. Structuring for speed often isn't just about creating a leaner, lighter faster set-up but putting the right people in those vehicles so they can (in the expression of one enthusiastic senior leader I work with) 'drive it like they stole it'.

The 'teeth to butt' start-up evolution story

It's not just the big corporates that suffer from 'bloat' too easily.

Maureen Taylor is the founder and CEO of SNP Communications, a consultancy which has worked with Silicon Valley start-ups for years (and has worked with companies like Airbnb, Transferwise, Google and LinkedIn). She brilliantly illustrates what can happen as companies grow in the 'teeth to butt' story, as told to her by Joe DiNucci from SGI, right before the tech crash in the late 1990s. A vivacious American with Irish blood in her, Maureen is a spellbinding storyteller (and this is a moment where I wish there was video in this book to share the way in which she tells this but I'll capture the essence here). It's about how start-ups evolve and the impact that has on their size and their agility and hunger.

When successful start-ups start, they are lean and they are hungry. Their butt is small, their pace is phenomenal and their teeth are sharp and effective. They are wolves, a little wild, a little feral but – boy, that speed and the desire to kill!

They then have some success and they become more confident – a little sleeker, if you like. They become tigers – powerful, intimidating, still dangerous and with sharp teeth.

The start-up grows and all of a sudden its bottom, its butt … becomes a major part of the animal. You need more people, you need more structure, you are trying to move at pace, still, so you add more to the company – and before you know it, you're an elephant. Strong, big and with a big old butt. But the hunger? The teeth? They aren't part of the beast any more.

Finally, you reach hippo status. Yes, you're still dangerous (in fact, the hippo is the most dangerous animal) but you attack infrequently, you move slowly and you wallow. The lesson? Keep hungry and keep lean. Watch out for that ever-increasing 'butt' – when it gets big, you can't move fast.

Structural foundations: considerations

Here are three approaches to provoke your thinking about team, project or company structure:

- De-layer or delay: go flatter to go faster.
- Breakthrough to breakout: extra agility means extra ability.
- Create plus iterate: be set up to polish, pivot and perfect.

De-layer or delay

If you want to run faster, a flatter structure will help.

Much has been written and much can be read about the various structural changes people make to increase speed. Passionate evangelists for Holocracy or Teal will tell you they are 'the future of organizations'. They're worth exploring, considering and discussing, but for most leaders there are practical, fundamental changes which can be implemented relatively quickly and which don't require a complete reorganization or reinvention.

One of the most common actions that the senior leaders I spoke to used as an acceleration tool was simple 'de-layering'. Liv Garfield, the CEO of Severn Trent, is a typical example, and she explains her rationale thus:

> When you're trying to work out what's holding back pace, it's not always the people. There are often other 'blockers' to speed. One of the most effective things we've done is to de-layer this organization. There are now five layers from top to bottom. When I arrived there were ten. It makes for simpler, quicker decision-making.

She goes on to explain how they restructured to compensate for this change:

> We've removed five levels of management. So we invest in the front line. For the 500 people we moved, we put 100 more in the front line. The 400 people we took out were all managers which meant we ended up with a smaller HQ – which in itself is probably not a bad thing because bigger HQs inevitably end up creating more internal work. We reduced the decision-making layers while making the workload fair – and all our performance measures got dramatically better as a result.

Structuring for speed is about accelerating decision-making (and enhancing ownership). Alibaba's UK MD, Amee Chande, explains her perspective:

> When it comes to thinking about speed, you need to look at the micro and the macro. Going from moment to moment worrying that everything is changing fast is unproductive but looking at the macro level

you absolutely must make sure you have a structure which is organized to speed up decision-making.

> **A word of warning:** in business, as in life, every action has a consequence. De-layering is excellent for accelerating decision-making but be aware that there's a motivation impact on many employees. Alex Davison, MD of L'Oréal Active Cosmetics, says: 'Delayering is a reality across all workplaces, so this means we all need to think differently about "career progression" and be more imaginative about what it looks like. For some that might be about developing incredible depth of expertise in an area; for others it might be about collecting new and different experiences to continually learn and stay agile.'

Liv Garfield's experience of speed is echoed by Paul Polman, worldwide CEO of Unilever. He heads up a company which reaches 2.5 billion consumers a day in 190 countries and has 171,000 people worldwide working to support that. He vehemently believes that delayering within Unilever had a dramatically positive effect on their speed. 'You have to work your organizational structure to be faster, which means de-layering. In Unilever now we have five layers. That's it.'

The speed that he's talking about is, of course, not just generic 'speed' but that holy grail of the modern business world – agility:

You can't anticipate what will happen next, so what you need to do is be sure that your organization has a certain level of agility. Within Unilever that meant us creating three different business units and de-layering the organization; as a result, we are more decentralized, which reduces decision-making time.

A simpler structure can lead to great agility and responsiveness to what's happening outside the company. It also helps with internal communication and change.

This is in no way a quick fix for most organizations, though; change does not happen overnight. Polman remains realistic and pragmatic about how long it takes for organizations to change but appreciates that too many layers can slow that down further: 'In many companies, the top level implements something and thinks the rest of the company will behave, which is not true; it takes a long time.' He has an interesting rule of thumb: 'For every layer in the company, you will need a year to change the culture.'

De-layering critically ensures that 'the feedback loops' from the market and consumers are quicker. The Chinese whispers effect will be reduced. Polman comments:

> The world is getting more volatile everywhere so you need a structure which can pick up the signals, one which is very externally focused and agile. That's why we've de-layered and decentralized to the countries more within Unilever. It's us moving from being a supertanker to a speedboat.

The Mosquito: a story about creating a winning structure

FIGURE 4.1 The Mosquito

Adding more people to a team often feels like the way to get things done. But remember that fewer can mean faster. The advertising legend Dave Trott believes in 'less is more' when it comes to strategy and uses the story of the British Second World War bomber the Mosquito as a kind of parable for his philosophy. The Mosquito was originally the Lancaster, with a crew of seven and weighing a massive 16 tons when empty. It moved slowly, too – with an average speed of 245 miles per hour – because (the logic went) it needed defensive armour to survive any attack. The Americans also had a 16-ton beast: the B17 Flying Fortress. This needed a crew of ten. The German planes, by contrast, were over 100 miles per hour faster than any Allied bomber.

Then a British man named Geoffrey de Havilland came on the scene with a different idea. He thought about things from a different angle. As Trott explains: 'You needed a lot of guns for when the enemy attacked you, but what if the enemy couldn't catch you? What if the bomber was too fast for German fighter planes?'

From this insight came the de Havilland Mosquito. Instead of adding more and more things to defend it, de Havilland got rid of everything that made a bomber capable of defending itself. The guns were taken off the plane. To make it lighter, it was made of wood instead of metal. It needed only two engines because it was smaller. It needed a crew of only two because he had got rid of the guns, although it still carried a 4,000-pound bomb load like the bigger planes. He managed to get the weight down to just 7 tons, less than half the original weight. The Germans couldn't catch it.

This story is told as a clear example of how a strategic approach means making choices – getting rid of things in order to focus. Trott sums his idea up as 'Strategy is sacrifice'. Start with what the ultimate objective is. De Havilland realized that the objective wasn't to defend the aircraft from attack, it was to win the war. Are there other ways you can look at how you're structured? Can the agile Mosquito inspire you to be lighter and faster?

Breakthrough to breakout

You expect stories of fast innovation from companies like Facebook and Google. But HomeServe, a home repair and insurance company based in the West Midlands, UK, might seem a less likely candidate for speedy innovation success. Nonetheless, it conceived, tested and launched a ground-breaking innovation for the business in under 24 months. The ingenious 'Leakbot' is a smart water-leak detector designed to help tackle the UK's £800 million a year bill for repairing household damage from mains water leaks.

A zero-to-launch timing of 24 months is impressive for an organization which doesn't specialize in innovations, tech or new product development. Greg Reed, the CEO of Homeserve UK explained the secret to the success of this: it was all in a key structural decision.

Welcome to The Shed

The success of this innovation is particularly impressive when you understand the context of HomeServe's recent business experience. The company hit a significant setback in 2011 when it was fined £35 million for mis-selling. The organization has worked determinedly since then to radically transform its culture and the focus for success, but inevitably this type of issue led to a greater caution internally; they now have a 'huge safety net' to make sure that things don't go awry again.

Greg Reed talks about the challenge that presented: 'You have these huge safety nets and then you want to innovate and you say, "This is what we're going to do, we're going to move fast, we're going to be agile, we're going to do this thing", and then you try to get it through all these committees and through this governance.'

Greg and his then boss agreed on a 'breakout' solution:

> So we did it a little differently ... We created something called The Shed. People from my team went to another place; it even looked different. I let them paint it, it looks and feels different; it's got different furniture; it looks like you could be in another company. We gave them a compliance person, a software engineer, architects, a creative person. We co-located them and then we gave them a budget. We promised not to interfere with them.

Creating 'jet-skis' on the side of your supertanker, creating smaller, more agile 'mini companies', is a smart speed structural tool if you want things to happen fast. 'That's how they were able to get LeakBot done because they were able to really think in a different way and to act like a start-up.'

Looking at your structure to ensure it has the power to move fast is not just about the innovation accelerators, the speed-boats or the jet-skis. It's about making sure that your structure is smartly set up to allow independence within offers, either to help the customer or help maintain independent structures that can move at the requisite pace. This is one of the key reasons Google gave for its Alphabet restructure, why Facebook has kept Instagram and WhatsApp as resolutely separate brands and experiences, and why companies like Octopus have very different structural set-ups for its different sub-companies.

The temptation is to 'borrow' attributes across different parts of the organization from a brand perspective and from a structural perspective. But the difference that different companies bring to a big parent brand is in terms of both cultural and consumer benefits. WhatsApp and Instagram reach audiences which might be alienated by Facebook's conglomerated dominance so, despite the fact that their innovative approach might give a halo effect to Facebook, the opposite is true. If you are adopting an acquisition strategy to help your business move faster, be careful to make sure that you preserve the speed of your 'jet-skis'.

> Moving fast and moving smartly isn't just about making decisions and launching new things. Agility is not just speed and lightness of structure; it's about being able to flex quickly.
>
> Don't just focus on finishing something; focus on being ready to improve and evolve. How can you set up a structure which allows you to respond to reality once it's 'out there'? Can you 'test a little, learn a lot'? Can you reduce the time to market but increase the ability to flex once there?
>
> Creating a structure which allows you to polish, pivot and perfect means you reduce the stress of decision-making and increase the possibility of getting it right.

'FIRE BULLETS FIRST, THEN CANNONBALLS'

We've looked at Second World War bombers in this chapter; it's time to move on to warships. In Jim Collins's comprehensive research on companies that were more successful than others in turbulent times (*Great by Choice*), he argues strongly that the right approach is to 'fire bullets first, then cannon-balls'. Imagine, he says, you have a ship that's being attacked. You have a limited amount of gunpowder on board. If you panic and let off the cannonballs and they miss … you are screwed. The right approach is to try first with bullets. Yes, they'll have less of an effect but the power of the cannonball is useless if it doesn't hit the right spot. If you try first with the bullets, you can see how close you get to the target, each time, improving, improving, testing, discovering … until you know you have the right angle to hit the attacker and you can let loose your cannonball.

Finding ways to spend a little and learn a lot is the same approach. You need to do it fast, clearly, or the attacking ship will get you, but act fast and learn and you minimize the risk and maximize your chances of success. L'Oréal has adopted this approach. Alex Davison, managing director of L'Oréal's Active Cosmetics division, says its speed has been increased with this move towards learning on the go: 'Test and learn is the new perfection.'

Paul Polman from Unilever was inspired by a Procter & Gamble leader when he was younger, the legendary Durk Jager, whose favourite saying was 'I have spent a little and learned a lot.' Paul recognized that Durk was hidebound in his ambitions by his short tenure at Procter & Gamble, but the validity of this approach has stuck with Polman throughout his career: 'That sentence has always stuck in my mind and I try to implement it.' Polman's financial background may drive this prudence, but it's not just about the financial sense of testing first but also the question of, as he puts it, how to create 'a culture where debate gets very quickly translated into action … where there is, in a global company especially, some intermittent risk-taking of testing, not arguing …'

If you don't have the fearlessness to take risks in the super-tanker, you test quickly or you set up a less risky jet-ski on the side. Or you allow natural selection to take place in the marketplace and you buy up those who survive – like Unilever's acquisition of Dollar Shave Club or T2, the premium Australian tea company, or Facebook's acquisition of Instagram, or Google, which, in one estimate, has been acquiring a staggering one company a week since 2010 (including YouTube and Waze). In Dave Egger's satire on the dominance of the tech giants, *The Circle*, he includes a scene where a senior exec refers to the start-ups as 'plankton' lining up to be consumed by the big whales: there is a natural selection going on that many of the plankton intend from launch.

MOVE FAST, LEARN FAST

It isn't just unicorn start-ups that have the power to disrupt the business world. Cedric Donck, entrepreneur and business angel, is here commenting on the beast that is IBM:

> Everyone is always talking about Amazon or Zalando, but some conventional companies have been engaging in disruptive innovation for decades. IBM sold mainframe computers in the 1970s and personal computers in the 1980s and 1990s. After that they moved to consulting. In the next four years they will be investing 1 billion euros in the artificial intelligence of their supercomputer Watson. IBM is sometimes considered a dinosaur, but that's not the case: it's a company that reinvents itself every ten years.

When Paul Polman became global CEO of Unilever, he focused quickly on looking at trade stock because he knew that 'you have to create a business model that helps you to be faster in the market'. He moved to make sure that the company was in a position to run different models to allow agility and to cross-fertilize ideas:

And then it's important to give people the opportunity to test things, I always find. I ask them, 'What are you testing? What are you learning? What is in the marketplace?' But it's difficult because people don't like to fail; it's still a risk when you're associated with doing something new. You have all these elements in that. You have to have a culture of intermittent risk-taking, with a fast feedback loop.

Whether you are risking your life savings to find out what works or whether you can persuade your organization to run a rapid beta test, the only unifying factor here is the bias towards action. You don't know whether something will or won't work until it's in front of the audience.

Amazon's Bezos talks often about the importance of being skilled at rapid course correction: 'You need to be good at quickly recognizing and correcting bad decisions. If you're good at course correcting, being wrong may be less costly than you think, whereas being slow is going to be expensive for sure.'

The answer comes from the customer but they won't ask for it. Research can give you some indication but research itself will never tell you the answer you need to hear. An amazing planner I worked with in my first job, a woman called Martine Marchand-Mader, had a fabulous French accent and a particularly original mix of cynicism and passionate enthusiasm. She once explained clearly and memorably to me the limits of asking consumers for the answer: 'Darlink. You don't ask a chicken how'e wants to be cooked.'

You will know stories like the one about the ATM machine, which was an innovation that completely bombed in research with consumers. Anything too different needs time and trial to work. Get the customer insights to inform what you do but don't use them to stop you making brave decisions. Make it, test it in action, learn quickly.

LISTEN, LEARN, ADAPT

Beta testing is the model used in software development which has proved helpful in developing the 'testing a little, learning a lot' concept. Otherwise known as 'user acceptance testing', it's the way to get the product out and get feedback before total launch. Outside the software world, companies like Procter & Gamble and Unilever used to do the same with a test market in a geographical region. In today's world, these test markets feel slow and unwieldy as it takes too long for the data to come in. The faster-moving world is therefore pushing companies to take bolder risks.

The truth is that, no matter how 'close' we feel to our customers/consumers or clients, we can't accurately predict how they will respond until something is in market, especially if it is new and different. We need to find ways to test something out and learn from it. It doesn't have to take for ever – Google Venture's 'Sprints', as pioneered by Jake Knapp, are week-long 'ideahacks' which use injections of consumer input to help them iterate an idea quickly. This speeds up the process of idea development dramatically – and always features consumer insight as part of what is included.

The power of three

Consider a 'triumvirate' to head up teams or organizations. In ancient Rome there were at times three people in power: a triumvirate. The Roman Senate engineered two restructurings that created triumvirates to resolve personality conflicts among pretenders to the throne. The first comprised Julius Caesar, Pompey and Crassus, and then, many years later, Octavian, Mark Antony and Lepidus. Both attempts were utter failures that led to war.

In business, however, this model can work well. Three can be a magic number.

Sara Tate, now CEO of TBWA, was Managing Director of Mother London for a while and was very positive about its unique triumvirate that headed up Accounts – she says it allowed for great debate and discussion. Adam Balon, Richard Reed and Jon Wright, who founded Innocent together, are also positive about having three in charge. Adam cites this as a real secret to their success:

> I am in awe of people who launch stuff on their own. There is no way I could have done that; I do not think the others could have either. We bring different things from different perspectives to it, which helps the business – there's a blend of skills. But the other thing is just the emotional support you get because you could be having a bad day and thinking this is never going to work, we are never going to get this off the ground, but one of you has had a result and you have found a wholesaler that is really going to fly and he is coming in, and so you get that balance basically. If you are doing it on your own, you are going to do it all in your own head, which is almost impossible. Some people do it but we would not be able to do it. So, actually flipping to where we are now, as investors, we look for teams. It is very rare occasions when it is all about one person. Actually, we look for teams and that is our learning influence.
>
> Three is a great number. Because you've often got one person with a very strong opinion here, one person with a strong opinion here, and someone who comes around who doesn't feel that strongly but could kind of see the middle ground. It's much easier for us than two. It's a triangle; it's a very specific sort of shape, actually. The best handbooks say you shouldn't have a three-headed leadership, you know that's a terrible thing, you want one person accountable, but actually it really worked for us.

Google's senior management is a triumvirate as well – Page, Brin and Schmidt, who bring different perspectives but have shared values and mutual respect.

Iterate and evolve

There are a number of structural models which companies have adopted to help speed up their approach to get things to market and to constantly iterate. Many involve accelerating the insight from the product or the customer experience to the decision-making person. Alibaba, the world's largest retailer, is hyper-aware that this is a challenge with a big organization. Jack Ma, the co-founder and Executive Chair, promotes an internal culture where the management should 'make friends with the guys testing the product' because, of course, as the UK MD Amee Chande says, 'the worry is that in some ways the more senior you are, the less likely you are to make the right decisions – who is actually touching the code? How close are you to the engineers? You need to walk over there, find it out, get it done.'

Lean start-ups and tech companies have embraced a more iterative approach as a fundamental part of their culture. Where it's becoming more interesting is where this pivot-and-polish thinking begins to infect every part of the business mix: where GV – Google's investment arm – uses its week-long 'sprint' to work on communication plans as well as product development, where general decisions are made with an eye on how they can be reversed or reviewed quickly.

Clearly, this is more possible with some decisions than others. If you run a multibillion-dollar consumer goods company and your decision involves capital investment and the lives of many employees, you can't treat it with the same relaxed attitude as a decision about a new button on a social network. The publisher for this book pointed out charmingly that it was worth taking the time to get this book right as it's not a beta-software launch that can be edited and tweaked once published. However, the principle of building in feedback loops to make sure that you can improve and iterate, and find ways to make decisions as flexible as possible, is a smart and solid consideration – not just to take away the stress of decision-making but to make sure that you can continue to improve what you are offering to your audience.

If you're finding your structure slow to get to market or slow to respond to the feedback loops, it's worth seeing how it can be altered to improve its 'loops'. Technology is the answer for many on this.

Anne Boden, founder of fintech disruptor Starling Bank, moved from the big corporate world to the fast-paced full-on world of working to set up a mobile bank from scratch. She believes strongly in the agile structural approach Starling adopts and the way in which technology supports that:

> What makes Starling stand out is that, unlike any of the big banks, we are entirely situated in the cloud. We are essentially a technology company that has banking as a product. So, for us, that means that technology and implementation of technology run throughout the entire company rather than acting as a support function to the business. Most legacy banks, by contrast, treat technology as a cost centre. The trends there are all around cutting costs while spending more on middle management and on offshore teams. That's a false economy and we are challenging that model by keeping technology at the core of the business.

As she points out, 'these great tools are all something like five years old; we are doing things you just couldn't do a few years ago.' The tools and visibility can turn work on its head:

> Everything we do is all about visibility and seeing the process and having very clear schedules of what we're going to do today. So traditionally people have figured out: 'We need this work to be done. We'll break it down into how many days we need and we'll figure out how long it's going to take.' We do the opposite.

In the film *The Social Network*, Aaron Sorkin's sprightly 'story' of Mark Zuckerberg's chequered start with Facebook, he uses the morally ambiguous risk-taker Sean Parker character to lure Zuckerberg into aiming for something that's 'cooler than a million-dollar valuation': 'And that's where you're headed, a billion-dollar valuation. When you go fishing you can catch a lot of fish or you can catch a big fish. You ever see a guy in a den standing next to fourteen trout?' However, the truth is that there are plenty of organizations which make a lot of money and live well on a variety of smaller fish.

The attractive allure of the entrepreneurial world is that those big fish are such powerful stories: the billion-dollar acquisition of Dollar Shave Club in 2016 after only three years and with no profit or the $19-billion acquisition of WhatsApp in 2014, with only 52 people and with a $50 million annual revenue, which would need to be increased a hundredfold to hit the valuation of the deal. The speed trajectory of such stories is intoxicating for those who want to move fast − and it inspires people to believe that moving fast is possible. Which it is. But an evolving, test-and-learn set-up means that everyone can believe it is possible to grow, bit by bit, learning as you go.

> Structure it right. De-layer and break out; create, iterate, evolve. Set up a framework which will help everyone move fast.

A final story about structure

'When time is of the essence − play, prototype, pivot.'

Lessons from the Marshmallow Man

Tom Wujec, an innovation expert and pioneer in business visualization, was interested in understanding more about how senior leaders work together and how they innovate. To help his understanding, he used the 'Marshmallow Challenge', which was devised by designer Peter Skillman.

In 18 minutes (the time a TED talk takes), teams of four are asked to build the tallest freestanding structure out of

20 sticks of spaghetti, 1 yard of tape, 1 yard of string and one marshmallow. The marshmallow must be on top.

It seems simple but it's hard; it forces people to collaborate very quickly; it's a great way to discover personal lessons on how you innovate. Having run over 70 of these challenges with designers, architects, students and Fortune 50 leadership teams, Wujec made some interesting observations. The worst-performing groups of people were those who'd just got their MBAs. School-age kids, by contrast, were among the best-performing groups. Their spaghetti and marshmallow structures averaged almost three times the height of the recent business school graduates.

Why did the kids do so much better?

They started trying to build a structure straight away; they tested, they tried, they learned quickly. There was no hesitation. They didn't hold back because they were worried about getting it wrong.

Meanwhile, the MBAs discussed plans and assigned roles and responsibilities. In business, we are educated to create a single right plan, then execute it. But by the time the business school graduates executed their plan, they'd spent all their time planning and had no time to fix it when it failed. Time and again, Wujec saw people carefully drawing up plans, debating and then trying to put the marshmallow on the top with a 'ta-da' (which quickly became an 'uh-oh' moment instead). The kids worked differently – they play, they create prototypes as they go.

So whatever your structure, creating a set-up that encourages speed of trial, play and getting stuck in will get you there faster.

A **side note:** this experiment also produced interesting skill diversity findings. The tallest structures
were normally built by engineers and architects,
who are specialists in this area, so you'd expect this
to be the case. CEOs do a bit better than average,
but, interestingly, Wujec found that if an executive
administrator worked with the CEOS they always
did better: 'Any team member who pays close
attention to the process of work – encouraging
timing, improving communication, cross-pollinat-
ing ideas – increases the team's performance significantly.' Make sure that you include the right
people in your team to accelerate the progress of
the work as well as setting the direction.

Espresso takeaways

Check your structure

If you are having a problem with speed, check whether it's the people or the process. A structure which slows down ideas and action is far too easy to create.

ASSESS YOUR STRUCTURE FOR SUCCESS

1 Fashion your vehicle to achieve the results you need. Think of your team or organization structure as a vehicle. In general, light and lean will create speed.
2 Delete levels to reduce decision-making delays. Layers make things long-winded.
3 Consider how you might vary your vehicles. Create Mosquitos that fly fast or make sure that you have jet-skis on the side.

SPEED UP YOUR STRUCTURE

4 Allow the front line to be empowered – they can see what needs to be done.
5 Use technology to drive visibility as part of the structure to help give you pace.
6 Consider how sparks fly – look at anti-silo thinking, the serendipity of different perspectives and the power of diverse thinking.

7 Create an action bias and the confidence of trial (either by making fast testing easier – using beta testing or sprints, for example – or by creating the confidence that the biggest risk is inaction).

CREATE AND MAINTAIN STRUCTURES WHICH EVOLVE, ITERATE AND CAN PIVOT EASILY

8 Consider what happens if you turn the thinking around from 'What can we do to reduce the risk before we launch/try?' to ask 'How can we be set up to respond quickly to improve when we do?'

9 Build in immediate, responsive feedback loops.

10 If you're acquiring new companies, work out how to preserve their speedy structure.

5

Editing is expediting

The 'less' lesson of Superfast

'The first draft of anything is shit.'

Ernest Hemingway,
American writer

Many successful authors will tell you that it's the *editing* of their work that's the tough bit. The same is unequivocally true in business. Editing means cutting out some of what you've done or want to say. It's about simplification and sharpening. Focusing on less is a radical way to make you better and to make you faster.

To better lead at speed, you must become an effective editor. You have to learn to expedite processes, edit plans, edit schedules, edit communications. Cut things out. Eliminate. Prune. Prioritize. Curate. Choose. All these incisive verbs are relevant here.

Generating ideas is not the hardest part of business. It's patiently, persistently pruning those ideas and then pursuing them with a relentless discipline ... and it's this that will give you success.

A great leader needs to be a great editor. This chapter is a lesson in less.

Why is 'the edit' so important?

1 A more minimalist approach inspires confidence.
2 It takes away distractions and drives up discipline.
3 It reduces the 'brain-load' for others. Make things simple, memorable and easy for people to focus on what action is needed.

These three things will expedite your success. Let's look at each in turn.

Why edit? A more minimalist approach inspires confidence

Have you ever noticed that the most expensive shops frequently have little in them? Luxury is often about scarcity – and space. The talented Middle East-based creative director Steve Harris once told me the one secret of creating a luxury or premium look in communications: 'Put plenty of space in.' You need to give room for the visuals and words to breathe, create space around the logo, create a look where there is less. This is how to make something feel premium. Focus on less. It implies great confidence.

A smartly edited business approach can equally be extremely powerful. It shows confidence to your team, your investors and shareholders, and to the market. It is a sign of great decisiveness, which is a surprisingly rare and precious attribute in a leader. When Gary Coombe took over as president of Procter & Gamble Europe, the business was (in his words) 'stuttering' a little. Around the time of his move into the role, Procter & Gamble announced the sale of its beauty business to Coty because it wanted a simpler, nimbler organization. This was a dramatic move after years driving the beauty business. As a shareholder in the business, I watch what they do carefully. It was the first thing I'd seen in a while that felt bold and brave. And surprising – to divest their business in order to achieve growth.

Gary and the European Procter & Gamble teams applied the same rigour and ruthless editing approach to looking at the European portfolio of brands. Within 18 months the organization cut down its number of SKUs (stock keeping units/products including variants) by 30 per cent, including selling off non-core businesses like Pringles. It focused in on its strengths and simplified the offer to consumers, significantly improving profitability and growth. To walk away from having more, to prune down your offer, is a bold and confident move.

It's not just about editing your products (which may or may not be right for you); it should also be about editing your plans and priorities. If something is classified as a priority, someone has made a choice that it takes precedence in rank of importance or urgency. There are plenty of organizations where people feel that 'everything is a priority'. This is a dangerous brake on progress.

Always check with your teams, with your people – are they crystal clear on the organization's priorities? Whichever acronym-laden model you use to share your strategy (e.g. your OGSMs – Objectives, Goals, Strategies, Measures – or VMOST – Visions, Mission, Objectives, Strategies, Tactics), can your people actually articulate the priorities themselves in their own words – do they understand what is most important? 'If we do nothing else this year, we *must* …' And are they being measured on what's important? What gets measured is what gets done.

It would, of course, be somewhat unnatural to look at this idea of 'editing' in business without referring to Steve Jobs. Jobs was a supreme editor. This was beautifully demonstrated when he returned to Apple in 1997. The organization he'd founded was then on the brink of failure. Sales in the final quarter of the previous year had plummeted 30 per cent. *Fortune* magazine described the organization at the time thus:

> Apple Computer, Silicon Valley's paragon of dysfunctional management and fumbled techno-dreams, is back in crisis mode, scrambling lugubriously in slow motion to deal with imploding sales, a floundering technology strategy, and a hemorrhaging brand name.

Jobs very quickly reduced the number of products by an incredible 70 per cent. He had to hold his nerve – in the year after he took over, the company still lost $1.04 billion and was, in Jobs's own words, '90 days from being insolvent'. But the rigorous reorganization paid off and the following year the company posted a profit of $309 million.

Jobs was a bold, brave editor – someone who knew that it was about choices, that it was about less. He was someone who said: 'Deciding what not to do is as important as deciding what to do. It's true for companies, and it's true for products.' That type of decisive action is supremely confident and requires chutzpah and conviction. Leaders who make choices about what they *won't* do are worthy of respect. 'People think focus means saying yes to the thing you've got to focus on,' Steve Jobs told writer Walter Isaacson, 'but that's not what it means at all. It means saying no to the hundred other good ideas that are out there. You've got to pick carefully.'

Don't just look at your business to look at what you will do to make it grow; be clear on what you choose not to do. Removal makes what's left incredibly strong, punchy and powerful. Taking something out highlights what's left in so it's absolutely clear to everyone.

This is also a rule for negotiation. When preparing your 'reasons' in negotiating a point, expert negotiation consultants Scotworks teach you to choose fewer arguments. Including weaker arguments in a case dilutes the power of the strongest ones. So it is in all communications: editing down to the best and most important makes it more likely that that those communication points will connect and be effective and remembered.

Deciding what you should focus on requires time and discipline – annual business planning processes, long and short-term vision setting, strategic overviews – but once that time has been invested you will achieve greater speed. Time, money and resources are all finite and need to be deployed wisely and well. Help your team by making the choices around 'what' so that that they can focus more on the 'how'. Help yourself and your profile by showing decisiveness and focus.

> Be confident. Show your confidence. Be a chooser.
> Be a curator. Edit.

Why edit? It takes away distractions and drives up discipline

A better-edited business creates momentum because you are creating fewer distractions internally. This allows people to obsess about quality and hone the execution, focusing on what their client, customer or consumer needs rather than internal management, as they struggle to deal with a million different priorities and distractions. The tighter the edit, the more you take away the 'excuses' from people because you aren't asking them to do too much.

> Being clear on what the priorities are also helps manage the scattergun optimism of individuals.

In a world where 'innovation' is the most overused aspiration of every business leader, the idea of not pursuing new and shiny ideas is really tough. Take it from the man who's 'shaved lives', Will King, who founded King of Shaves in 1993, the UK's highly regarded challenger brand. In 2014 he stepped down from his CEO role and now advises other entrepreneurs (moving to being a 'Kingmaker'). Part of his role is always to help people to make sure they keep the focus on 'the main thing':

> I work with other people, I want them to be great. Mainly what they need is help with their focus. It's a singularity thing. It's concentrating on what you've got to do. You have what's a singularity of purpose, or as Mohammed Ali would say, a singularity of greatness. Now, you think it's very hard to be truly great at one thing. Actually, it's really easy to be truly great at one thing. You just need to be truly great at one thing and make sure it's one thing only. I'm working with the CEO of Pavegen – people-powered payments. He needs to focus on Pavegen being the Tesla of people power. That's what he needs to do. Not get distracted by all the other stuff he gets distracted by. Just do that. Just keep walking.

Focusing is a confident approach. Andrew S. Grove, the founder and CEO of Intel and semiconductor pioneer, explained his philosophy of confident choice: 'I tend to believe Mark Twain hit it on the head when he said, 'Put all of your eggs in one basket and WATCH THAT BASKET.'

If you focus on fewer things, you can focus on evolving them, on practising and perfecting. John Zeratsky, designer at GC (Google's start-up venture fund) and co-creator of its sprint process, is inspired by the idea of 'reps' to practise and improve designs and products:

> A few years ago I saw Mike Kriege, co-founder of Instagram, speak at a conference in San Francisco. I'll never forget what he said. During the early days of Instagram, he and Kevin Systrom built a new prototype every week. Each weekend, they'd install the prototype app on their phones and share it with beta users. They'd use it all weekend, and then on Monday, begin work on an improved prototype for the next weekend.
>
> You already know how the story ends: Instagram became one of the most successful mobile apps of all time. It's not a coincidence that they got there by getting in lots of reps.
>
> What does it mean to 'get in reps'? It's shorthand for the idea of structured learning through repetition. Think of a musician doing scales, or a basketball player practising shots, or a software designer testing a prototype and fixing the problems. Simply putting in the time is not enough. To truly learn, you need to structure your 'reps' with a clear goal, feedback, and a chance to try again.

If you focus on fewer things, you have the space and time to get them right. Sam Altman, the serial entrepreneur, Co-Chair of Open AI with Elon Musk and president of Y Combinator, knows a lot about what works for entrepreneurs. His advice is to 'stay focused and don't try to do too many things at once. Care about execution quality.' To really deliver, leaders must make choices. Once you've made them, stay focused.

Explorations are allowed, though, as part of this. This isn't to say that you must keep focused only on the big prizes. It's likely that you will want to explore possible new product development or options for sister businesses. It is likely that these will be part of your strategy and choices generally. But it's smart to work out how to avoid all the new shiny ideas that take up time, money and attention in your organization. Mark Parker has, since 2006, been CEO of Nike Inc., an organization he describes as rich in ideas. A great problem to have, you'd assume. Ideas are great but making them happen is the challenge. At one stage in the organization he noticed that there were 350 initiatives R&D was working on; he whittled that down to 50. It's a matter of numbers. You can't prioritize everything. Someone has to be the editor, the curator, the simplifier. As Parker puts it: 'The ability to edit and amplify is so critical.'

The complication is that you need to work out how you can explore the viability of options without throwing all your cash and brains at the wrong idea. Within a focused framework, you can still experiment and explore a myriad of options. So, if you are exploring innovations, for example, you will need to try a few different things. And sometimes you need to throw a few things at a wall to see which ones stick (like cooked pasta). Choosing to have some experiments is a choice in itself. Having hundreds of different untested initiatives is just clutter.

You may choose to have a Moonshots fund like Google. You may choose to have a VC fund and invest in a number of start-ups like the data company dunnhumby (which can explore at minimal risk and learn while doing it). You may decide to develop to MVP stage a number of different initiatives. However, be constantly aware that people, focus and money are finite. So what's the trick? Make these areas ones where you can test and learn with the minimum risk before putting all your focus and financial firepower against them.

When we are working out how to move at a smart pace, we know we need to take risks but judging when it's right to do so requires testing and learning.

> Do less and invest less to start with, as you learn.

Pots of practice

Choosing to focus on less does not necessarily mean going slowly or necessarily producing less. In the tech world, many people cite the following story as an argument in favour of doing a lot (the story was originally from a book called *Art and Fear* by David and Ted Orland).

The ceramics teacher announced that he was dividing his class into two groups.

All those on the left side of the studio, he said, would be graded solely on the quantity of work they produced, all those on the right solely on its quality. His procedure was simple: on the final day of class he would bring in his bathroom scales and weigh the work of the 'quantity' group: 50 pounds of pots rated an A, 40 pounds a B, and so on. Those being graded on 'quality', however, needed to produce only one pot – albeit a perfect one – to get an A.

Well, come grading time and a curious fact emerged: the works of highest quality were all produced by the group being graded for quantity. It seems that while the 'quantity' group was busily churning out piles of work – and learning from their mistakes – the 'quality' group had sat theorizing about perfection and in the end had little more to show for their efforts than grandiose theories and a pile of dead clay.

This story is used as a clear metaphor for the power of practice and the power of learning by doing. These are 'reps'. Some use it as a way of saying 'Try lots of things and some will work' but it is clearly a metaphor for focus. By doing the same thing repeatedly, we learn and we improve.

There was still a real simplicity in the task (the choice was simply to focus on pots). They'd edited the focus, not the output. The brief was simply 'lots of pots'.

So 'more' *is* more sometimes.

Why edit? It reduces the 'brain-load' for others

I'm repeatedly struck by how the cleverest people I know have an innate ability to make the complicated stunningly simple. Longer words, more waffle, 250 different projects – that's what we see from leaders who lack the confidence to edit their words and their plans. Simplicity is often incredibly beautiful. The calm minimalistic look allows you to focus on a few beautiful, important things. Simplicity also makes it easy for others to understand what to do.

Editing is hard, for you and your senior team, but it should be your consistent objective and approach. As the simplicity-obsessed Steve Jobs explained: 'Simple can be harder than complex: you have to work hard to get your thinking clean to make it simple. But it's worth it in the end because once you get there, you can move mountains.'

In our Superfast world, where the average person's brain is blitzed with messages from different sources from the moment they are awake, when they are balancing personal, political and professional worries every day, you'll always get a better result if you can give them less. Give them the edit.

> The art of simplicity is certainly not about dumbing-down. Albert Einstein got it just about right when he wrote: 'Everything should be made as simple as possible, but not simpler.' The trick is to boil down your ideas, thoughts, plans and so on to their purest expression but without sacrificing anything of their richness of meaning or implications.

In the 1980s John Sweller, who was researching problem solving, argued that learning could be improved by improving instructional design to reduce the 'cognitive load' in learners. Cognitive load is a phrase used to refer to the amount of effort used in working memory – that is, the effort the brain needs to go through to understand and process. Think of cognitive load as the total amount of mental effort that's used in our working memory.

In *How to Have a Good Day*, the behavioural economist Caroline Webb explains more about the way our brain is divided up:

> The brain's activity is split across two complementary systems: one deliberate and controlled, the other automatic and instinctive. The *deliberate system* is responsible for sophisticated, conscious functions such as reasoning, self-control, and forward thinking. It can only do one thing at a time and tires remarkably quickly. The brain's *automatic* system lightens this load by automating most of what we do from day to day, but as the brain's deliberate system becomes more exhausted, the automatic system increasingly takes the reins, leaving us prone to making misleading generalizations and kneejerk responses.

The 'deliberate system' that allows forward thinking without misleading generalizations must be looked after if you are a busy leader. Reducing the complexity of messaging or the tasks you need to do means that your brain will be less tired and can tackle what is important.

Think complex, speak simple

Great oration through effective editing has a history that reaches back across time. Maureen Taylor, CEO of SNP, a global communications company, works with the leaders of highly futuristic tech companies like Airbnb, Google, LinkedIn and Transferwise and she uses inspiration from a man born in 384 BCE to help them with the simplification of their public speaking: 'Simplifying does not have to mean dumbing down. Aristotle's rules remain as relevant as ever – seek understanding, make content clear and delivery understandable.'

Sara Bennison, chief marketing officer at Nationwide, believes in simplicity but she also believes in telling a story. She reacts against the dominance of PowerPoint in developing ideas:

> Writing is important, for me and my team. I do believe that PowerPoint has destroyed our ability to tell stories. It means that everyone tries to reduce everything to a bullet point and some infographic that they've learned to master. I think that's really dangerous because it stops you telling a story. If you start by writing a paragraph or a page of longhand explaining an idea it comes to life far more vividly than five bullet points ever could. It might be longer but is more nuanced and accurate and takes people less time to understand.

> Simplicity without simplification means working out your story. What's the message you want people to be left with? What's the end, the start and the middle (deliberately thought of in that order)? Why should people care? What words can you use to connect – words that are unpretentious and jargon-free, and will capture the attention of your audience? If you want people to remember, tell them a story.

As Robert McKee, who has acted as a storytelling consultant for years for companies like Microsoft, Nike and Hewlett-Packard, would tell you: 'Stories are how we remember: we tend to forget lists and bullet points.' The business journalist Jon Card explains how entrepreneurs and businesses can use a storytelling archetype, the 'Hero's Journey', to help bring to life their otherwise fairly dry business success case – the classic story in literature and film where the hero starts from relatively humble or relatable beginnings, goes on an adventure and faces drama or challenges, and finally achieves their goals and success. The use of this makes it relevant, appealing and engaging for the audience and it provides a template for telling the tale which is of interest to the person hearing it. A simple tale, well told, is highly effective.

Curating and crafting your messages is about powerful, decisive editing and empathy for the audience. There is such beautiful elegance in simplicity when It's done well. Antoine de Saint-Exupéry, who was a pioneering aviator as well as one of France's most celebrated authors, was an ardent supporter of this approach: 'Elegance is achieved – not when there is nothing more to add – but rather when there is nothing more to take away.'

Getting to 'the edit': ways to focus and sharpen your business plans and communications

There are three main areas for you to explore leading as an exceptional editor: business plans, communications and your life. The last, your life, has been covered in depth in Chapter 2: Time is finite – energy isn't. I focus here on what you choose to do (your business plans) and what you want to say (your communications), and look at how a sharp editing approach can help both.

Editing business plans

When looking at any type of business plan, there are ways in which you can ensure that it's as sharp, simple and effective as possible:

- Create constraints
- Be clear on your 'we don't' and 'we won't' rules (and the 'not now').

GIVE YOURSELF (OR OTHERS) CONSTRAINTS

Be brave. Be brief. There is enormous value in being forced into brevity.

Moving fast does not mean moving without a plan. There are many different flavours of strategic planning in different organizations, however, and some accelerate progress and others can make progress falter. Sarah Wood, CEO of Unruly, has an approach that is fast and focused:

> Whatever project, launch or initiative you're trying to deliver with a team, you need a plan. That doesn't mean you should sit down and write a planning document that rivals *War and Peace* or build a 10,000-cell Gantt chart that maps out a project inch by inch over a period spanning months. In today's business environment that would be commercial suicide and a waste of time that you simply can't afford.

She believes in 'MVPs' all round – not just the agile approach of 'minimum viable product' (getting something to a level where it requires the minimum input to be testable or workable) but specifically, when it comes to strategy and planning, working on a 'minimum viable plan' – the simplest plan possible that will get your team aligned around what you're trying to achieve, who's doing what and when it needs to be delivered.

The MVP should be a compass, not a map – this is a key distinction. You need to build resilience, agility and flexibility into the project from the outset, while at the same time bringing absolute clarity as to the purpose, process and people involved in delivery.

> Restrictions can help you focus. Constraint drives creativity.

Many people in the design world have long understood that giving people a constrained brief helps focus their creativity on what matters. Marissa Mayer, when she was VP of Search at Google, believed that 'Constraints shape and focus problems, and provide clear challenges to overcome as well as inspiration.'

Psychological research conducted at the University of Amsterdam's Department of Social Psychology supports this, demonstrating that tough obstacles can prompt people to open their minds, look at the 'big picture' and help make connections between things that are not obviously connected.

> Restrictions and focus can help with the speed of communicating.

Amazon's way of communicating is via a six-page document. Simon Calver, who sold LoveFilm to Amazon for £200 million in 2011 and then moved into a role where he attended Amazon board meetings, was delighted by the smart way they used time in those meetings. The meetings start with proposals being shared and everyone reading them then and there. They have 15–30 minutes' silence to do so. Those proposals can be no more than six pages long, a constraint that speeds up communication. This 'Study Hall' start to meetings is an initiative from Jeff Bezos, who explains that it is more effective than Power-Point: 'If you have a traditional PowerPoint presentation, executives interrupt. If you read the whole six-page memo, on page 2 you have a question but on page 4 that question is answered.'

This is also a very insightful acceptance of the reality of busy business life. Those minutes at the start ensure that people read the document. When asked why he doesn't just get everyone to read them in advance, Bezos says: 'Time doesn't come from nowhere. This way you know everyone has the time. The author gets the nice warm feeling of seeing their hard work being read.'

There are many organizations where PowerPoint proposals/plans can run to hundreds of pages. This is a great way to slow down comprehension and adoption. It's easier to understand, approve or action plans when they are short and focused. Procter & Gamble's unrelenting focus on the 'one-pager' has saved hundreds of hours of management time over the years and has also driven writers to prioritize what goes into it and really polish the way in which their argument is presented.

Austin Lally, Group CEO at Verisure, spent many years at Procter & Gamble and took with him some of the lessons he'd learned there into his new role, including the focus on the 'one-pager':

> Our strategy is not a long document or a set of PowerPoint slides. It is a single A4 piece of paper. P&G alumni will see some similarities with the classical 'OGSM' document that spelled out Objectives, Goals, Strategies and Measures. We came up with a different acronym. Our document is called a SOAP, which stands for Strategy On A Page. It's a little amusing since my new colleagues saw me coming to security from a 'soap' company.

SOAP – clean, clear thinking on a page. Using a restriction like this in your documents helps you focus on the words that matter and helps the reader understand quickly.

> Make it simple. Make it easy to read. Make it easy to understand. This makes it more likely it will happen.

You may joke about 'writing a strategy on the back of a fag packet', but if you did just that at least it would be focused. Many entrepreneurs use the 'Can it fit on the back of a napkin?' idea as another way to get that focus. Groupon's original business plan was done that way. 'Can you describe the main points using the fingers of only one hand to represent the five most important elements?' is another way of ensuring brevity, clarity and memorability. You may have a wonderful strategy but if people don't remember it and act in alignment with it, it's a total waste of brainpower. Your vision is just a velleity – a great word to describe the weakest form of a wish, something that should be avoided in a world where you want to keep the pace going. Weak wishes will not give you the acceleration you need.

Another 'impatient' leader who saw the value in brevity was Winston Churchill who wrote a memo on the subject in 1940 fuelled by a desire to conserve time and energy (see Figure 5.1). He asks for 'short, crisp paragraphs' and points out that 'often the occasion is met by submitting not a full-dress report but an aide-memoire consisting of headlines only'. He asks for the end of 'woolly phrases' but makes the point that people should not 'shrink from using the short expressive phrase, even if it is conversational'. That's timeless advice.

CREATE YOUR ANTI-GOALS

For most of us (myself included), saying no to interesting things is hard. Humans are eminently distractible; life and work are packed full of distractions. To move forward fast we need to make choices.

The power of focus and making clear, sustained choices is consistently associated with some of the world's most powerful business brains. Let's look at Warren Buffett, the world's most famous investor, as a great example. Buffett has a simple strategy for working out what deserves his attention. His personal pilot, Mike Flint, once asked Warren Buffett which of his career goals Flint should prioritize. The business magnate suggested this method:

- **Step 1:** Write down your top 25 career goals on a single piece of paper.
- **Step 2:** Circle only your top five options.
- **Step 3:** Put the top five on one list and the remaining 20 on a second list.

Easy, right? List A and List B. With this exercise done, Flint confirmed that he'd start working on List A – his top five goals – right away. But then Warren Buffett asked Flint what

(THIS DOCUMENT IS THE PROPERTY OF HIS BRITANNIC MAJESTY'S GOVERNMENT).

S E C R E T.

W.P.(G)(40) 211.   COPY NO. 65

9TH AUGUST, 1940.

WAR CABINET.

BREVITY.

Memorandum by the Prime Minister.

    To do our work, we all have to read a mass of papers.
Nearly all of them are far too long.   This wastes time,
while energy has to be spent in looking for the essential
points.

    I ask my colleagues and their staffs to see to it
that their Reports are shorter.

    (i)   The aim should be Reports which set out
          the main points in a series of short, crisp
          paragraphs.

    (ii) If a Report relies on detailed analysis
          of some complicated factors, or on statistics,
          these should be set out in an Appendix.

    (iii) Often the occasion is best met by submitting
          not a full-dress Report, but an Aide-memoire
          consisting of headings only, which can be
          expanded orally if needed.

    (iv) Let us have an end of such phrases as these:
          "It is also of importance to bear in mind
          the following considerations......", or
          "Consideration should be given to the
          possibility of carrying into effect.....".
          Most of these woolly phrases are mere padding, which
          can be left out altogether, or replaced by a
          single word.   Let us not shrink from using
          the short expressive phrase, even if it is
          conversational.

    Reports drawn up on the lines I propose may at first seem
rough as compared with the flat surface of officialese jargon.
But the saving in time will be great, while the discipline of
setting out the real points concisely will prove an aid to
clearer thinking.

                                        W.S.C.

10, Downing Street.

    9TH AUGUST, 1940,

FIGURE 5.1 Winston Churchill, an impatient leader, lays down the rules for brevity in communications in a Downing Street memorandum from August 1940.

he planned to do with the second list, a question to which the pilot replied: 'Well, the top five are my primary focus, but the other 20 come in a close second. They are still important so I'll work on those intermittently as I see fit. They are not as urgent, but I still plan to give them a dedicated effort.' Buffett shook his head: 'No. You've got it wrong, Mike. Everything you *didn't* circle just became your Avoid-at-All-Costs List. No matter what, these things get no attention from you until you've succeeded with your top five.'

The 'Avoid at All Costs List' comprises your second-tier priorities. That's focus. They're what you *don't* do. It's what you have the focus and determination to not do. It's saying no (or at least not right now). Eliminate the distractions.

One last thought on communicating your business plan: tell people and tell them again and stick to it. Be clear, too, on what you won't do as well as what you will do. And stick to it.

Some things need to be done now. Some can come later. Some need to be considered or tested. Share your choices and your timeline with your organization and your board: 'We aren't ruling out x …' 'We will test whether x might be an option.' 'We will consider this again at such and such a stage.' That way you don't waste time with people filling in the gaps. Share the choices and the edits you made.

> Leadership is often about managing expectations –
> with shareholders, with your teams, with yourself.

Sheryl Sandberg tells a revealing story about the need for forceful reiteration of 'what you won't do' when she and Mark Zuckerberg realized that Facebook had to respond quickly to the move from browser dominance to handset technology. They knew that it meant they had to make Facebook work first and foremost on mobiles and they had to switch away from testing everything to work on a big computer screen. They realized how fast the move away from desktops was going and they knew something had to be done.

But their knowing this was not enough. They had to make sure that others understood and acted, too. Sandberg tells the story:

> Mark did this all-hands [meeting] and said: 'We are going to be a mobile-first company.' And do you know what happened? Nothing, nothing happened, everyone went back to their daily lives as they normally did. And what they did, they would come to product presentations and they would present: 'Here's our desktop app ...' and the last screen would be a mobile screenshot. And so Mark one day said: 'No more meetings until you come in with a mobile screenshot first' ... and he did not have any product meetings for a couple of weeks.

Editing your communications

This is an area where you will be more used to seeing editing at work (at your work). But that doesn't mean you can be complacent. Never underestimate the power of focus in simplifying communications for your audience:

- Get to the point. Make it. Repeat it.
- Check that 'Granny would get it'.
- Make it about the message, not the medium.

GET TO THE POINT. MAKE IT ...

Getting to the point is often seen as a particularly contemporary need in a world where Twitter, with its 280-character limit, is now the megaphone of leaders. But it has always been the case. Brevity is so often better. Over 150 years ago the Gettysburg Address – one of the most powerful and memorable communications in history – was delivered by President Abraham Lincoln in less than three minutes and was just 272 words long. With a few carefully chosen words, Lincoln summarized his view of the American Civil War in just ten sentences, including the well-known definition of democracy as 'government of the people, by the people, for the people'.

Mastering the ability to make the complex simple is a huge speed skill for leaders. Using a Twitter-style word count as a constraint that forces you to summarize an idea is an excellent test. It's an even more espresso version than the 'elevator test', where you work out what your pitch would be if you found yourself in an elevator with someone who could launch your career. The beauty of editing down your communications message is that it makes it memorable and therefore repeatable by others.

Brevity and simplicity have enormous power, but it's also about choosing the *right* words. Great communicators have the ability to find words to describe their aspiration that are human and distinctive – and therefore memorable – whether it's sharing the fact that they 'have a dream', want to 'put a dent in the universe' or 'not be evil'. The speed and efficiency of a (meaningful) soundbite which gets repeated is a real tool of the Superfast.

Give your employees or customers some 'pub currency' – a great story or line to use when chatting to friends in the pub. Or give your investors or the press something they find easy to remember and pass on. If it's too complicated, you'll forget and they'll forget. If anything is clumsily written, people won't repeat it.

Chris Anderson and 'the idea worth hearing'

Chris Anderson is the 'dreamer' head of TED and therefore has credibility when it comes to communication, having made it possible for millions to communicate ideas effectively, spreading them in a succinct and effective way. He's also an entrepreneur who, at the nadir of the dotcom bubble burst, personally found himself in a situation where he was losing $1 million every day for 18 months. He knows the challenges of leadership and he knows how tough it can be to communicate well. A stutterer, he is not a confident orator and happily jokes about it while confidently sharing how he has learned how to help others speak with impact. Anderson's recommendation when it comes to TED talks is to focus on 'an idea which is worth hearing'. By this he means sharing an idea or a story which the audience will find interesting (and, he warns, not boasting about how great you've been but rather what you've learned).

This is a guideline rule for communication generally, whether advertising, emails or speeches: start with thinking about what it means for the audience. Then share that. Don't tell them what you have or what you've done; tell them what it means for them.

And keep it simple – edit it down to the one big idea. What's the headline? Once you've identified the killer idea, Anderson suggests that you articulate it in no more than a headline or a (short-form) Twitter message (Sheryl Sandberg's TED talk and book, for example, could be summarized as 'Women Need to Lean In') and then make sure everything in it reinforces this point. 'Less is more,' Anderson points out. 'Once you have found something worth saying, focus. Strip it down to a single core point. Everything about your speech – stories, jokes, statistics, graphics – should connect to that point.' His guidance is then that there should be no more than three points to support that core idea.

A note on timing: TED talks are no longer than 18 minutes. Anderson reminds people that Martin Luther King's 'I have a dream' speech was 17 minutes 30 seconds. If Martin Luther King can inspire generations with his speech, which was shorter than a TED talk, you can manage to keep your speech to less than 20.

... And now repeat it

Let's take inspiration now from someone who really knows how to deliver a successful TED talk. Dan Pink's motivation talk is one of the top ten watched TED talks of all time, with 19 million views. This is not surprising as he is a great speaker (as well as a behavioural scientist, author and thought provocateur). His career has included political speechwriting (for Vice President Al Gore among others), so he's often asked what makes a good speech. This is what he has concluded:

> The three things you need for a good speech are:
>
> - brevity
> - levity
> - repetition.
>
> Let me say that again ... I said repetition. I'll repeat that. Allow me to make that point over and over again. I want to be sure that you will remember the repetition point. It's important I reiterate it for you.
>
> I will repeat the important stuff over and over again until you want to scream.

A strong reason for editing your message to focus it is the knowledge that you will need to repeat it. If you are trying to get a message across, you will need to give the audience repeated opportunities to hear it, understand it, hear it, believe it, hear it again. Persistence is key here. Media agencies and marketing companies have spent years assessing the number of OTHs or OTSs (opportunities to hear or opportunities to see) needed to get a message across to consumers.

Creating change in organizations requires working with distractible, distracted, divergent people and, just because you've said (or done) something once, it doesn't mean it will be remembered or get changed for ever. Lazlo Block, the SVP of People Operations at Google, gives a classic example of how making change happen once is not enough.

In 2008 Google noticed that women were being promoted at a lower rate than men in engineering. They realized that it came down to a very simple reason: the default way in which promotions happen. At Google at that time, to get promoted you raised your head and said, 'I'm ready to get promoted.' Women were nominating themselves at a lower rate than men (a gender trait that's often seen from the earliest years of education, where boys will raise their hands more in class). The People team partnered with the head of engineering who sent a communication to the company to highlight this issue, transparently sharing data and explaining what was happening and urging the women to 'raise their hands'. They did. The results were great – for a while. After about a six-month cycle, the issue happened again – no one had sent another email and people had forgotten or just reverted to their old behaviour.

Remember this when you are trying to create change in your organization or trying to get investment and commitment from shareholders or outside partners: when you are communicating your message, once is never enough. A number of interviewees for this book have come to this realization: just because *they* get an idea and get it fast doesn't mean that telling people about it once has the desired effect.

You need to repeat your message – and you need other people to repeat it. If you can edit it so it is powerful, simple and memorable, that is a start. You will then need to accept that you need to repeat it over and over again in order to create the change or belief needed.

Information is not transformation – you can't just share an opinion or an idea and expect things to happen. Remember these steps:

- Edit your message, polish it, perfect it.
- Get it simple and then rinse, repeat, rinse, repeat.
- Persist, be patient but weigh the odds in your favour by taking time to polish the message to perfection – take

time and increase the speed of understanding, adoption and belief.

> Editing is about working out what is the minimum you need in communication. Make it easy for your audience and take out what's not needed (which gives you space and time to repeat it).

Check that 'Granny would get it'

If you have seen the crisp tone of voice and appealing communications that surround Innocent's food and drink offers, it will come as no surprise that Adam Balon and his co-founders believe strongly that simplicity is critical for communications and for business itself: 'Like most business ideas, ours was clear and simple. The world of commerce rewards simplicity and their associates, clarity and focus.'

One of Innocent's golden rules to help continue simplicity, clarity and focus was to apply the 'Granny Test' to everything they do: 'The theory behind the Granny Test is that, if you need three paragraphs to explain your idea and strategy, it's probably too complicated or unclear to take root in the business world.' There's an intellectual snobbery for many about simplifying messages. And, of course, there's a huge danger in reducing complex issues to Twitter headlines or snappy soundbites all the time. The worry is that making it fast can make things seem facile. The key here is that your communication mode should fit the audience, their time tolerance and the situation.

We must never assume that fewer words mean that there is less opportunity to genuinely connect and communicate something meaningful and memorable; there is often greater power in brevity. Here is a perfect example of that: Ernest Hemingway's (or somebody else's) six-word story – a masterpiece of impact. It may be shorter than many a book title but it delivers piercing emotion:

For sale: baby shoes, never worn.

A way to edit: force focus with the Rule of Three

If you are simplifying or wanting to create something memorable, remember this: the Rule of Three. Many people agree with the Rule of Three, not just me ...

There's something satisfying about threes. It's an ancient rhetorical technique that can be traced back to the Greeks, is featured in the Bible and Shakespeare, and is still used to great effect by orators and business leaders alike today. *Omne trium perfectum* is a Latin saying about the beauty of things that come in threes that is roughly translatable as 'Every set of three is complete'. Good speeches are peppered with lists of three items. Look at the speeches of Martin Luther King, who frequently used phrases with three elements ('insult, injustice and exploitation'), or those of Pope Francis. Thomas Jefferson introduced the concept of 'life, liberty and the pursuit of happiness', and the French revolutionaries aimed for 'Liberté, égalité, fraternité'.

Things that come in threes are often perceived as more satisfying and more effective in many ways. This means that people are more likely to remember them. It is argued that it creates a rhythm that is easy to remember (and, of course, brief enough to help the brain retain it). You will, if you've been reading carefully, see how frequently this technique occurs in this book. Businesspeople and entrepreneurs also swear by three. Steve Jobs used the Rule of Three in almost every product launch, with the most memorable being the time he announced that Apple would be introducing 'three' revolutionary products – a new iPod, a phone and an Internet communication device – and repeated this statement until his audience realized he was referring to just one device that encompassed all three functions. Leadership researcher and guru Jim Collins says that 'if there are more than three priorities then you don't have any'. Simon Hay, when CEO of dunnhumby, cut dunnhumby's values from seven down to four. He wanted three but it didn't quite happen – but he noted that everyone could easily remember only three of them.

So the editor's Rule of Three is: make it simple, memorable and nicely balanced. And the business leader's Rule of Three is:

- Divide a presentation into three parts or make three points in your speech.
- Give yourself three things to achieve per week or set three agenda points in a meeting.
- Communicate three priorities or three values.

Many of the interviewees for this book swear by this – including Adam Balon from Innocent, who subscribes to the power of three. He then actually broke the rule, but set up another one which helped give the organization real focus:

> At Innocent, we have a rule of … five. Whenever we write a strategy, a series of objectives, a set of tasks for the day, or even just a shopping list, we always remember the highly scientific Rule of Five. The theory goes something like this:
>
> Everyone can remember one thing.
>
> If they can't they are a doofus.
>
> Most people can remember three things.
>
> And no one can remember more than five.
>
> The Rule of Five.

Make it about the message, not the medium

When thinking about communication, it's important here to pause and reflect on the perils of PowerPoint. Naturally, Power-Point can be used to enormously positive effect in business. Like any piece of technology, however, it can be used for good or for evil. Used without discipline, PowerPoint has destroyed the souls and lives of many a business executive who has spent hours watching people read bullet points gradually drowning in 'deck' after 'deck'. It can be dull and time-wasting for the audience and it's also a time-stealer in the amount of preparation it demands.

If you want to use PowerPoint, a great discipline is to ask for it to be used 'PechaKucha' style. PechaKucha is Japanese for 'chit-chat' and it's a smart, Superfast style of giving a presentation, started by Japanese architects wanting to hold evenings where people presented designs and ideas in a short, sharp and stimulating way. If you're based near Orlando, Florida, you can see it being used at incredible PechaKucha evenings run by Eddie Selover, who discovered this global phenomenon when he personally was finding it harder to communicate (https://www.youtube.com/watch?v=qM4TXMBGLdY). PechaKucha follows a rule where the presenter shows 20 images for 20 seconds each. The result? Six minutes of an engaging, pacey and interesting presentation. This is a great creative challenge for presenters – and of course it's easiest for designers – but we've seen a CFO present his business financial update effectively in a similar style.

You can always back up plans and communications with more detail for those who want it … but the truth is that most people would always rather have less detail to start with. Life is too short to drown in PowerPoint preparation or to be bored to death by slide overload. PowerPoint has to be edited and thoughtful. It must be short, it must be smartly planned, and it must be stimulating. Or it should not be used.

One of Gary Coombe's first actions when appointed as Procter & Gamble's European President was to ban PowerPoint in meetings with him:

> I want a meeting to be a meeting – for us to discuss things. I do not want to sit and listen to people presenting. So I now ask for a one-pager in advance of any meeting. This means I can have thought about the issue/the proposal in advance and then when we meet we can discuss and decide.

That rule can apply to anything you are doing from a communications point of view. Start simply. Start with the takeaway.

We work with a number of senior leaders at Caffeine on their 'Pitchcraft', ensuring that they can win pitches (whether financial, legal, marketing services or whatever), and we also help craft speeches for leaders to deliver at conferences or major meetings. In both cases, we firmly encourage people to be ready to present or speak in the event of a technical blackout. They should know their message and be able to deliver it even if they find themselves without PowerPoint or even without much time.

David Kean, one of Caffeine's 'pitch doctors', will regularly challenge the writers of speeches and pitches to continually ask a question made up of two simple little words. As you make each point, ask yourself 'So what?' How does this matter to the audience? What should they feel? What should they think? Are you telling them something that is relevant?

Get to the point and get connected with that audience. That's all you need.

How to be a better editor: fall in love with laziness

It's unlikely that you are someone who would be described as lazy. If you've gone to the effort of reading this far, you're probably not afraid of a bit of hard work. However, if you want to speed up the success of your organization, then you should consider adopting a conscious, ingrained habit of being 'strategically lazy'. This is not me advocating laziness of the kind meaning 'a lack of care'; you should still care but you should focus that care on where it matters. It's not about doing nothing. It's not about doing little. It's about consciously doing less in order to achieve more.

Warren Buffett has spent a lot of time with successful people. As the second-wealthiest man in the world, he is one himself and one whom many people revere for his investment success as well as his philanthropic principles. His view is that 'The difference between successful people and really successful people is that really successful people say no to almost everything.'

Here's a story from history about a leader who appreciated laziness. Kurt Gebhard Adolf Philipp Freiherr von Hammerstein-Equord was the German Chief of the Army High Command until he resigned his office in 1934 due to his opposition to Hitler. In assessing how to make a success of dealing with his army, he classified his officers into four simple groups:

> There are clever, diligent, stupid, and lazy officers. Usually two characteristics are combined.
>
> Some are clever and diligent – their place is the General Staff.
>
> The next lot are stupid and lazy – they make up 90 per cent of every army and are suited to routine duties. One must beware of anyone who is stupid and diligent – he must not be entrusted with any responsibility because he will always cause only mischief.
>
> Anyone who is both clever and lazy is qualified for the highest leadership duties, because he possesses the intellectual clarity and the composure necessary for difficult decisions.

It takes one to know one. Hammerstein himself had 'a reputation for independence and indolence, favouring hunting and shooting over the labours of administration' and was described by Field Marshal Erich von Manstein as 'probably one of the cleverest people I ever met'. Laziness for Hammerstein did

	Lazy	Hard-working
Clever	Make him a commander.	Make him a staff officer.
Stupid	You can always find something for him to do.	Fire him.

FIGURE 5.2 Von Hammerstein-Equord's four types of officer

not mean idleness, it meant doing what was most efficient and effective to do – and no more. Hammerstein's clever classification is as relevant as ever today. Take time and think about those around you and where they fit into each group.

It's also worth being conscious about the personal power that comes from being smart and lazy. These leaders are natural delegators who look for simpler, easier things. Ask yourself – do you personally 'possess the intellectual clarity and the composure necessary for difficult decisions'? Do your future leaders? We are talking about the people with the mind – and the mindset – to be a good leader and to cope with the challenges it brings.

Michael Greenlees was the tough and charming Chair of Scoota. He's recently stepped down from being Chair of Ebiquity, the AIM listed marketing and media specialist, which he joined after selling his first agency, Gold Greenlees Trott, to Omnicom. Before that he was Ebiquity's CEO, and he freely admits that as CEO he made sure he added maximum value during the meetings he went to, but that his objective was as far as possible to ensure that he limited his 'to do' list between those meetings. His objective was to empower others and thus give him the freedom to focus on the things others were less good at. This is not a lazy man but one who chooses smartly where he applies his skills.

So ask yourself, 'Do I have to do this?' and only do it if you are the only person who can.

Bill Gates is alleged to have said, 'If I want a job done I give it to someone lazy. They'll work out the fastest and easiest way to do it.' A 'consciously lazy' mindset helps you to think about how to scale things, about how to make them easy so you can do them more and do them more often. It's smart and it's so much easier in today's world. Use the machines. Remind yourself that in 1930 Maynard Keynes believed that by 2030 there was likely to be a system of 'technological unemployment' with people working 15 hours a week or less. You may not be ready for that but it's definitely true that wasting time tweeting again and again when Tweetdeck or Hootsuite can do it is as mad as choosing to wash up by hand or get the mangle out.

It's your duty as a leader to find ways for your team to automate and accelerate by using smart tools.

Save your brainpower for what really matters

Decision fatigue is to be avoided. Be lazy about things that don't matter. Save your firepower and your brainpower for decisions that make a difference.

There has been much interest in Mark Zuckerberg's and Barack Obama's simplification of wardrobe choices. Obama, in an interview with *Vanity Fair*, explained that managing life as President required taking away decisions which could distract – which was why he wore only grey or blue suits. 'I'm trying to pare down decisions. I don't want to make decisions about what I'm eating or wearing. Because I have too many other decisions to make.'

The billionaire founder of Facebook wears (a version of) the same thing every day. 'I really want to clear my life to make it so that I have to make as few decisions as possible about anything except how to best serve this community,' Zuckerberg said, after clarifying that he had 'multiple same shirts'. He said that even small decisions like choosing what to wear or what to eat for breakfast could be tiring and consume energy, and he didn't want to waste any time on that. 'I'm in this really lucky position, where I get to wake up every day and help serve more than a billion people. And I feel like I'm not doing my job if I spend any of my energy on things that are silly or frivolous about my life.'

You know that 20 per cent of what you do is likely to create 80 per cent of the results. The Pareto Principle has proved to be true so frequently. So be ruthless. Allow yourself to be lazy by identifying that 20 per cent. Work out what has to be done first and fast. Tim Ferriss has been a living, breathing evangelist of this approach since publishing *The 4-Hour Work Week* (2007) where he extols the virtues of outsourcing daily tasks to virtual assistants and focusing on the work that delivers the greatest returns. In a world of incredible automated help and technology that supports on-demand connection with others who can get things done, it's simply daft to overwork and get overwhelmed.

Andy Milligan, the co-founder of the Caffeine Partnership, reflecting on the ten-year anniversary of the company, shared one of the earliest pieces of advice he was given by a successful entrepreneur: 'Don't do today what you can put off till tomorrow – because by the time tomorrow comes, you may not have to do it anyway.' Milligan treasured this advice because:

> Time is our biggest challenge. We all struggle with priorities. We've all got a list of things to do as long as our arms, each of which demands equal attention. And we've all had the 'false deadline' request; you rush to do something for someone only to discover it could have waited. We have to focus. Do less and do it better. So only do today what really needs to be done. Then relax.

Laziness is an excellent leadership trait. If it doesn't come naturally, nurture it.

Think strategic laziness but don't choose lazy thinking

Any work on speed in business could not exist without referencing the thought-provoking work of Daniel Kahneman: *Thinking, Fast and Slow*, a must-read for many of today's most considered thinkers. This seminal work divides thinking into two kinds:

- System 1 thinking – the faster cognitive 'short cuts' including stereotypes, emotions, intuitions and cognitive biases
- System 2 thinking – the more logical, in-depth and 'effortful' thinking that is slower and harder.

The first is 'lazy' and has a role to play as it is speedy but it is less logical, rational and considered. It's critical, too, to understand and recognize why people will default to System 1. It requires less cognitive exertion and it is only human that people prefer to take the lazy short cut. System 1 operates automatically and so is hard to turn off. An awareness of this helps us understand why we might make cognitive errors, to be hyper-aware of cognitive biases and drive us to put more effort into the important thinking questions that we need to answer.

Because of the complexity of the world around us and the amount of information in the environment, it is necessary sometimes to rely on some mental short cuts that allow us to act quickly. These mental short cuts are also known as heuristics, which can lead to errors in thinking. Social pressures, individual motivations, emotions, and limits on the mind's ability to process information can also contribute to these biases. Psychologists believe that many of these biases serve an adaptive purpose – they allow us to reach decisions quickly and they are not always bad.

A knowledge of the respective strengths and weaknesses of System 1 and System 2 thinking is essential for the Superfast leader. To create speed in others' decision-making, a knowledge of where emotions can persuade and influence will help you. To create quality in your decision-making you may need to create time and space to think a bit more slowly.

Kahneman's writing shows that constant vigilance around thinking is not always smart and it's certainly tiring and impractical. As a compromise, we should work together to recognize where mistakes can happen when the stakes are high. (Incidentally, it's easier to recognize System 1 thinking in others.)

Love laziness but not where thinking really matters.

Espresso takeaways

The editor's top ten

HOW TO EDIT

1 Think 'less' – aim for minimalism.
2 Reduce decisions for others.
3 Make it easy; reduce the brain-load.
4 Create constraints.

COMMUNICATION

5 Get to the point. Make it. Repeat it.
6 Think complex; speak simple.
7 Make it about the message, not the medium.

BE STRATEGICALLY LAZY

8 Aim for automation and delegation.
9 Know your priorities and your 'Avoid at All Costs' list.
10 Save your brainpower for what really matters.

6

Human understanding

Know your audience, know your team,
know yourself

'When you start to develop your powers of empathy
and imagination, the whole world opens up to you.'

Susan Sarandon,
American actor

Dame Helena Morrissey is one of the UK's most successful business executives. She is Head of Personal Investing at Legal & General Investment Management and former chief executive of Newton Investment Management. The super fund manager has had phenomenally positive results managing £54.6 billion in assets as well as nine children. She also created the 30% Club, which calls on businesses to drive up the representation of women in the boardroom. She quotes the actress Susan Sarandon (see above) to explain what she feels is important in leadership – empathy. One of her frustrations is the slowness of the UK's leadership to take this on board: 'People see other people and they don't empathize. I want to see more empathy in business.'

In this chapter, we will see how empathy and understanding are formidable speed tools and that to be a powerful pace-setter you need to understand who you are talking to and who you are working with.

Human-centred innovation has long been key to progress. A human-centred approach to everything will make your

GET CLOSER
KNOW YOUR CUSTOMER

Leadership

– Human understanding

GET STRONGER
KNOW YOUR TEAM

GET SMARTER
KNOW YOURSELF

FIGURE 6.1

organization work faster; an understanding of how people work and a knowledge of specific people helps you take smarter short cuts and communicate more easily:

- Customer-centricity increases the speed of decision-making – whether broadly in your organization on a day-by-day basis or as insights into the creation or development of an idea or product.
- Teams also work better when members understand one other's strengths and preferences.
- Leaders who have taken a long hard look at themselves are better positioned to work out how they can move faster.

Developing your human understanding and thinking about how people work, how to persuade them, how to communicate effectively, how to get the best out of their performance – all this will dramatically accelerate your progress. In a world where we are moving towards 'artificial' intelligence, the skills of human intelligence and the ability to navigate with empathy will become increasingly important to hone and preserve.

Get closer: know your customer

Note that I'm using the word 'customer' here but it can be substituted with 'consumer' or 'client', depending on your business audience (whom do you sell to or who needs to buy you or who needs to buy into your approach?).

Without customers, nothing will happen. They are the most important people in your organization. Everything you do and plan should be customer-centric. Organizations can get caught up in spreadsheets, roadmaps, improvements and 'strategy' but never talk to, see or truly remember the customer. A human understanding of the customer is not a nice-to-have extra; it's essential for a business to drive its success fast. It also unifies people internally by providing a shared focus which helps circumvent any internal 'politics' or distractions. Paul Polman, Unilever Global CEO, comments:

> The world we live in now requires us to solve internal company conflicts and these are being solved by putting the consumer first. You put the consumer on the table, so it's not about product supply, it's not about finance, it's not about HR, it's about the consumer.

Get closer to move faster

> So we decided to think about problems, problems that we have, as humans, and then ways of potentially solving them. Smoothies were just one of those problems about life: living in London, going out a lot, not eating enough good stuff, feeling guilty but no time to do too much about it. We thought that's a problem we have got, and loads of other people will be very similar.

This is Adam Balon on the idea behind the launch of Innocent smoothies. He and the co-founders *were* the customer. One of the classic reasons start-ups move fast is because they're often set up to meet a need the founders have perceived themselves – they frequently start in a situation where they are the customer. The further you are from the customer in terms of demographics, psychographics, habits and understanding, the more you need to get close to them. This isn't because they will tell you the answer but because they will help you make a quicker, clearer decision. This is not just about research but about your personal knowledge – how close you are to the audience.

Charlotte Vicary is a co-founder of the Customer Closeness Company, which works with companies like eBay to help senior leaders accelerate decision-making by gaining a more intuitive understanding of their audience. Vicary explains how closeness to the customer helps improve the speed and confidence of business decisions:

Clarity begins with understanding. The most successful companies recognize that being connected to customers means they can make better, informed decisions. Many businesses have masses of data but it's difficult to create the type of insight on which staff feel compelled to act.

Sam Altman, the Co-Chair of Open AI with Elon Musk, advises entrepreneurs simply to: 'Always have a direct relationship with your customer.'

Developing this customer instinct is a leadership priority. Amazon's Jeff Bezos, one of the most high-profile customer-centric leaders, talks about the critical importance of understanding your audience:

I'm not against beta testing or surveys. But you, the product or service owner, must understand the customer, have a vision, and love the offering. Then beta testing and research can help you find your blind spots. A remarkable customer experience starts with heart, intuition, curiosity, play, guts, taste. You won't find any of it in a survey.

Jack Ma, the co-founder of Alibaba, controversially but firmly always insists that for his company 'It's customers [who are] number one; employees, two; and shareholders, three.' He goes on to explain why: 'It's the customer who pay us the money, it's the employees who drive the vision, and it's the shareholders who when the financial crisis came, these people ran away. My customers and my people stayed.'

The customer, then, should be at the heart of your culture, considered and thought about in everything you do. This is infinitely harder than it sounds, and it's scarily rarer than it should be in business. Customer closeness helps with decision-making, helps you anticipate what is needed from them, and allows you to respond to their issues with the speed of responsiveness that is required today. It is perhaps obvious that customer-centricity has a role to play in marketing but it drives smart decisions around everything else in your business, including product development and service priorities. Focusing on the customer can also empower your front line to be more responsive, and is thus a highly effective speed tool.

And in a world of corporate cynicism and where technology makes people uncomfortable and sometimes believe that business is inhuman, customer-centricity allows your organization to be seen as human – a distinctive, appealing attribute.

Anticipate, don't just ask

We operate in a world where the amount of data and knowledge that can be generated is powerful, exciting and almost overwhelming. Data on the customer gives us clues and helps us to listen. But data can be useless unless it gives you genuine insight. Chris Britton, serial investor and business accelerator, puts it like this: 'Always remember the difference between information and insights. Insights are information you can leverage.'

The question to ask about what you hear and see about your customers is always 'So what?' What does this mean for us and how do we use it? It's not what they do or say that's important.

Where it works, customer closeness reveals an insight into how people feel and how they will respond in the future. Where it does not work, data is used to prove something … in a world which is changing so fast that it's already dramatically different before you can respond to the data.

The real danger of thinking that customer-centricity is about data and research is that, in our Superfast world, as soon as that data reaches us it is no longer current. A rear-view mirror is no good for working out where you are going.

Paul Polman is the sort of leader you'd expect to like data. He comes from the rigorous data-driven traditions of Procter & Gamble and he is, by original training, a financial brain, before his career heading up the Unilever global empire. Nonetheless he'll firmly and provocatively say to his teams: 'All this research is useless.' He goes on to explain:

They get a shock. I challenge people 'Why do you pay for news? Tell me why you pay for news. Do you subscribe to a newspaper that's 30 days old?' Research and data explain what is happening, not what you want to change. Basis testing is killing things in the world because every basis test will be different when you're in a marketplace. It's based on past behaviour that doesn't count any more. It's just not the world we live in any more.

It's not a question of asking the customer; it's about anticipating them, about helping them and about being driven to delight them. There has been a seismic shift from companies 'telling and selling' to passive consumers to companies connecting with what matters to customers and interacting with them in conversations and in communities. Technology has allowed us to be even more personal about that, so companies need to understand these people and how to build relationships with them.

Simon Rogerson, the successful founder of the Octopus Group, has a simple test of a strong brand (one with integrity). 'If this brand was a person,' he asks, 'would you invite them into your home? Would they be your friend? John Lewis, for example … yes, I would. If your answer is no, then don't do business with them.'

Part of understanding your customer is understanding your relationship with them – what role can you play?

Understanding your audience: communication principles for pitching and presenting perfectly

If your role includes 'pitching' to people in any way, always start by thinking about them before you think about what you are going to say:

- **Pitching for business?** If your business is B2B, if you are dealing with 'clients' rather than consumers, taking time to understand your audience is particularly important.
- **Pitching for investment?** This could be fundraising for your organization or just signing off a budget for something you are doing.

- **Pitching for support?** Perhaps you want to win ambassadors and allies behind your cause – charitable or commercial.

Thinking first about your audience before you think about your message can transform your effectiveness fast. What does your audience want to hear? What is their problem that you can solve? What type of people and what kind of language will resonate?

This works brilliantly if you're pitching to new people: always find out in advance what they are like. It's easier than ever to do. If you've not met them before, investigate any digital footprint they have – sometimes people have written about topics in a way which is hugely revealing. Or look on LinkedIn for their history – you can easily make assumptions about the person you are meeting (have they, for example spent their career as an entrepreneur or in the corporate world?) and you should use an appropriate style of approach.

Find mutual friends or colleagues and ask them 'What are they like?' You can often get very useful tips ('He hates people who are late', 'She loves research', 'She is worried about the tech implications of this initiative'). Often, you can ask them directly – before the meeting there might be a phone call or an email trail where you can ask two or three smart questions to really understand them (such as 'What does success look like for you?' or 'What do you want to make sure we cover?').

Audience understanding is sometimes about finding the right language to communicate in a way which resonates. Sue Unerman and Kathryn Jacob, in their excellent advice for women in the corporate world, collected in *The Glass Wall*, tell the story of a senior woman who had proposed a 'role exchange' between two parts of the organization to help them work together well. She hadn't managed to convince her boss until she found a foot-balling analogy which brought it to life for him. She explained that it was like Dutch Total Football (a 1970s story of success when the Dutch team trained to be able to play in every position) and lo, the initiative was sold. She spoke his language. She created a story which resonated. She understood her audience.

The Dutch Total Football example is also an excellent story for us all about the importance of understanding others. The team played like a team because they could appreciate each other's pressures and pain and what it felt like to be in the other positions. 'Walking in other people's shoes' to get closer to understanding people and anticipating their needs and their likely moves can work wonders with consumers, clients and colleagues.

Customer understanding takes time – to watch, listen and think

You need to get into the heads of your customers to understand what their real desires and expectations are. One of the best ways of doing that is through observation.

A. G. Laffley, the erstwhile Procter & Gamble CEO, explained his approach by sharing what he did while on a regional assignment in Asia:

> Every time I travelled to China, I always went to stores to watch people purchasing our products. Then I went into homes. I always went in the evening because the woman almost always works outside the home. My routine was stores, homes, then the office. It gave me a current snapshot of what was going on. Of course, you can't generalize from a single qualitative experience, but over five years of doing this regularly, those experiences add up, combined with reading whatever you have access to, as well as the 'harder' data. You develop a feel. You become more of an anthropologist. Your power is observation, your listening skills; your ability to read non-verbal cues gets a lot better. Your ability to observe increases. There are so many subtle things to read, understand, react to in a foreign country.

Lafley liked to think about the questions that really got to the heart of what customers needed. Rather than thinking 'How do we help consumers get their floors clean?', it's 'How do we help customers get their Sunday mornings back?'

Jeff Bezos is the king of what he styles 'Customer-Obsessed Culture': 'We're not competitor obsessed, we're customer obsessed. We start with what the customer needs and we work backwards.' In his 2017 letter to shareholders explaining how the business will stay vital, he identifies 'True Customer Obsession' as key to this:

> There are many advantages to a customer-centric approach, but here's the big one: customers are always beautifully, wonderfully dissatisfied, even when they report being happy and business is great. Even when they don't yet know it, customers want something better, and your desire to delight customers will drive you to invent on their behalf. No customer ever asked Amazon to create the Prime membership programme, but it sure turns out they wanted it, and I could give you many such examples.

The closer you can get your organization to understanding your audience, the quicker its responses will be to opportunities or threats, the more accurate their innovative punts, and the more confident their decision-making about what really matters.

Getting closer to your customer: eight top tips

Internal debate and discussion, strategizing and word-wonking – all this can slow down business. Focusing in on 'what will the customer see' and 'when will this make a difference to our customer' are questions which will cut through all that, accelerate and focus the decision-making. Finding ways to remind people of their audience and to provoke their thinking about them are important tools for speeding up decision-making, increasing confidence in actions.

1 **Keep the customer experience a constant, visual presence – every day.** Airbnb have meeting rooms designed like the rooms they rent out.
   - *Where could you share the experience your customer has with people – visually, verbally, with film or live?*

2 **Have no doubt who the most important person is. Never forget.** Jeff Bezos uses an empty chair in board meetings to remind people that the most critical opinion is that of the customer.
  - *How is your customer represented in your offices and in your decision-making?*
  - *Where is the insight fed in and the opinion fed back (fast) in your project process?*
  - *Do you make sure that there is customer insight (not just customer information) as part of key decisions?*

3 **Bring in 'the voice of the customer' live.** The visceral impact of having real customers as part of management events makes it easier for those making decisions to feel less disconnected.

4 **Shopfloor and road thinking.** Executives need to understand what the real impact of decisions will be – on the shop floor for retail, on the road for the automotive industry …

5 **Co-create and innovate.** Companies like Lego and Airbus involve customers in innovation sessions and competitions to help co-create new product ideas.

6 **Walk in their shoes – choose moments of delight for your customers.** You can understand your customer journey better by watching them doing it and doing it yourself.
  - *How can you prioritize sorting some of the irritations?*
  - *How can you add in moments which delight and improve the memory of the experience?*

7 **Articulate your customer focus.** Words matter, so signal your priorities. For example: Ritz-Carlton's 'We are ladies and gentlemen serving ladies and gentlemen.'

8 **Work out the 'piss-off factors'.** Sam Altman, the entrepreneur guru behind Y Combinator, points out

that 'more painkillers are sold than vitamins'. Work out what the problem is that you can solve; find their pain. Or find the 'piss-off factors' as O2 did when it launched and made a better customer experience for telecoms customers.

- *What is it that irritates customers about your category? Can you solve it?*

Get stronger: know your team

When Peter Williams, the co-founder of Jack Wills, returned to the business as CEO in 2016 to accelerate its success, the first thing he focused on was rebuilding the way the team worked together. When José Neves realized the potential for Farfetch to hyper-scale, he looked at how the leadership team could become a 'superteam' to drive through this growth. Understanding the strength of how a team can work more efficiently and more effectively will allow you to do more (and do it faster).

It's not how good the individuals are; it's how well your team works

One of the most fascinating pieces of research in the last few years is the Google re:Work study where they undertook rigorous analysis into what made teams work effectively. Code-named 'Project Aristotle' after Aristotle's dictum 'The whole is greater than the sum of the parts', it had the goal of working out 'what makes a team effective at Google'. The research team started with an assumption that it was about the quality of the individuals, but the data showed them this startling conclusion: 'Who is on a team matters less than how the team members interact, structure their work, and view their contributions.'

How many 'superteams' have you seen in your career? How many exist in your organization? They are frustratingly few and far between. Patrick Lencion, author and board-level team-building analyst, comments: 'Not finance. Not strategy. Not technology. It is teamwork that remains the ultimate competitive advantage, both because it is so powerful and so rare.'

High-performing teams are rare because they don't always happen automatically. The Google Project Aristotle findings seem incredibly simple but require time to apply and build; this is rarely something that happens by chance but can be developed with practice, patience and determination. Google's research concluded that there were a few critical components of a successful team. These included the following:

- **Psychological safety.** The researchers identified this as the most important finding – the sense that people could share ideas without being judged. This type of positive relationship often requires teams to know and understand and show respect for one another.
- **Everyone working to the same (high) standard.** If the first point is about being supportive, this is about knowing that there is accountability in the team and achievements that spur on the others.
- **Individuals thinking that their work is meaningful and that what they do counts.** There is a personal element here about motivation and also a link to the greater purpose.

Google 'open-source' its management findings in the same way as Facebook do; we have moved far away from the world where companies jealously guarded their insights about working, so it's easy for you to explore more about how Google approached team optimization. And for your competition to do the same, of course …

FIGURE 6.2 The All Blacks haka: a 'superteam' in action

When Peter Williams, CEO of Jack Wills, wanted to step-change his team, he took stories from a legendary rugby team as stimulus – perhaps not the most obvious choice to help cata-lyse an acceleration of growth for a global premium fashion brand. But the inordinate world-class success of the All Blacks came from a story which is relevant for anyone fighting in a competitive marketplace.

The Kiwi team's rugby victories defy statistical probability and are a great example of the importance of team discipline and unity. There are no superstars in the All Blacks. Though there are some players who have led their team to victory more than others, have more seniority, have better skills – at the end of the day they all pitch in to clean up. All the players sweep the dressing room at the end. They all work together towards the higher purpose of 'leaving the jersey in a better place'. They are also all teachers who share their knowledge widely and pass it on. The collaborative approach of the All Blacks means that everyone has a turn to speak, so that all have an equal voice and make an equal contribution to the team.

Williams has applied this approach to his team at Jack Wills, and the Google Aristotle study supported the importance of this contributory value: 'On the good teams, members spoke in roughly the same proportion, a phenomenon the researchers referred to as 'equality in distribution of conversational turn-taking.' The 'human understanding' on the good teams went one step further: 'The good teams all had high "average social sensitivity" – a fancy way of saying they were skilled at intuiting how others felt based on their tone of voice, their expressions and other nonverbal cues.'

This argues in favour of recruiting people who have a good human understanding. At the Caffeine Partnership one of our recruitment checks is 'EQ as well as IQ'. It's worth bearing in mind that within a team social sensitivity can be built the more you get to know each other and understand each other as individuals. We work with senior people to build them into high-performance teams, and we always see the value of 'breaking bread together' at senior off-sites (time to get to know each other) and the development of a culture of candour which encourages a constructive fast feedback mechanism, both of which will help you and your team avoid misunderstandings.

The former Chief Executive of TalkTalk, Baroness Dido Harding, takes a different inspiration from the formation of rugby teams. A determined advocate of the power of diversity on executive teams, she says: 'Businesses should be more like rugby teams than rowing teams – made up of different shapes and sizes.'

It will come as no surprise that, like Williams and Harding, Alan Gilpin, the CEO of Rugby World Cup and COO of World Rugby, also inevitably takes lessons from the sport to help his team understand what needs to be done. 'Rugby is all about the team and how it works together. You have to know that when you pass the ball you can totally rely on the next person.' He also argues that rugby (the traditional 'gentleman's game') is a good example of principles and manners – a sport which hasn't been tainted by the doping scandal of other sports, a family game and a game where people work together and the team is more important than the individual.

Tech entrepreneur Sarah Wood from Unruly highlights the critical nature of a strong team in business – to deliver business and to retain talent:

> Your team is the single most important aspect of your leadership journey and legacy. More important than the speeches you give. More important than the recognition you receive. More important, even, than the new business you bring in. The first, best and most important investment you will make as a leader is in your team – whatever your circumstances as a leader, you will come to rely and depend on your team. And that's exactly the way it should be.
>
> We live in a competitive, highly networked world where it's highly unlikely you're the only business in your field. In that context, your team brings competitive advantage. The company that wins in the long term will the one with the best-organized, motivated and clearly aligned team. In a constantly competitive talent market, you need to lead like a politician running for election: continually seeking to win the vote and endorsement of your people.

Building a team takes time and commitment. But it's important every day at work, and it's particularly important when crisis hits. Katherine Bennett, SVP for Airbus, knows this is paramount: 'Knowing your team is critical – understanding each other's pace, understanding strengths and weaknesses means that when a crisis hits you can respond at speed.'

So, if you're ready to go faster, start with your team and work out how to turn it into a superteam where ideas are shared without fear and where members still constructively challenge each other but care about what they are doing and who know that, when they pass the ball, success will happen. Patrick Lencioni, an American writer of books on business management, says: 'I honestly believe that in this day and age of informational ubiquity and nanosecond change, teamwork remains the one sustainable competitive advantage that has been largely untapped.'

We measure what we treasure

Seeing a visible indication of progress drives belief and a sense of mastery. If you want your team to continue to feel motivated, measure what matters.

Michael Saunders, CEO of Bibendum PLB, presided over the growth and consolidation of the business where five companies came together, and he believes that the introduction of OKRs to his organization helped everyone deal with the transition to being a bigger company without losing any pace. OKRs provide a framework to define and track 'objectives and key results', normally on a quarterly basis. They were first introduced at Intel before being adopted by companies like Google, Uber and LinkedIn. Advocates say that they show clearly the relationship between individuals' objectives and the overall company objectives and purpose (something Daniel Pink in his seminal work on company motivation *Drive* believes is critical). Keeping everyone individually focused on their OKRs and making sure that those OKRs were visible to everyone else in the organization as a symbol of transparency, trust and shared endeavour helped people continue the pace through great change at Bibendum PLB. These OKRs were shared in an accessible online forum which meant that everyone could see everyone else's objectives and progress (and know that their progress was visible). Saunders points out that 'the shared visibility made a phenomenal difference'.

Visible ways of sharing progress are highly effective for motivation, even if transient. The behavioural economist Dan Ariely conducted a study where students were paid to build Lego figurines called Bionicles (they were paid $2 for building the first one, then slightly less for each subsequent one):

- In Group One, those involved saw their Bionicles dismantled as soon as they were built.

- In Group Two, they were told their work would be dismantled at the end of the study. They placed each completed Bionicle on a desk before continuing on to the next one.

Group Two out-built Group One, 11 to 7. Group Two were driven to keep building, encouraged by the visible indication of progress provided by the accumulating Bionicles even with diminishing monetary returns and knowledge of their Bionicles' eventual fates. That sense of 'We're getting somewhere' is powerful, even if it's transient. (As I write this, I'm tracking my word count to encourage me to keep on writing.)

Tech tools which can visualize the progress of a team can be highly powerful. Recently, there has been an explosion in the adoption of 'people metric' tools applied to both customers and employees. Jackie Lee-Joe, Chief Marketing Officer at BBC Studios, introduced Officevibe, a simple cultural tracking tool. Another fast-growing alternative is Culture Amp, used by Airbnb, Slack, Pinterest, Box and Etsy. The development of start-up fast-feedback tools has not gone unnoticed by the bigger tech players, with Microsoft snapping up Volometrix, a company that had raised $17 million before being acquired at the end of 2015. Volometrix can tell CEOs how long people spend on emails and meetings (it's anonymized, so it's not an individual productivity check). Tools can show progress – and they can show productivity.

One of the appealing elements of these tools is their capacity for speedier updates. In a world where things are moving fast, annual employee surveys are too little, too late. For Airbnb, which at one point was tripling its growth year on year, annual surveys could not possibly reflect the 'state of the nation', so using something like Culture Amp allowed it to get a quicker, clearer sense of how employees were feeling. Jackie Lee-Joe from BBC Studios sends weekly quick questions to get the 'pulse' of the organization because she knows that, in the world of TV, things move fast and you need to be able to listen regularly.

> If you know more quickly that there is an issue,
> you can act and anticipate.

Measurement is symbolized by career progress and financial results for many. Eric Ries, author of *The Startup Way* and an expert on how to apply the pace of start-ups to bigger, slower organizations, points out that big corporations often say they value risk and innovation. They put it on posters, and they speak about it regularly as part of their vision, but, as Eric says, 'People listen with their ears but also with their wallets.' If innovation isn't linked to remuneration, and if executives who are seen to fail get fired, people won't take the risk.

If the goals to be measured are too complex, they lose impact. Oliver Tress, founder of Oliver Bonas the retail store, has one KPI only for himself: he measures success on the percentage of his employees who are proud to work there.

Know your team: sea legs

Technology can provide brilliant insights into fast-changing trends, but don't forget the old, face-to-face methods, too.

UK government advisor and naval commander Rear Admiral Neil Morisetti has used some advanced technology in his career, but he picks 'legs' as the most useful tool in a leader's armoury:

> Walking the ship was the most important thing I could ever do – to get a sense of what was really going on, to listen and to observe – you can't get that by sitting behind email. As leaders, you need to walk around, you need to talk – or you need someone to do this, although it really should be you as the boss, for you to learn (fast) where there are problems and where there are opportunities in the organization.

So walk your ship. Connect. Face to face drives pace.

Know yourself

This is not an indulgence; it's not navel gazing. An engineer takes times to understand a machine, assessing its strengths and weaknesses. You are more complex than a machine, with fears and dreams, insecurities and emotions. You have things you enjoy doing, things you are good at doing and things that challenge you more. Taking time to work out a clear understanding of how you function at your best will save you time every day and costly mistakes all the time.

Self-knowledge in leadership reduces complexity. The most senior and successful leaders I spoke to talked about the importance of knowing themselves, recognizing their strengths and weaknesses, and understanding how to manage themselves so they could be the best they could be. This may be as simple as learning how to overcome inertia in themselves or it might be a fundamental assessment of what they are truly bad at. Most frequently, it's understanding and playing to their strengths; self-knowledge reduces time-wasting as well as a lot of personal pain which can distract from the job in hand.

Navigate strengths first. Chris Britton, ex-big corporate CEO and now a serial investor, is a dramatic example of someone who moves at great speed. Having had success being involved with a series of food, drink and wellness brands including hits like Graze, Ella's Kitchen, Aromatherapy Associates and Hippeas, he now runs an 'accelerator' company in Los Angeles and London as well as being chair of a number of different companies, staying fit and dividing his time between his home and his two company bases. He's near retirement age but has three times the energy of any twenty-something I've ever met. As an investor, he gets approached hundreds of times a year to get involved in companies and he's a shrewd people assessor. He told me that he learned years ago to be guided by the strengths of people first:

In corporate life, you're taught to manage people by developing their weaknesses. Which is great for a learning culture and for long-term well-rounded people. But I learned that the key to success for me and for other people was starting with strengths first. Work out what you're really good at and do more of that. You choose your role and your path in life based around that knowledge; it's more efficient to compensate around the weaknesses. If you can do what you're good at, you will feel positive and you'll move faster.

You may have a burning desire to improve some things. Certainly, developing some core leadership skills with practice and help can't be a bad thing – perhaps prioritizing public speaking or financial literacy, for example. But knowing what you're good at and shaping your role or choosing roles that suit you is the way to move fast.

IBM founder Tom Watson set great store by personal knowledge and accountability: 'Nothing so conclusively proves a man's ability to lead others as what he does from day to day to lead himself.' And he had an understanding of his weaknesses and what to do about them: 'I'm no genius. I'm smart in spots – but I stay around those spots.'

Never be blind to your weaknesses, though, and make sure that you appreciate them and compensate. In Chapter 7: Truth, you'll learn how truth will help keep you humble and smart.

Knowing your strengths allows you to calmly adapt your plans and your ways of doing things to best suit you. Of course, there is no one model of a perfect leader. We are bombarded with images of extrovert, flamboyant leaders of business because they often appear in the press and in stories. Jim Collins's *Good to Great*, which assessed which companies outperformed a similar organization by ten times or more, concluded clearly that a 'charismatic leader' was not a factor in determining success. Rear Admiral Neil Morisetti realized one day that he wasn't great at the big podium-style *Henry V*-style speeches but that he was highly effective one-on-one. So he just did more of those one-on-ones and got on with it!

Start with your strengths. Focusing on these will build your confidence but also your competence. Daniel Goleman, the journalist and originator of the term 'emotional intelligence' (EQ), made a big point of comparing the importance of EQ to IQ. He quoted studies, in his chapter 'When Smart Is Dumb' in *Emotional Intelligence: Why It Can Matter More Than IQ*, for example, proving that many high-IQ-scoring students end up failing miserably in their practical lives. In contrast, many 'average' people, Goleman pointed out, go on to phenomenal success. His analysis also shows that EQ is not just about managing others but about understanding yourself:

> Self-aware people can also be recognized by their self-confidence. They have a firm grasp of their capabilities and are less likely to set themselves up to fail by, for example, over-stretching on assignments. They know, too, when to ask for help. And the risks they take on the job are calculated. They won't ask for a challenge that they know they can't handle alone. They'll play to their strengths.

It starts with knowledge about what your strengths are.

Choose a 'super' model

So how do you accurately identify your strengths (and your weaknesses)? Truth-tellers and critical friends in your lives are important for constant updates. But a significant majority of the leaders I interviewed referenced one personality profiling/psychometric model or another in their conversation.

When I was growing up in the UK, magazines like *Cosmopolitan* did personality profile quizzes that put you into humorously labelled 'types'. Personality profiles at work can sometimes feel a bit like that. There are doubts sometimes about their scientific rigour and certainly some have been criticized for the 'So what?' nature of them. However, I, and a significant majority of the interviewees I spoke to, would say they have a very valuable role. Not necessarily as a 100 per cent accurate piece of unchanging analysis or a detailed guide to being better, smarter or faster, but as a stimulant for thinking and as a tool for debate and the understanding of others.

Like much in this book and much in business, personality models will not tell you the answer to how to achieve success but they will stimulate discussion and stimulate thinking. The Myers–Briggs Type Indicator is the most celebrated and was the most quoted by the Superfast leaders in this book. Other people swear by the Gallup 'Strength-finder' (which supports the 'strengths first' approach) and the DISC model. Finding a model which helps stimulate your thinking about your strengths and your understanding of other people will help you move faster to understand others.

Tech tip

Want to try something fun? Want to meet someone new? Want to understand a human? Ask Crystal. The start-up 'Crystal Knows' will give you a prediction about the personality of the person you're about to meet at https://www.crystalknows.com

This works best when that person has a digital footprint, as it takes data from that person's records available online – their blogs, Twitter, Facebook and other online records. Anyone with a LinkedIn account can be checked and Crystal will suggest how to speak, email, work with or sell to them. It will suggest a tone of voice and language to connect effectively with the target.

Clearly, a tool like this will have vulnerabilities (although it can be fun), but getting quickly to know what type of person someone is (someone who values directness or someone who needs data, for example) will short-cut your communications and help you build relationships more quickly.

Start with yourself, and then share that with others.

One of my ex-bosses sat me down on our first day together and outlined clearly what he respected and what he admired in people and what was guaranteed to irritate him as well as what he expected. That saved me time in working out what he was like and avoided awkwardness and inadvertent upset.

Gallup, the American research-based performance management organization, studied the best entrepreneurs to understand the actions and decisions that lead to venture creation and growth. After years of research, Gallup identified ten innate talents that define the best 'builders' of business success:

1 **Confidence:** You accurately know yourself and understand others.
2 **Delegator:** You recognize that you can't do everything and are willing to contemplate a shift in style and control.
3 **Determination:** You persevere through difficult, even seemingly insurmountable, obstacles.
4 **Disruptor:** You exhibit creativity in taking an existing idea or product and turning it into something better.
5 **Independent:** You are prepared to do whatever needs to be done to build a successful venture.
6 **Knowledge:** You constantly search for information that is relevant to growing your business.
7 **Profitability:** You make decisions based on observed or anticipated effect on profit.
8 **Relationship:** You have high social awareness and an ability to build relationships that are beneficial for the firm's survival and growth.
9 **Risk:** You instinctively know how to manage high-risk situations.
10 **Selling:** You are the best spokesperson for the business.

Note the number-one factor: human understanding. 'Know thyself' and understand others to deliver the confidence that people need.

Electric eels and catfish

An understanding of yourself is critical for helping you connect with people if you are pitching for something or interviewing. Louisa Clarke, 'Pitch Guru' at the Caffeine Partnership, uses a great metaphor to capture the awful feeling when you don't connect in an important meeting:

> Edith Sitwell, the British poet, critic and eccentric who died in the mid-1960s, once described herself as 'an unpopular electric eel set in a pond of catfish' and anyone who's ever pitched for business knows that sometimes, despite your best efforts, you're the electric eel and the catfish ain't buying.

Her advice is to work on understanding yourself and how your style comes across to others and to work on using a behavioural profiling model to help understand the 'archetypes' of people. In years of working with professionals, she has taught them successfully to understand human behavioural archetypes better to give them insights into how to pitch and present more effectively – winning over people and winning faster.

She explains why this helps and why it is important:

> Is knowing this and flexing your style to build better rapport manipulation? Am I asking you to abandon your own personality and become chameleon-like? No. I am only interested in helping you get your message across effectively. You can use these insights to get a sense of who you will be pitching to and how to best communicate with them – couching your idea, your solution in a way that has the greatest chance of being understood by the client. It puts your thinking into their language and removes any distractions that could get in the way.

> Clarke points out that
>
> It turns out that the electric eel is not related to true eels but is a member of the neotropical knifefish order, which is actually more closely related to the catfish. With a bit of effort, I bet they'd find they had lots in common after all.

The value of critical friends

To accelerate your understanding of yourself, it's worth allowing yourself the indulgence of a 'critical friend' to talk to (a coach is ideal for this) and work on identifying more about yourself. 'Our lives teach us who we are,' says the novelist Salman Rushdie, who has certainly had an interesting life. Some of us learn more quickly than others, though.

In a recent edition of BBC Radio 4's *Desert Island Discs,* the multi-award-winning songwriter and musician Ed Sheeran confessed that he'd made some mistakes when his monumental fame hit him at an early age and, to help with this, his entourage now included a number of his childhood friends to give him balance and make sure he had people to challenge his behaviour. It's a contemporary version of the Roman emperors who employed slaves to whisper 'Thou art mortal' on triumphal marches. Such challenges to your thinking will improve the quality of your approach.

Heidrick & Struggles, the C-Suite recruitment experts, published a report emphasizing the need for challengers at a senior level: 'One of the most important things is having people around you telling you how wrong you are.' The more senior you become, the more you can inadvertently believe the hype of your own success. And that means there are more people around you who see you as a title rather than as a human being. A senior agency head I interviewed said that he was able to build relationships with client CEOs mainly by asking 'How are you?' before he discussed business. He said: 'When you become that senior, people see the title first, not the person. So they tell them things, they ask for things, rather than connecting as humans.' Another company head told me how taking the top job resulted in a tangible, noticeable change in the way people around him treated him, even people who'd worked with him for years.

It is only human to enjoy the sensation of being treated as special, as important, as infallible. But if you want to survive the knocks of leadership, if you want to keep learning, you do also need to make sure that you have those around you who will challenge you and those who will make you think or help you to think differently.

You need people who will give you the radical candour you need, who will be your friend but also ready to challenge you constructively. It's likely that you need a few of these – people who are trusted advisors whom you trust to be honest. Most senior leaders have a coach who will push them further; someone who is on their side but also on their case. Most have built up a team of people who sharpen their thinking, their whetstones. Build up a practical team of those who will be able to push your thinking and feed back on your behaviour.

This could be informal – or you could formally invite critical friends on to the board. At Coca-Cola, when Sprite was positioned as a youth brand, the team had a 'cool advisor' – a skateboarding champion who gave a refreshingly non-corporate perspective.

Like any situation where you want to move faster in a certain direction, sometimes this starts with small actions, regularly practised:

- After key activities or meetings, practise quick reflections with trusted partners where you discuss 'what we could have done better' as a team and make sure that you ask someone who you know will be direct. 'Is there anything I could have done that might have helped more?'
- Reward the 'voices': people who speak up constructively and who are able to build and develop ideas should be praised and encouraged. When you

talk to Karen Blackett, now one of the most highly respected leaders in the agency world, about her trajectory to success, she says, 'That's an interesting question, what accelerated me? I genuinely think it was just speaking up. It was saying a nugget of insight and speaking up about it and knowing who to go to speak about it and I suppose it's my bosses at the time observing.' As a leader, you need to find ways to reward those who contribute with passion and who are prepared to say something which may not always be in total agreement with the voices of power.

- Provide forums for voices to be heard more within the organization. As Patrick Lencioni, the high-performance team analyst, puts it, 'If people don't weigh in, they can't buy in.'

Your network is a support network

There aren't that many people in business who are truly lovers of 'networking' as an activity. I happen to be one (I'm curious about people and quite happy to talk to strangers) but I know so many friends, clients and colleagues who curl their lips in horror at the thought of doing it. However, most successful people I speak to have built a 'network' outside their immediate work team which has contributed enormously to their ability to move fast and win things.

I spent some time recently with the managing partner of an early-stage VC fund talking about why female founders/entrepreneurs receive less funding in the UK than they proportionately should. There are many frustrating challenges involved here but his perspective or perception was that one of the challenges for female founders is often that they'd spent less time building up their network (either because networking was something women did less or – his theory – because the women had been focusing on children in the evenings rather than building their careers). I certainly know a number of incredible women whose network is extensive and impressive (despite having children and spending time with them), so I suspect this view is somewhat simplistic. Nonetheless, based on my observations and the feedback from a number of the interviewees for this book, I'd strongly suggest that building your network is an extremely helpful speed tool.

Here's the fantastic Sarah Wood, the Chair of Unruly Group (yes, a female entrepreneur who has succeeded in building a global business), sharing her point of view on this:

> If you want to be an effective leader, you'll want to be well networked both within your organization and beyond, across your sector. You don't network because it's fun to collect business cards; you network because you need to meet people to build business context, procure market intelligence, spot patterns, meet potential clients, source the best colleagues, influence decisions and look around corners to see where the next big ideas are coming from.

Sometimes people are uncomfortable with the 'schmoozy, use-y' side of networking where people assess how useful you are, but the reality is that, with the right attitude, networking can introduce you to new friends with new perspectives and ideas, people you can learn from and people you can help as well as those who can help you.

Building up relationships with key people whom you respect and enjoy spending time with so that they become 'your network' can be a real support for helping you make key decisions or speeding up unlocking doors. The more senior you are, the more important networking is in finding new roles as you move careers or in asking people for advice on who can help consult in your business – or invest in it. We talk about a 'hive mind' to help with thinking; your network is a hive of help.

The Chinese business market is growing Superfast in terms of its influence globally. In China, there is a concept known as *guanxi*, which is a central idea in society, broadly translated as either 'connections' or 'relationships' but which has much wider implications which are hard to translate. Originating in the social philosophy of Confucius, it conveys the sense of the implicit mutual obligations, reciprocity and trust which come from networks and relationships. Those looking at the phenomenal growth of China in business quickly understand that this concept remains seminal in their speed. Amee Chande, the UK MD of Chinese mega-giant Alibaba, the world's largest retailer, describes the importance of relationships, connections and networks within an organization (and understanding how much 'relationship capital' one has) like this: 'In a rapidly changing world where things are quite uncertain and changing quickly, relationships facilitate success where process can get in the way.'

Building friends, allies, connections and a network can be great for your sanity, for gaining access to a diversity of ideas and learning, and for getting things done. Relationships take time to build but save you time in making things happen.

There are so many ways to meet people that aren't just 'networking events'. These might include asking people you trust to introduce you to interesting people or people in a certain field, or getting involved in charities or giving back to the community, and are a wonderful route to broadening your contacts.

You can meet people in the most unlikely places. I first met one of my favourite people, the co-founder of Azoomee, entrepreneur Douglas Lloyd, when he was sitting next to me on a train: he looked over my shoulder at an investment deck I was writing and ended up offering to invest in my business. Your network isn't about *using* people, it's about *choosing* people you'd like to carry on being in contact with. You have to be realistic and resilient in building up a network: not everyone you meet will love you or have time to be part of your network; move on and don't take it personally. Those you do meet and you stay in contact with can be incredible allies and accelerators for you.

Know your personal brand

Craig Kreeger is the CEO of Virgin Airlines and has presided over an impressive turnaround in the business. He had the challenge of coming in as a new CEO (traditionally, incumbent CEOs perform better and faster because they understand how to navigate the organization). One of the keys for him was working out what his 'personal brand' was – what kind of person he was and what worked about that. His 'genuineness' in communication was at the heart of this. When you meet him, you immediately understand this – he is naturally very open, a strong listener and with a real predilection for candour and the truth of a situation. Knowing that this was what he was like and what he wanted to be, he relaxed into this and helped convey a real consistency in the experience of being with him which allowed people to build trust and openness themselves.

Karen Blackett was lauded as 'the most admired chief in UK ad land', according to research that *Campaign* magazine did into the chief executives of British agencies, and, meeting her, it's easy to see why. One of the things that has helped her, the self-described 'exhausted mum', get to the top of her game has been thinking about her own personal brand. Authenticity may be a phrase that people are tired of in the marketing world but it's tremendously important to her:

> People understanding their own personal brand and how that helps the company is what's important. In any business that's moving, and especially in this industry when it's so dynamic and fast-paced, your role isn't to wait for HR to tell you what your job should be, your role should be to tell your managers how you can contribute and what your job is, so people understanding their own personal brand is important. I think the more senior you become, the easier that becomes.

There will be those who react cynically to the idea of a personal brand, but if you think about how brands work, it's just about creating a short cut for people to understand you, a way to make it clear what type of person you are from the start. Blackett's advice is to work out the simple questions about yourself:

1 What am I good at?
2 What do I really enjoy?
3 What contribution can I make to the organization I'm in?

The first question might benefit from a critical friend's point of view – ask others, look at your appraisals, be honest about your real strengths. The second question is very important – if we do things we really enjoy, we tend to be better at them and we certainly are more likely to have the mental energy to keep at them. And, lastly, being able to show how you can contribute and what role you can play makes it quicker and easier for people to believe in you. 'Knowing my own brand,' Blackett comments, 'and my bosses or stakeholders or decision-makers knowing what my personal brand was, that definitely sped up my own career progression.'

One note on your personal brand: once you've worked out what it is and what your strengths are, get comfortable with communicating it confidently. I'm often frustrated by seeing smart people in business who derail their own progress with self-deprecation. Marlène Schiappa, the French Secretary of State for Equality, is a fascinating 'brand' in herself. She is an eloquent speaker and committed reformer who moved from writing novels and blogging to politics, and she refers to this issue specifically when she talks about women needing to take responsibility for communicating their own strengths. 'Please,' she says, 'do not belittle yourselves with the language you use. I never want to hear "I have a *little* job" or "I have a *little* project". If you must use an adjective, make it 'great' or 'important'.

There are many small changes like this that can be made to improve how you communicate your personal brand effectively;

once you know what you are and what you want to be, you can make people's acceptance of who you are faster and clearer. Know yourself, and share that knowledge with others positively.

Working out the fit

Understanding yourself also helps you make the right decision about what type of organization you will sail fastest in. There are brilliant people who just can't move fast because they are in the wrong context and culture for what they like, are good at and flourish in.

If you are used to a highly organized structured environment or need the reassurance of full data studies, a more intense entrepreneurial 'wing it, try it, risk it' approach might make you uncomfortable. If, by contrast, you love the ability to get things done and prefer working on direct projects where your individual input has an impact immediately, then a risk-averse multinational bureaucratic approach will kill you. Are you someone who thrives on a team culture or prefers to achieve individually? What personal values are important to you?

> If you want to be able to move at the right speed, you need to be in the right environment that challenges you enough for stimulation but supports your values and your skills so that you can fit in and fly from the start.

Know how little you know

We exist in a world crammed full of knowledge, data and constantly changing contexts. You can't possibly know everything, so part of a leader's self-knowledge is working out how and what to learn and how to do it quickly. It's also about being ready to 'unlearn'. Gary Coombe, President of Procter & Gamble Europe, talks about the importance of 'unlearning' – by which he means not continuing an arrogant attitude of thinking that what worked five years ago is the only answer; the world is changing too fast. Andrew S. Grove from Intel places importance on this, too:

> Admitting that you need to learn something new is always difficult. It is even harder if you are a senior manager who is accustomed to the automatic deference which people accord you owing to your position. But if you don't fight it, that very deference may become a wall that isolates you from learning new things. It all takes self-discipline.

Know who you need to help you move faster

It's not all about you, you know. Other people will help you deliver at speed. And it's not just the obvious people – your team and the brilliant people you hire and retain – but other people who have been there before, those who have grappled with the same problems, those who have therefore developed strategies or software to help.

Use 'laziness' to find and be smart about who can help. It's about standing on the shoulders of those who have gone before or using the brains of others to get you where you want to go more quickly. It's about listening to people who can challenge, stimulate and advise. It's about looking for the algorithms, the code, the ideas that can be used for your mission and your goals and making them work for you.

Beg, borrow, steal, hack, modify and build on what has gone before. Borrowing, stealing or whatever you want to call it is a key secret of success – demonstrated perhaps most visibly in the tech companies that have dominated in the last 30 years. Steve Jobs was clear about this: 'We have always been shameless about stealing great ideas.'

To lead, read …

You can't connect to everyone. You can't consume all the knowledge that is available. But you can sharpen your mind with an easy habit. As part of writing this book, I have spoken to successful leaders of all kinds. Some lead large corporates, some lead start-ups, some lead opinion, some lead government policy, some lead charities. All are very different, and each has their own approach to leadership. However, as you'd expect, there are some recurring themes.

One recurring theme is their inquisitiveness, their total commitment to continued learning and their interest in the views and opinions of others. I found surprising their interest in me; how they questioned me, keen to listen and learn as well as to impart their own point of view. And a surprisingly high proportion of them read widely.

Many people feel that they simply can't find time to read in a ridiculously busy life. But it's vital that people do, especially if they want to 'lead at speed'. Chris Anderson, as the owner of TED, could be said to have popularized a great alternative to books – the worldwide phenomenon of TED Talks. But he is also an author of a 'real-life, old-school book' and asserts: 'I believe in books. I do not see a talk as a substitute for books. I see it as an alternative to watching kittens.'

Anne Boden, the ambitious founder of Starling Bank, has an office like a library, which is not surprising as she reads three to four books a week. 'I read three or four books a week. I love ideas; I love grappling with anything I can grab out there, any wisdom to apply.' Her story is not atypical. Lee Hodgkinson, the CEO of OSTC, the global trading firm, is clearly a busy man. He is also a man who sits in an office surrounded by books and a conversation with him pans through a wealth of literary and business references; he makes time to continue to learn, to read and to think: 'Find some time every week to reflect every week on what is going around you.' Other leaders support this approach: Mark Zuckerberg ran a 'Year of Books' from his personal Facebook account and Bill Gates's well-documented love of books supports the 'learners are earners' phrase. Bill Gates even released a 'How to' YouTube video to help people read books better.

Richard Kilgariff, the founder of Bookomi who tracks the reading of CEOs through Bookomi's Monthly Most Wanted chart and connects non-fiction authors to leaders in clubs and companies like Soho House, Google and Facebook, says:

The time versus reading problem is a myth based on a common misconception that leaders read hundreds of books a year. They don't. Nobody does. Except possibly literature students or the retired. Leaders choose what they read carefully – news, information, fiction, non-fiction – and make time for new knowledge, rather than playing catch-up with endless reading lists. Once selected, the right books are actually an efficient shortcut to long-term thinking that has taken decades to acquire. Socrates advised his pupils to 'improve yourself by the writing of others, to gain easily what they have laboured hard for', and we too can access brilliant minds in text, video, audio and live events easier and faster than ever before.

If we want to lead interesting lives and interesting business, we need 'leadership peripheral vision' – that is, we need to not just be looking ahead but be aware of what is around. A thirst for knowledge and a lust for reading develops that like nothing else. The most innovative and creative thinkers find stimulation in an inquisitive, curious approach. Reading sharpens your mind.

Espresso takeaways

Knowledge is power

KNOW YOUR AUDIENCES

Get closer to your customer. Work out your stakeholders, your partners, your allies, your accelerators. Communication is quicker, anticipation is better, innovation and inspiration are more likely to occur. Read. Observe. Listen.

KNOW YOUR TEAM

Get to know your team members' skills, strengths, personalities, ways of working together. Build a superteam that works together to make the boat go faster. Listen. Spend time understanding one another and working on your team cohesion and interaction.

KNOW YOURSELF

Take time to work out how you work best. It always starts with you. Surround yourself with feedback and critical friends.

All these things require time, but time for them can be incorporated into other things and in bite-sized pieces. It will pay numerous dividends for your pace.

Truth

Candour, conflict and the helpfulness of honesty

'When you've got candour … everything just operates faster and better.'

*Jack Welch, Chair and CEO of
General Electric (1981–2001)*

Jack Welch was CEO of GE for 20 years, during which time the market capitalization of GE rose from $14 billion to $410 billion, making GE the most valuable company in the world. Like all leaders, he has had his critics but his achievements certainly mean his opinions on leadership are worthy of consideration. He was a great believer in 'candour', and he applied this belief to every element of his business, to every business meeting and to every appraisal. Candour, says Welch, generates ideas and speeds things up:

> I've always been a huge proponent of candour … but I've come to realize that I underestimated its rarity. In fact, I would call lack of candour the biggest dirty little secret in business. What a huge problem it is. Lack of candour basically blocks smart ideas, fast action and good people contributing all the stuff they've got. It's a killer. When you've got candour – and you'll never completely get it, mind you – everything just operates faster and better.

Twenty years after Jack Welch left GE, the question of how to stimulate and nurture candour remains as topical as ever for organizations who want to operate 'faster and better'. In this chapter, then, we look at the how honesty really is the best policy in business, and we explore the ways in which truth is a powerful tool to help get you places faster.

Radical candour

Developing a culture of candour is a highly effective tool – for teamwork, for innovation, for greater speed. Instant candour and fast feedback helps working relationships. Candour improves the quality of work. Candour encourages ideas to develop.

The truth? This isn't an easy fix and Jack Welch acknowledges the reality of not ever being able to achieve total transparency. Getting candour into an organization is challenging. People are human, people are afraid, people are nervous of offending people.

Speaking up and speaking out require bravery or recklessness or a very specific culture. If you want a truth-based organization or team, it needs to be looked at, person by person, leader by leader, as well as finding ways to make it part of the culture.

Here's some ideas for how to instil candour in your culture and communications to 'make the boat go faster'.

Kim Scott was a Google employee working with Sheryl Sandberg when she worked out the power of what she's memorably christened 'Radical Candor' (Americans operate without the 'u' – a leaner version of the word!). Scott had just joined Google and presented to the founders and CEO an update on how the Adsense business was doing. She thought it had gone well, so at first she was slightly irritated to find that Sheryl Sandberg, her boss and erstwhile mentor, didn't seem so positive. Sheryl took her for a walk and gave her all the positives she saw in the presentation but then made a comment about how Kim's presentation had contained a number of 'ums'. Kim brushed this aside but Sheryl persisted with the point and then got to the crux of the matter by telling her honestly 'You know, Kim, I can tell I'm not really getting through to you. I'm going to have to be clearer here. When you say "um" every third word, it makes you sound stupid.'

Ouch. Truth hurts.

Truth also helps.

Sandberg was able to make this kind of comment to Kim with credibility because she herself was a successful leader already. In addition, it was taken as a constructive comment which would be listened to because she'd already shown that she cared about and supported Kim, helping her throughout her career. She wasn't being rude for the sake of it; she was being candid because she wanted to help her improve.

Scott went on to deliver a successful TED talk on the subject of Radical Candor and advises companies on how to implement it, having gone on to see what a powerful tool this type of constructive feedback can be in organizations. The most important thing a boss can do, Scott believes, is to focus on guidance: giving guidance, receiving it and (vitally) encouraging it. 'Guidance, which is fundamentally just praise and criticism, is usually called "feedback", but feedback is screechy and makes us want to put our hands over our ears. Guidance is something most of us long for.'

You might expect that bosses give this kind of guidance all the time but the truth is, they don't. This is the reason it's radical. It's not the standard, it's not the norm and it's not easy. It's awkward. Bosses worry about the impact, they forget about doing it ... and/or they don't know how to do it well. Helpfully, Scott sets this in the context of the ways in which you can get this wrong.

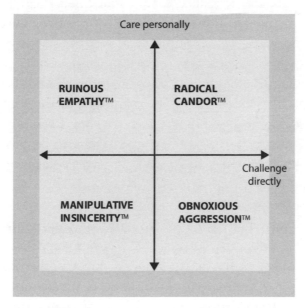

FIGURE 7.1 The Radical Candor tool

The forms of feedback or guidance are set on two axes to show you where it can fall short. The horizontal axis is about 'challenging directly'. This is where you need to be honest and communicate candidly even when it is uncomfortable. Too much and you are 'obnoxiously aggressive'. Your guidance must always be accompanied by thinking about the vertical axis – caring personally. If you don't care, you are manipulative and/or insincere.

> Radical Candor is important when you are thinking about the need for speed. It is radically time-saving.

Candour and teamwork

The benefits of this approach do not just enhance the boss–employee relationship. Implemented thoroughly, it is about peer-to-peer accountability and is crucially, about a powerful tool to avoid the backstabbing and bitchiness that can occur in a workplace environment. It is also your best weapon to reduce your complicit support of office 'politics'. The best-selling American author Patrick Lenconi defines this type of mendacious manoeuvring in the workplace: 'Politics is when people choose their words and actions based on how they want others to react rather than based on what they really think.' That is, words are actions which are likely to be manipulative or insincere, obnoxious or aggressive instead of being radical enough to be truly candid.

You'd assume that a less political, more open culture might be a more constructive place to be generally. It's not just more constructive but it's also a place where things can move forward faster because, if this culture of candour is rolled out across the team, there is no time wasted on second-guessing what the other person is thinking. Iterative, improving, marginal gains are a shared goal. Everyone can 'commit to making the boat go faster' through honest conversations which highlight the opportunities to improve.

Making the boat go faster: committing to candour

In 2004 the British Men's Coxless 4 won gold in a nail-biting photo-finish result. They had spent four years training for a race which lasted only six minutes and Great Britain beat Canada by a time of only 8/100ths of a second. It is perhaps unsurprising that the British rower Matthew Pinsent wept at the medal ceremony. They were coached for this event by Jürgen Gröbler, who has worked with gold-medal-winning teams for an eye-watering 11 consecutive Olympic Games. One of the keys to their success was a very simple question: 'How will we make the boat go faster?' This provided a powerful focus point when giving feedback and making tough decisions. They made the commitment to one another: 'We must say and do what it takes to make the boat go faster.'

It's an unrelenting focus on improvement, and by fixating on how to reach that target the crew had a context in which they continued to provide world-beating performances day after day, even when the big day was still years away. That winning time of only 8/100ths of a second led to gold. When reflecting on their success, the team said that a significant factor was their commitment to one another as a team – they'd promised each other that they would call out and say what was needed to make their boat go faster, no matter how uncomfortable it was.

The British Men's Coxless 4 were united by their focus on their shared goal. There is a reason why sports teams are so often cited as examples of teamwork; you can see the results of what they do and their shared goal is normally crystal clear. In the workplace environment, people's personal goals are frequently at odds with the team goal or the prioritization of individual attainment challenges the team goal. If you want to go faster, this is where candour helps force a shared debate about the positive results of unity.

Talking to Alan Gilpin, the CEO of Rugby World Cup, about the power of candour as a speed tool, he agrees vociferously. As he says, the fixed date and global importance of something like a World Cup brings a very focused perspective to the need to lead at speed:

> Those who work on the Olympics or sporting events like this have to be people who understand that the event is happening on that day whatever … and we have to be ready. No ifs, no buts, it has to be done on time and done brilliantly.

He talks about the importance of teamwork in delivering this type of pressured event and the need for a highly connected superteam working together, and he references rugby as a genuine inspiration. Everyone on a team has to be fit, everyone has to work together. Honesty, truthfulness, feedback and candour play a role in maintaining that positive sense of team.

Rugby has strong lessons for those wanting to understand teamwork. In discussing a commitment to honesty, Alan has taken inspiration from one of the most inspiring teams in the world, the consistently successful Kiwi team, the All Blacks, who as a team encourage each other with candour: 'In the front, not in the back', they say – that is, if you have something to say, tell it to us straight. You want the ball passed directly to you; you want the challenge or the question and the feedback to be given just as directly.

Other phrases used to describe this approach include 'front-stabbing' and 'fierce conversations'. Related here, too, is the term 'mokita', which is a great Papua New Guinean word to describe 'that which everyone knows but no one speaks of'. It's about encouraging people to talk about 'the elephant in the room' even when that feels personal or tough to discuss.

Airbnb has been a hyper-fast-growing company, so the culture has always changed quickly. The organization's leaders wanted to understand and get feedback, so they adopted 'Culture Amp' as a fast-feedback tool (it's a data-driven platform to track employee morale). When results from Airbnb's Culture Amp survey suggested that they weren't as open and honest as they wanted to be, one of the founders, Joe Gebbia, threw out an idea that he called 'elephants, dead fish and vomit' – a nomenclature the company has adopted to open up a dialogue. As Mark Levy, Airbnb's Gloval Head of Employee Experience, explains:

> Elephants are the big things in the room that nobody is talking about, dead fish are the things that happened a few years ago that people can't get over, and vomit is something that sometimes people just need to get off their mind and you need someone to just sit there and listen.

By giving a fun name to this and raising it openly, it encouraged more of a two-way dialogue between management and their teams.

When candour is absent, what can occur instead is resentment or stalled projects. This happens if people don't confront the issues that need to be called out and corrected. You then get a terrible waste of time where people are second-guessing others or circumventing the issues instead of tackling them head-on.

Candour avoids confusion but it can lead to conflict. Handled skilfully, it allows constructive, open communication in teams. The language used is important, however, and it needs to be set in a balanced, positive culture – otherwise, it's just the workplace equivalent of those slightly annoying bores who delight in proudly claiming to 'call a spade a spade'. Being prosaic and obvious, being mean, being brutal – that's clearly short-sighted and ineffective. Speaking up about improvements and also about achievements – that's an acceleration opportunity,

Candour and feedback

At the Caffeine Partnership, we've committed to a culture of candour. This is made real in a pragmatic way through the repeated disciplined habit of reviewing everything we do immediately after the event. We do a 'polish' after every key event and meeting where we cover what has gone well, what bits were wobblier and make suggestions: 'perhaps next time we could …'. This includes those involved giving direct feedback on each other, where they highlight the strongest parts of what was delivered or done and highlight areas where next time they might consider doing something differently.

> The discipline of feedback reminds us of our duty to each other, our responsibility to help each other improve and be the best version of ourselves we can be.

You do need your friends to help you grow. Remember, you can't see yourself as others see you, so we need our 'critical friends' to hold up a mirror to how we are communicating. That person can also judge more effectively than you how you are interacting with others – they may catch the rolling of eyes or sense your reaction more easily than you can. They can listen clearly to what you say and how you say it. A critical friend must always point out what went well: they are a friend and they are helping you.

The human tendency (particularly in the ambitious among us) is to only really focus on the 'improvement areas' in feedback, but it's equally important to make sure that you are conscious of your strengths and where you are improving, so do make sure you adopt a balanced approach and listen fully.

If you are lucky enough to have a critical friend prepared to play this role, listen carefully and tell them how useful this 'guidance' is. If you don't, start to implement it in your team and your culture – encouraging people to give direct, frank feedback … to help the boat go faster, to help the team be stronger and to help the people they work with improve and master their abilities even more.

Effective feedback *has* to be fast – that's where it has an accelerating effect. Seek feedback after a meeting while the experience is crisp and clear in your mind. Ask for feedback while an important project is under way to help you at a time when you have the opportunity to improve. This guidance will allow you to polish your performance, to pivot, to perfect while you are in play. Like so much else in life, 'little and often' when it comes to candour and feedback has a cumulative effect which is phenomenally powerful.

'Micro-learning' is a way of teaching and delivering content to learners in small, very specific bursts. It has been formally developed for training courses, but it's also useful as a way of thinking about your leadership role in providing guidance and part of sustained commitment to ongoing candour between colleagues, managers and teams. You are helping people 'master' their skills by guiding them with your praise and your feedback. Done well, it helps make people feel they are improving; the psychology of this – the confidence and the sense of mastery – is highly motivating.

The idea of mastery is strongly linked with the concept of 'grit' – the patience and perseverance to keep practising until you improve. That grit is needed to take the micro-learning opportunities and the (sometimes tough) feedback that people give you and use them as growth opportunities.

For those who want to develop their mastery and to grow, sustained practice and experience are necessary and the ability for 'learning' to be delivered in nuggets (and at the right time) makes it most effective. Feedback works better when it is fast and the messages can be delivered in a more digestible way.

> A mindset of micro-learning is much more relevant in a fast-moving world and much more efficient for a busy brain to digest.

Telling the truth is simpler and easier

A constant theme of this book has been finding ways to make life easier for you and reducing your 'cognitive load', that is, reducing the brain effort. As Mark Twain pointed out over a hundred years ago: 'If you tell the truth, you don't have to remember anything.' Lying is tiring. Obscuration is, frankly, onerous. There's a real release to be found if you consciously focus on candour and on telling the truth: frankness is faster and being more direct is a more direct way to get there.

Speak up – speak out

Candour is not just a manager's responsibility, and the need for honesty in a rapidly moving world is about all employees feeling empowered and encouraged and enthusiastic about speaking up and speaking out. Too often, people don't say what they are thinking. It's a prevalent problem in many businesses. They don't suggest ideas. They don't comment or criticize.

The idea of speaking up and being frank can be intimidating to the natural diplomats among us, the ones who like to avoid conflict, the ones who love being 'nice and encouraging'. However, being nice and encouraging is infinitely less effective when you are that way all the time. Radical candour works when you are candid, not just mindlessly supportive. And, in addition, you have a duty to be candid, not just to help the people you work with but to help the product(s) you are delivering.

Evidence suggests that greater diversity on a board or a team leads to stronger ideas and innovation, but this only works if everyone speaks up and speaks out (and listens to others). A drive and a commitment to candour among a broad group of people supports a feeling that criticism isn't personal but is part of a team or general desire to iterate and improve.

We need ideas in business. We need suggestions. And we really need debate. Frankness, speaking up, contributing opinions, ideas, thoughts – these are what add to inspiration, accelerate the discussions, improve the product. Jack Welch puts it this way: 'Candour generates speed. When ideas are in everyone's face, they can be debated rapidly, expanded and enhanced, and acted upon.'

Creative abrasion

Truth and speaking up lead to the 'creative abrasion' which gets ideas to their most beautiful and polished state, by subjecting them to debate and argument. If everyone gets on and agrees all the time, then that leads to a lovely comfortable environment – but it is, incontrovertibly, not good for innovation. If you all agree, then you are agreeing to mono-thinking, groupthink, an anorexia of ideas. Embrace some abrasion as part of your workflow.

'Creative abrasion' is a term first coined by the founder and president of Nissan Design International, Jerry Hirshberg, who has spent a lifetime dealing with the creative process and aiming to deliver innovation. Creative abrasion describes an environment where ideas are productively challenged. Creating a situation which allows opposing approaches to scratch and rub up against each other is seen by many who foster innovation as critical. It forces people to think and evaluate their approach. However, it can be unsettling for managers, those who are uncomfortable with conflict and those who don't feel that heated debate is appropriate or constructive. Jerry Hirshberg writes in *The Creative Priority*:

> Friction between individuals and groups is typically thought of as something harmful ... Creative abrasion recognizes the positive dimensions of friction, the requisite role it plays in making things go. Without it, engines would not work, a crucial source of heat and electricity would be eliminated ... Recognizing, marking, and transforming pregnant moments of friction and collision into opportunities for breakthroughs are the work of creative abrasion.

You may remember the 1980s and 1990s approach to 'brainstorming', where the person leading the session always said:'Don't judge: every idea is a good idea.'This was formed from a positive intention, the desire to help people overcome their fear of being judged and the knowledge that a rubbish idea can be built on or can spark a better one. More recent thinking suggests that vigorous debate is valuable in the creation of ideas, that arguing about and critiquing ideas can lead to better development of those ideas. Get passionate people in a room arguing about ideas and you get 'creative abrasion' – that magical, robust conflict which can polish and improve ideas. It works best when set up well, as part of the culture, as a clear sign of the shared commitment to quality.

Steve Jobs's desire to ensure diversity of viewpoints in his team, coupled with his own willingness to 'embrace conflict', allowed creative abrasion to support his quest for perfection. Greg Brandeau, who worked with Steve Jobs at NeXT Computer before helping to build Pixar Animation Studios as SVP of Technology and Chief Technology Officer at Walt Disney, explains how he's seen it work:

> Creative abrasion is the ability to have difficult conversations. It's like taking sandpaper and polishing something. You have a number of diverse points of view in the same room, and everybody is riffing off each other's ideas. You're doing [the improvisational comedy approach of] 'Yes, and' instead of 'Yes, but.'

And when you don't agree? Take a leaf from Jeff Beos's playbook. The Amazon dynamo, when talking about 'high-velocity decision-making', suggests that in some situations leaders should 'use the phrase "disagree and commit"'. He explains:

> This phrase will save a lot of time. If you have conviction on a particular direction even though there's no consensus, it's helpful to say, 'Look, I know we disagree on this but will you gamble with me on it? Disagree and commit?' By the time you're at this point, no one can know the answer for sure, and you'll probably get a quick yes.

Honesty combined with the trust in a team, together with a united willingness to move forward – this gives you the abrasion needed to polish something brilliantly and also the continued momentum you need for speed.

ZOUD: the zone of uncomfortable debate

The 'zone of uncomfortable debate' was identified by Professor Cliff Bowman as part of his research into the nature of high-performing teams at Cranfield School of Management but was popularized by John Blakey and Ian Day in their seminal *Challenging Coaching* book as a tool for executive coaching. Here they write:

> Often in our coaching we will be in the zone of comfortable debate, the outer circle of the diagram. This is natural and serves our purpose for considerable elements of the coaching need. However, there will come decision points in the coaching conversation where the coach can decide to enter the ZOUD, the inner circle, in the pursuit of discovering the 'elephant in the room'.

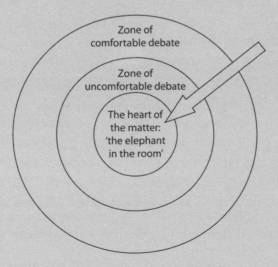

FIGURE 7.2 The zones of debate

This awareness of the need to enter the ZOUD can help accelerate progress in executive coaching but it can also be planned into meetings, idea generation sessions and team approaches. You can signal it in advance to those who are in the room if it makes you more comfortable – challenging doesn't have to be done aggressively and can be done with humour – but getting into the habit of making it part of planning and understanding the need for it can be a remarkably useful tip.

The ability to argue is an essential quality in employees, says Sir Martin Sorrell, the founder and erstwhile CEO of WPP plc, which when he was in the role employed 200,000 people in the group. He knows the danger of being surrounded by 'yes people':

> It's annoying when people disagree with you, but an argument is usually a more constructive exchange than a conversation in which everyone wholeheartedly agrees with each other. If a leader is surrounded by yes people they learn nothing. Good people know how to stand their ground and make their case – even (especially) when others don't want to hear what they are saying.

Within Amazon, this candour is embedded in its leadership principles; the received wisdom of those who have worked at Amazon is that the people who do well there are often those who enjoy a more adversarial atmosphere. The guidance is explicit – this, according to John Rossman, is the 12th principle of 'The Amazon Way':

> Leaders are obligated to respectfully challenge decisions when they disagree, even when doing so is uncomfortable or exhausting. Leaders have conviction and are tenacious. They do not compromise for the sake of social cohesion.

Candour from others is great when it's volunteered and should be encouraged, but candour and frankness have to be modelled from above. So being aware of when it's time to move the debate into a more uncomfortable zone is an opportunity for courage and an opportunity to accelerate progress.

The leader as listener-in-chief

Ursula Burns was CEO of Xerox, the $22-billion enterprise giant, from 2009 to 2016 – the first African-American to run a Fortune 500 company – and was appointed to Uber's board in 2017. Regularly featured by Forbes as one of the world's most powerful leaders, she has also been a highly visible and vocal one. She has been described often as someone who doesn't mince words. She says this is something that comes from her upbringing: 'My personality was formed by my mother, my brother and sister, and my community. New York is a tough place. You have to speak up, you have to be a little gritty.'

One of the seminal moments early in her career at Xerox was when she attended a company meeting on work–life balance and openly criticized the executive who was leading the meeting for displaying a lack of passion and principles. When Burns quickly discovered that the executive was an executive vice president she thought that her career in the company was over and that her salary would go 'poof in the wind'. The man, Wayland Hicks, did reprimand her for her tone, telling her that 'There's a way to disagree', but went on to have more meetings with her, before offering her a role which would step-change her trajectory.

Burn's direct approach continued when she became a leader of the organization, describing her role as 'a listener-in-chief'.

Candour in admitting mistakes

Evan Spiegel, the 26-year-old co-founder of Snapchat, has a reputation for an unfiltered leadership style. He admits that one of the areas that he is trying to improve is apologizing when he makes mistakes.

When I ran an e-commerce business, exceptional customer service was our focus. One of our recruitment tests for customer-service people, therefore, was giving them a 'Grumpy Gertrude' test phone call to see how they dealt with a difficult customer complaining about a situation. The situation given was always one which was completely an error on our side (or certainly could be seen as such). For example, the loss of an expensive cashmere baby blanket intended as a gift for a much-wanted first grandchild was actually the error on the part of our shipping agents, but to the 'Grumpy Grandmother' the most important point was that it wasn't her fault and she'd paid for a luxury service which had not been delivered. The successful applicants were the ones who quickly and charmingly admitted how frustrating the situation was – and then apologized for the error. Saying sorry cost nothing but helped express empathy and showed shared disappointment that the service hadn't been perfect, thereby accelerating the relationship with the customer.

Microsoft CEO Satya Nadella made a comment in an interview around the question of women's pay, which generated a huge backlash (he suggested it might generate 'good karma' if women didn't ask for pay raises). Within 24 hours he'd issued a total apology, saying 'I answered that question completely wrong.' This smart, quick response and the rapid realization that he'd made a gaffe is typical of a highly eloquent leader who has written and spoken consistently about the importance of empathy in a world where technology is transforming everything we recognize at a phenomenal speed.

If you're leading an organization or team, your 'sorry' needs to be set in the context of what is being done to 'move and improve' after the apology, to make sure that it feels genuine and that you are still controlling the story. Now, of course, when you are the CEO of a multinational company, this can get more complex – frequently, there is litigious risk in saying 'sorry' – but for many in a workplace environment where things move at speed there's far too much time spent on trying to uncover cover-ups. In teams, there is something highly unsettling about those who refuse to admit mistakes. The quicker you can have a culture where mistakes are acknowledged, acted on and moved on from, the less time is wasted and the less potential there is for uncertainty to fester.

Listen to the quiet ones

If you really want ideas and if you really want to know the truth, you do need to find ways to hear from those who don't have the loudest voices: the introverts who are exhausted by the conference 'brainstorms'; the less-than-confident executives who are fed up with being interrupted so just shut up; the crazy ones whose opinions are so unusual that they never share them but whose ideas are so original that they could change the shape of everything.

Don't rush your listening so much that you don't allow people time to think individually (try building 'pauses' into team sessions to allow for individual reflection), and try to create environments where feedback and ideas can be canvassed in different ways. This is particularly important for global organizations where there may be some cultural norms which make 'speaking up' less comfortable. Sometimes anonymity can give you more chance of hearing 'other' voices. Glassdoor – the online company review site written by people who work in the companies – is an example in itself (although, of course, the self-selection of those who choose to write reviews on there can, as with TripAdvisor, skew things sometimes).

Laszlo Bock, the ex-head of Google's People's Operations, started a company called Humu whose mission is to 'make work better everywhere through science, machine learning and a little bit of love'. He believes that looking at 'voice' is one of the most important factors in making work better … and smarter. The Google People analysis demonstrated that teams which exhibit 'conversational turn-taking' (where everyone's voice is heard) are more effective. As companies like Google have learned, psychological safety – whereby people are comfortable about speaking up without the fear of being shot down or feeling judged – is the number-one factor in high-performance teams, and so smart leaders have looked to find ways to encourage an environment where voices are encouraged and listened to. In a swirling, whirling, constantly evolving world, you need all the brains you have available to you.

Candour is about encouraging people to speak up – but to do that, and to make that useful, you also need to listen. Showing that ideas are recognized – demonstrating that ideas (even when they aren't used) are welcomed and add to the mix, demonstrating, in short, a 'listening leadership' – is a way to motivate your teams and make sure that you are giving yourself a smart competitive advantage. Are you listening? Are you being honest about that? Because if you aren't encouraging the voices to speak up, speak out and speak the truth, you are missing out on opportunities to learn and develop.

It's fine if you disagree with people's perspectives, but allowing them to vent or make suggestions makes them feel more involved and allows you to know what your audience (your internal, employer audience) is thinking.

And, of course, sometimes they might be right and you might be wrong.

Manners maketh the manager

Those who espouse the importance of 'telling it like it is' can often come across as rude. If you are navigating as a leader in a rapidly moving world, I would argue that courtesy is as important as candour and that the two are not mutually exclusive.

I worked with a French senior manager once, who on our first meeting told me that I would be 'too British' – by which he meant 'too polite to call out the problems'. He soon changed his mind. One of Caffeine's core values is to be respectfully disrespectful. We believe it's possible to be candid without being obnoxious (and we believe it's important to be that way). You can challenge people but you can do it with charm.

The stereotype of what the successful businessperson is like – straight-talking, ruthless and, frankly, rude – is, I think, dated and it makes me incredibly uncomfortable. Writing this book has meant interviewing some extremely senior global business leaders, people who are ridiculously, crazily busy with huge pressures on their time and lives. What became clear during my research is that the more successful a person was, generally the more courteous was their approach. It's really striking. I've seen it time and again. The global FMCG CEO? Communicates with charm and shows principles. The famously 'nails' female business leader? Delightfully prompt and polite in emails. The successful entrepreneur? Human and helpful.

All of them straight-talking, direct and clear … and surprisingly candid and open. But all of them courteous.

Grace under pressure

It strikes me as no coincidence that most of the smartest people in business realize that consideration for others is not something to ignore. They don't perceive respectful behaviour as a fundamental weakness. In fact, it's a highly valuable trait. The most motivating managers show empathy (see Chapter 6: Human understanding) and it's also amazing to be led by people who stay calm in the face of constant challenges. The world of business is volatile, uncertain, complex and ambiguous, so I think 'grace under pressure' is an incredibly desirable trait in a leader which should be praised, lauded and role-modelled consistently.

It's good for business to have leaders who are human and respectful. And a consistent diet of considerate behaviour is definitely good for individuals. All the experience I have in business always demonstrates the 'tremendously small world' we operate in (helped even more so by LinkedIn). People talk. People ask. People like to work with decent people. Yes, you have to be smart and savvy, but if people trust you as well then you're on a highway to winning friends and finding success. Conversely, if you behave badly to others in business, it does rebound on you. I won't share the stories here but you'll all have your own examples of where people have lost out on jobs or opportunities because they have alienated people in business.

Now, please don't misunderstand me here. I'm not advocating weakness. As a leader, you have to make tough decisions and you have to fire people, and I'm a firm believer in the challenging but important value of radical candour as a cultural approach. If people are messing you around, being courteous does not mean putting up with insolence or poor performance from them.

As a woman in business, I feel this is particularly important; I worry that sometimes people will push the boundaries further with 'nice'-seeming female bosses. Karren Brady is a fantastic role model of someone who is smart, tough and incredibly full of grace – one of the most courteous, loyal and dignified people in business I've met. But being a diplomat does not mean being a doormat. I love this story about Brady: when she was on a bus with her players early in her career as MD of Birmingham City FC, a player shouted, 'I can see your breasts in that shirt', to which she replied – quick as a flash – 'Don't worry, when I sell you to Crewe, you won't be able to see them from there.' And, reader, she sold him.

Courtesy is not about advocating the pernicious attitude of 'wanting to be liked for being liked's sake'. Anthony Wreford, ex-CEO of Omnicom's marketing services division, described 'leaders wanting to be liked' as one of the most dangerous traps in business. He added that 'It's much more important to be trusted and respected. If people like you as well, that's a bonus, not an objective.'

Don't say sorry but do say thank you …

I get irritated by people (including myself) saying 'sorry' too much but I definitely think we should all say thank you a little more.

Business – and life – can be challenging. To feel appreciated and to see someone showing consideration for you is warming and inspiring. It takes seconds, it costs nothing and it can have a bonding, boosting power that should not be underestimated.

We are drowning in a sea of too many emails but acknowledging important ones with a short message or putting thought into your response is incredibly powerful.

It's part of a world where most smart businesses are moving towards 'purpose before profits' and where people like Tim Cook, the CEO of Apple, can say: 'You don't have to choose between doing good and doing well.'

You can be truthful while still being thoughtful. You can behave with courtesy without losing the ability to be candid. In fact, it's always better if you can be both.

Espresso takeaways

Truths to remember about truth

A culture of candour will accelerate positive relationships and the likelihood of faster idea generation. It is not always simple, and it needs to be developed with an understanding of how people interact, culturally and psychologically. It is a radical way to make a workplace culture simpler and speedier.

Ways to accelerate candour	Action suggestions
Be radical. Help others with constructive, considered candour. Help yourself by saving time. If you are leading, mentoring and developing people, consider how you can practise radical candour and help them develop and build confidence as they grow. If you care (about the business and the people), then well-framed, considerate honesty is a way to accelerate development and your team unity.	Assess your feedback processes, formal and informal, with your line manager or mentees. Share the theory of the accelerating power of candour and consider what more you can do to show that you care.

(*continued*)

Ways to accelerate candour	*Action suggestions*
Commit to candour together. A culture which encourages radical candour will make relationships clearer, save time and encourage people to grow and flourish. It needs to be constructive and balanced, not manipulative or abusive. The truth helps 'the boat go faster' but only if everyone in the boat is committed to it and to rowing in the same direction.	Take time as a team to explore what roles greater truthfulness and transparency could take on. Make it part of your 'charter'.
Ask, listen and understand the real story. Create easy, open ways to share ideas and opinions to get full value from all the brains in the organization. Consciously and frequently ask: 'Is there something we aren't saying here?' What is the 'mokita' – the unspoken thing that everyone knows but no one mentions. Be brave and supportive of each other in your candid relations, with a clear awareness that you are all aiming for the same goal.	Designate people who are listeners-in-chief or whose role it is to amplify voices. Practise clarifying what you are thinking with others in order to encourage them to do the same.
Set up a fast feedback loop wherever you can. Set in motion ways to get 'fast feedback' as you go – by using technology or through people interaction.	Whenever a plan is put in place, ask what the feedback loop will be. Is it timely? Is it truthful? Is it going to be used to inform and evolve your approach?

Ways to accelerate candour	*Action suggestions*
Embrace creative abrasion and zones of uncomfortable debate. Progress is made through creative abrasion, debate and discussion. If you want to make things happen fast, make it as easy as possible for your customers, employees and team. If you want to improve the quality of thinking fast, make time for arguments to take place and create an environment that relishes diversity and development. Recognize the value of entering the zone of uncomfortable debate in one-on-one discussions, and enjoy the ability to review ideas in psychological safety. Accept the difference between agreement and alignment in your team. Be prepared to 'disagree and commit'. Have the backbone to debate, but the discipline to make things happen once a decision has been made.	Look at product and strategy development to understand how creative abrasion can be used as a consistent part of the process. As a team, discuss who will have the final say on key decisions and allow time for input and uncomfortable, vigorous debate.

8

The power of the pause

Thinking slow, smartly

'Stop for a minute, cease your work. Look around you.'

Leo Tolstoy, Russian writer

A regular regret I hear from a number of leaders and managers I know and work with is: 'I don't have time to think.' It's fun to go fast. People feel important being busy, and it's easier to move from meeting to meeting and follow the flow than it is to consciously carve out thinking time and moments to go slower but deeper.

Elsewhere in this book we've explored where practice and action help you learn. Thinking by doing and observing is a highly valuable approach in start-ups, as in life. But there's a difference between being in a hurry and being in a rush.

In a productivity-obsessed world, pausing feels unnatural to many. Delaying and dithering because you are indecisive is one thing and is irritating for those wanting to move forward. Taking a considered decision to apply some focused thinking to a situation, or scheduling time to dream and think is a very different matter. Pressing pause deliberately (rather than faltering) can give you a boost of ideas and energy to accelerate problem-solving and your progress.

The busiest, smartest interviewees for the research for this book have all spent time working out how to steal time to pause to think. Miles Young is a great example. This erudite man crowned a successful career in the capricious world of advertising with his role as Global Chair of Ogilvy & Mather, the international media, PR and advertising firm. Remaining a non-executive for the company, he has now taken a refreshingly different role as Warden of New College, Oxford. Impressively charming manners go hand in hand with an intellectual ferocity in Young, and his analytical nature has led to years of considered thinking about how best to 'make work work'. In conversation with him about the ways in which he helped people do well in a relentlessly competitive world, he zones in immediately on his belief in the accelerating power of taking teams offsite for focused thinking time. He's learned the power of people pausing and firmly believes that creating space for this should be a priority for leaders: 'More important than the idea of pace is the ability to create "space". Space to plan, to dream, to talk together.'

This chapter looks at how to find that space, by managing pace to allow that all-elusive 'time-to-think' and also to explore why a little more 'percolation' can help ideas brew better.

There is magic and logic in chiselling time for planning, dreaming, talking, thinking; it will help accelerate the doing.

Make like a pickpocket: take time (don't make time)

Here's the reality about the squeezed nature of our world of hurry worry and our workplace. You can never really 'make time to do something'; you have to be ruthless and 'take time'. You have to steal it; you have to pick pockets of time; and you have to be ingenious about finding time to be creative.

In April 1928 a journal called *The Forum* published an interview with Henry Ford, the disrupter who brought the world an alternative to a 'faster horse'. In this interview, he commented on the apparent increase in the complexity and rapidity of life (yes, it was ever thus – this topic is not a new one for anyone). Ford expressed cynicism about whether the acceleration of thought had matched it: 'But there is a question in my mind whether, with all this speeding up of our everyday activities, there is any more real thinking. Thinking is the hardest work there is, which is the probable reason why so few engage in it.'

Thinking is hard. It really is. It's far easier to tick things off a 'to do' list than to make structured time to consider options, review ideas, allowing pauses to reflect or review. If your team is doing and running but not ever pausing to think, then you must stop, pause and work out how to steal some proper pauses. It may be that you have a life where you can indulge in fabulously creative time to think over a long period (take that sabbatical!), but most people need to plan a heist to think properly. The smartest people I interviewed for the book consistently discussed how they made time to do this – to plan, to pause, to parley, to ponder, alone or together. In a Superfast world, this won't happen organically, so you as a leader need to plan (and help others plan) considered pauses.

Some implement systematic solutions for the whole organization (the reason why Dropbox bans meetings on Wednesdays is to drive a culture of thinking time); other interviewees have developed personal productivity hacks to manage this. Karen Blackett, one of the most Superfast leaders I've ever met, is Chairwoman of MediaCom UK and Ireland, a fast-paced company working with hyper-fast clients. She carves out time on Fridays for writing time and thinking time, off-site, undistracted and focused. Others block time together with 'brains in a room' to think more deeply and discuss issues more effectively. At Caffeine, we work with a number of global leaders on their senior leader 'summits', which is where they create a focused two-plus days to work through strategic issues; they allow intense debate and thinking to feed into progress. John Allert, global CMO Board Director of McLaren Technology Group, believes this is a smart way to help 'unstick the stuck'.

Other people have reshaped their businesses to drive thinking and decision-making to be more effective – Jake Knapp from Google Ventures (now GV, part of Alphabet) has pioneered the 'sprint' process across a week for just such a purpose. A two-day summit or a week-long focus on accelerating thinking and decision-making may feel like a luxury in the diary but it allows the amplification of 'slow thinking' within a relatively fast period.

Whatever the mechanism, if you are conscious that you are firefighting and reacting rather than taking time to work things through, you need to find the spaces and places to allow people to pause and ponder. This is because planning 'time to think' is one of the most valuable speed-tools your organization will discover – it allows ideas to coalesce, build and evolve, it allows people to make precious connections (sometimes with each other but mainly with ideas from different parts of their life of business) and it delivers fresh and original thinking.

Give yourself permission to 'pause' or 'percolate'

Pulitzer prize-winning *New York Times* journalist Thomas Friedman's latest book is called *Thank You for Being Late*. It's a book on thriving in what he calls 'the age of accelerations'. When asked about where the inspiration for his title came from, he tells the story about an experience he'd repeatedly been having. All over the world he'd have appointments set up and he'd find that meeting after meeting would start behind the scheduled time. He'd receive the inevitable text with the 'Sorry I'm late – traffic/trains/dog-ate-my-homework' excuse.

A considerate man with a considered approach, Friedman got into the habit of making the first thing that he'd say to the other person as they arrived, breathless and apologetic, 'Thank you for being late', and he would tell them what he'd done with that time. The first time it happened he explained to his flustered tardy guest that

> I had minted time for myself. I had 'found' a few minutes to just sit and think. I was having fun eavesdropping on the couple at the next table (fascinating) and people-watching in the lobby (outrageous!). And more important, in the pause, I had connected with a couple of ideas I had been struggling with for days.

Friedman is smart here in three ways. One is that he successfully manages his own irritation. Secondly, he recognizes the positive power of relationships and that starting the meeting with good humour is essential. Thirdly, he transforms the experience into an opportunity to learn, and to 'pause' to think.

I love this story because it's a positive, optimistic reaction to something that was beyond his control. He controlled his attitude when he couldn't control what was happening – and it made him and his guests feel more positive about the situation. 'Like many others, I was beginning to feel overwhelmed and exhausted by the dizzying pace of change. I needed to give myself (and my guests) permission to slow down.' But it also makes a clear refutation of the 'I don't have time to think' excuse. We all need to find the moments and be ready to use them. He talks about it as a 'pause' to think.

There will be moments across your day which can be seen as 'wasted time'. Commutes, on the train, on the bike or in the car, moving between meetings; if you're ready for them, you can use these as thinking time. Novelist Rose Sandy uses an app on her phone to write as she commutes on a crowded underground train; she finds the environment strangely conducive to thinking (and it makes her resent the commute less). Wim Dejonghe uses his bike ride to work to think about problems he needs to solve. One interviewee for this book has a list of things 'to think about properly' ready for any moment where he finds peace and time to reflect. They are all stealing time for what really matters.

Percolation: why strategic procrastination helps 'brew' full-strength ideas

The urge to procrastinate is something we regularly fight with. The surprising truth for those who want to operate in a world moving at pace is that, used wisely, procrastination can be an invaluable tool when you are dealing with the creation of something different. Adam Grant spent time researching on what leads to the world's most creative ideas and published his findings in *Originals*. He discovered that sometimes we need 'to strategically procrastinate'. There are occasions when you need time to mull over and work through a difficult problem or to put together a creative approach to something.

The trick, of course, is not to use this as an excuse for being a 'last-minute Larry', but to consciously decide on what can be done quickly and what needs to have proper time to brew. Think of this as the process of 'percolation' – giving ideas time to brew to full strength, allowing them to steep and develop.

Grant tells the stories of two of the world's most memorable speeches of all time. Lincoln's Gettysburg Address (which at 272 words perfectly illustrates the power of brevity and the 'less lesson' covered in Chapter 5) was only half-composed the day before the address, despite Lincoln having received the invitation to speak two weeks before. The closing paragraph was written the night before and finalized in the morning. Martin Luther King similarly took his time to get his 'I have a dream' speech right for August 1963. He sought perspectives from others and, according to his lawyer and speechwriter Clarence Jones, 'said that this was such an important milestone in our civil rights struggle, we should make every effort to get the best ideas from key players in the movement'. At 3 a.m. the night before the speech, King had still not finalized it. Staggeringly, the script written the night before didn't even include the 'dream' idea at all; this was included by King 'on the hoof', prompted by a gospel singer shouting from behind him, 'Tell 'em about the dream, Martin!' In front of 250,000 people in the crowd, and with millions watching on TV, King, in the words of his speechwriter, 'winged it'.

Reviewing the idea of 'the discipline to delay', Grant points out that in ancient Egypt there were two different verbs for 'to procrastinate': one denoted laziness; the other meant waiting for the right time. Let us take inspiration from other people's language and other people's experience. The right pace sometimes includes planning to pause for thought and waiting for the right time.

> Sometimes good-quality things need to be slept on, debated, thought through.
>
> Ideas and plans need to percolate, to develop, to brew and strengthen.

Taking more time to think things through is also about giving time to make sure that you have all the information and all the insight available before you rush into a 'fast' decision. Input from your team, from advisors and from the market intelligence available will help result in a more considered decision. The 'creative abrasion' of debate helps develop thinking well and polish ideas. Sometimes we must pause, to percolate.

'The soak': start smart (the pre-change pause)

So you have a new challenge, a new role, a new project? You want to begin a process of company renewal? Pause before you make sweeping changes.

The multinational GE identified the need to be more agile, to be able to respond to the changes going on around it. Jeffrey R. Immelt, the organization's CEO from 2000 until 2017, talked proudly of the metamorphosis the business completed: 'We were a classic conglomerate. Now people are calling us a 125-year-old start-up – we're a digital industrial company that's defining the future of the Internet of things.' The man who has been awarded the title of 'World's Best CEO' a record-breaking three times, and who is consistently named as one of the most influential CEOs of recent times, articulates the need for great leaders, working in a complex situation to allow themselves time to percolate their ideas:

Good leaders, good CEOs, are curious. They are absorbing information about potentially important trends and developments all the time, but they don't instantly react to them. They contemplate them. They read about them. They listen to internal and external experts with a variety of perspectives. They engage in what I call a 'soak period' before they reach a conclusion about what the input means for their company and how to act on it.

This period of allowing things to soak in is particularly important for leaders moving into a new role. Pausing in the early days to connect with people in the business and listen to those around you, to read and reflect, to allow your brain to make connections as well – this is what will give you the creative, innovative edge and ideas that it may be harder to be able to focus on later.

A leader who put this approach into highly effective practice was Sara Bennison, the CMO of Nationwide Building Society. She prepared for her new role by indulging in one of her favourite habits – reading omnivorously – through the gardening leave she had available between roles. This supports the good advice a number of interviewees shared – if possible, take a break *between* senior appointments. Take it and use it as reading and thinking time; it's precious. Think of it as prophylactic preparation, measures taken in advance. Bennison used the time wisely:

> I was lucky, moving to this new job, I had four months of gardening leave, which was brilliant as it meant I could spend a lot of time then reading about the history of the building society movement and the history of Nationwide specifically. Because I was moving from a competitor, I knew the market in the sense that I knew the product set and the broad customer needs. What I didn't know and which was unique was the story of this particular brand.

Bennison stole the pocket of time before she started her role. She used it as a soak period, and this deeper thinking experience allowed her the unique insights around the history of building societies which quickly and effectively allowed her and her team to reposition Nationwide behind a powerful new purpose.

> Take a break. Use that break between roles to recharge and also to reflect.

Allow a pause, a soak before you make significant changes in your team or your company – allow that time to strengthen your thinking and fire up your energy to be sure and determined that the approach is right. Move too quickly and you will be less effective in conveying the 'certainty' of your approach or you may be less resilient in defending against the inevitable knocks and questioning you'll face. GE's Immelt explains this:

A leader needs a long soak period mainly because of the tremendous amount of personal fortitude required to drive lasting change in a big organization. You must be profoundly convinced that the company must transform itself – that it's a matter of life or death – because when you start the play, you will immediately get pushback.

Before you 'start the play', press pause. Pause at the start, or, ideally, even before you start. Make sure you tell everyone what you will be doing and explain your reasons. They will respect your desire for reflection. Pause so that you can allow yourself to be reflective, not reactive. Knee-jerking is not a good look in a smart leader.

> Slow down to think, then speed in action will be faster.

Take time. Take time to think. This is the time you need to create the strategy which will then allow you to move faster when crises hit, when decisions need to be made. Allow yourself the luxury of developing your thinking and getting ready.

The 'hundred-day hero'

The 'first hundred days' have become important for those moving into a new role, not just in politics but now in business. In a fast-paced world, there is pressure for leaders to achieve something and to communicate something as quickly as possible. However, managing expectations of those around you is critical when you move into a new role. Paul Polman of Unilever scoffs at the idea of the 'hundred days' as he says he's seen smart leaders put themselves under unnecessary pressure to achieve results fast. Typically, it takes new CEOs six months to start to affect business, so resist any urge to promise results quickly.

Many of the interviewees in the book reflect on the importance of moving fast at the start – but not rushing without thought, without input or without listening to others.

Here are three speed guidelines that can help new leaders achieve a positive impact in those first hundred days and firmly build the foundations for long-term success.

1 Manage expectations

You should do this up, down and all around. Tell your board, tell your boss, tell your team what you are doing and when. Make them understand that you need time to listen, learn and think before you act. If your board or boss is impatient for action, set a clear timetable for when you will present your conclusions or start to drive change but don't let them drive the timetable or judge too quickly. Tell people you are going through 'the soak'.

2 'Only connect'

Listen. Connect. Connect with people, connect the ideas, connect the past with the future.

Talk to the right people around you – your team, potential 'allies', people across the organization who have insights and ideas. CEOs promoted from within – 'incumbent' leaders – usually outperform hero outsiders in terms of results. Partly, this is because the 'outsider' lacks insight into the existing business. But it's also because they fail to properly connect with and consult those who do have insight (and the golden nuggets of knowledge that are essential).

Setting up a number of half-hour/one-hour interviews with people with smart perspectives will buy you supporters and furnish you with priceless insights into what the blockers and barriers to progress are. It will also show humility by indicating that you are willing to learn from others – often a very compelling trait. Lastly, it will allow you to connect ideas in your brain with points of view from different people and different experiences, to create unique and powerful solutions.

> If you want to hit the one-hundred-day deadline as a hero, don't be a solo hero. You'll achieve more by connecting more – both in a hundred days and for as long as you want to stay in your role.

3 Find your focus

You can't do everything. You *shouldn't* do everything. You need to give your team and yourself clear priorities and – as ever – less is more. Use this period to make choices:

- What is the most important thing the business needs to achieve in Year 1? Or what are the 'three pillars' of turnaround?
- What insights about your customer/consumer are most important – what are you going to do for them?

- How will you operate inside out? What changes within the culture will help deliver what you need?

You don't need all the answers and the detail at this stage, but by the hundred-day deadline you'll have a clear plan and usually some quick wins either in place or in progress. Articulate your goal or goals in a way which everyone around you can understand and believe in. Simple storytelling language is a potent way to share this. Clarity on the business brand and purpose will always help make this work – whether it's linking the goal to the agreed purpose, or more accurately defining it.

So when moving into a new role, press 'Play' and move quickly but make sure that you build in the pauses ... to communicate what you will be doing, to listen and, above all, to think.

Try 'speed-dating'

Soon after becoming the Norwegian MD of Hewlett-Packard, Anita Krohn Traaseth set up a series of candid, constructive chats, seeing them as a way for the people there to get to know her quickly and for her to get to know the truth about the organization in a thorough way. She wanted to ask people, one-on-one, questions like: 'What should not change or be messed with by me at HP Norway?', 'What should be changed?', 'Give me examples of bottlenecks' and, finally, 'Do you have a talent or skill you don't get to use now in your position?' It was these 'speed dates' that helped solidify the company's ambition to become known as Norway's top workplace.

'The ability to stop is as important as the ability to go'

W. Timothy Gallwey has spent more than 50 years helping corporates looking to manage change by helping leaders deal with mental blockers to success. He prescribes a single simple tool – 'STOP' – to help a person or team pause and disengage from the tunnel vision that can hit when working at pace:

- Stop
- Think
- Organize your thoughts
- Proceed.

This 'stop' can be a quick pause when the phone rings when you're in the middle of a piece of 'deep work' to check whether you want to answer it; a pause before you speak in a meeting, or a pause in a project. This pause always ends with an action but allows you to make sure that you've thought about the risks and likely consequences of actions and inaction, and nudges you to check that you can organize your thoughts coherently to help others.

This may seem like too obvious a tool, but for those suffering from excessive adrenaline and overwhelm, building in a quick stop has proved extremely helpful. Gallwey describes the perils of working at momentum without fully conscious consideration as like driving 'a Maserati without brakes'. He points out that 'when we are running on adrenaline generated by one crisis after another, it can be very hard to find, much less want to apply, the brakes ... but the faster the car, the more important it is that I know how to slow it down.'

Breathe: the power of the pause in speaking

So you want to speak or present with real impact and influence? Plan your pauses.

The 'less lesson' applies to your speeches, too. We have talked elsewhere about the importance of brevity in communications and in speechwriting. Brevity allows you to repeat key points, allows the audience to keep awake and – importantly – allows you the space to breathe. It allows you the space for powerful pauses.

Pauses are one of the most useful tools that powerful orators learn to use. They make speeches feel like conversations with the audience, not a monologue. They add drama. Just ask the British playwright Harold Pinter, whose career was based on the gaps between his words. It's frustrating to see people rush and stumble into speech; a pause can signify thought, consideration – and confidence.

> Pauses help the confidence of your delivery.

If you – like me – are naturally fast-speaking, pauses are vital. They slow down the pace, which increases the effectiveness of what you are saying by making it more digestible and also the sense of the relative importance of what you are saying.

Your speech tempo can help signify control and power. When working-class boy-done-good Michael Caine was working out how to play a more upper-class character for his first role in *Zulu*, he based his performance on his observations of powerful people – their gestures and the tempo of their communications. He slowed down his speech: 'They speak slower because you're not going to stop listening. The lower and the poorer people are, the faster they speak, because no one listens.'

Pause for attention

The most important moment to build in a pause is at the start of a speech. If you can, count for three seconds before you start.

Hold the room. Get people's attention. You may have to do a 'My name is' introduction at the start ... you may want to do that and then pause before you get into the speech proper. But own the room with that first pause.

Pause for emphasis

Have you made a key point? Pause. Make sure that the audience has heard it – scan the audience, watch their eyes. Make sure that it has landed. Give them a moment to reflect on the importance of what you've said. Let it connect in their brain. Let the idea breathe as you do. Let them understand how important it is by the 'space' you've given that sentence.

Researchers investigating the question 'Does the language of silence have any neurological value?' have found that a pause aids the working memory of your listeners. Speakers who don't pause negatively affect people's comprehension.

A pause can also denote a transition in your speech, giving the audience time to prepare to move with you as you move to another part of the message.

Pause to think

I've seen many great speakers in my career. For some it comes relatively naturally; others have worked to improve their fluency and their flair. But it's in the Q&A after the speech that a totally different test comes. Most smart people anticipate what the questions will be and prepare for them – it helps enormously to do that. But if you're not sure, or even if you are sure, about your answer, feel confident about pausing before you do so. This works in difficult meetings, too. A pause demonstrates that you are thinking about the question, not just rushing to make a point you want to make. It connotes respect for the question. It conveys a considered response. It increases people's interest in the answer. And, above all, it gives you a precious few seconds to construct the best articulation of the answer.

And then force yourself to pause once you've made the point. It's too easy to fall into the trap of rambling and repetition in answering questions. Pause to think. Say it and stop.

Pause to connect

Pauses aren't just effective in formal speeches, but in any critical conversation with another person or other people. For example, pauses are highly effective tools in a negotiator's or salesperson's arsenal. If you are a good listener, this is something you will have mastered – being comfortable with silence. Avoiding jumping in as soon as the other person has spoken reduces the risk of your interrupting if the other person has just stopped to gather their thoughts – they might be about to give you more information or suggest a way forward. In addition, pausing indicates respect for the other person's point of view; you aren't one of those hideous people who wants only to state their own point of view but instead you are someone who listens, thinks and respects others' opinions.

Slow fixes and caesuras

Graham Allcott, the 'Productivity Ninja', is full of ideas about making your day more effective in terms of getting things done. He's a great resource for helping you get to inbox zero, for example. He was also the person who introduced me to Carl Honoré, who has led a movement 'in praise of slow'. Allcott was curious to see how we would get on as my acceleration addiction would seem to be at first glance the antithesis of Honoré's point of view. However, on closer examination there are parallels between us, as I also believe that a fast pace is not always the right one.

Honoré believes that there is a danger in a quick fix and champions the idea of a thorough 'slow fix':

> Applying a Slow Fix means taking the time to: admit and learn from mistakes; work out the root causes of the problem; sweat the small stuff; think long and connect the dots to build holistic solutions; seek ideas from everywhere; work with others and share the credit; build up expertise while remaining sceptical of experts; think alone and together; tap emotions; enlist an inspiring leader; consult and even recruit those closest to the problem; turn the search for a fix into a game; have fun, follow hunches, adapt, use trial and error, and embrace uncertainty.
>
> All of this takes time, and in an impatient world that can seem like an indulgence or a luxury. But the Slow Fix is neither. It's actually a smart investment in the future. Put in the time, effort, and resources to start tackling problems thoroughly today, and reap the benefits tomorrow.

Honoré admits that this requires a mindset change for a world which is accelerating and which is full of people like me who love the thrill of getting things done fast. One of the most effective ways to tackle this mindset change with 'impatient leaders' is to consider deep thinking not as slowing down or taking it slow but simply building in pauses. There are natural moments when this occurs. I like to think of them as caesuras. A caesura is a break in the middle of a line of verse where one phrase ends and the following phrase begins, often shown by a comma. In choral works, it's a notation to help singers catch their breath. In business, moving from role to role gives you a natural pause, as does the end of a project or year, for example.

As a leader, building in pauses can be a strong symbol of your commitment to promoting rigorous thought (without losing vigour). It could be as part of your understanding of the need to maintain energy (see Chapter 2: Time is finite – energy isn't) but it's also a way to get input and insight into work or to allow reflection time.

There is a world of difference in the symbolism of talking about pauses versus slowness; psychologically, there is a chasm of inference between slowing down and pausing. Pausing is planned; it's deliberate. It's pressing 'pause' rather than just going slowly. A strategically planned pause or delay is very different from the torpor that bureaucracy, lack of direction or lack of commitment can deliver. It allows everyone to make sure that they are not just reacting and thinking with their 'automatic' and obvious minds but allowing ideas to connect and create sparks, which can be different, smarter and longer-lasting.

Espresso takeaways

Understanding the pause

PLAN FOR PAUSES; USE THE ONES YOU HAVE WISELY

Take time; don't make time. Don't believe you don't have time to think. You can steal time — those pockets of 'wasted time' when your lunch date starts late or you are on your commute. Give yourself a specific problem to tackle in your off-time and let your mind play with it. Dream about it. Daydream about it. Go for a run, a walk, a swim and get active. Find yourself a thinking partner to speed up the debate.

CREATE PROPER SPACE TO HELP YOUR PACE

Give your teams space and time together to work through plans, allow them time to make connections together and to make connections around ideas. This is about you and your team factoring in the planning and the reflection in a smart, time-optimizing way. Don't let overstuffed diaries be an excuse for not focusing time to be together to get things right. Run a sprint, a hackathon, a summit. Take them away, make it interesting, make it work.

GIVE YOURSELF A PROPER PAUSE WHEN YOU NEED TO DO SOMETHING SIGNIFICANT.

Decide to 'strategically procrastinate' when you are writing a speech, creating a new idea or working on your plans. Manage people's expectations if there isn't an already created deadline – when you're starting a new role, for example, tell them that they should expect you to start with a 'soak'. Get input, ideas and inspiration from those around you to help you make the connections – allow a pause when you know something shouldn't be rushed.

9

Hire smart, fire fast

How to say hello to the best and goodbye to the worst

'First-rate people hire first-rate people; second-rate people hire third-rate people.'

Leo Rosten, American writer and humorist

There are few more satisfying and positive experiences as a leader than watching the impact of a great hire in an organization. It's a glorious feeling when someone is able to anticipate what is needed, inspire their team to be better, and to challenge those around them constructively – someone who fits the company but reshapes it at the same time.

Efficient, brilliant hiring will save you energy as a leader. Adam Balon, the co-founder of Innocent, talked about

> that moment quite early in most start-ups when you realize that you've got a really great person in a role that makes your life so much better – someone with the skills, aptitude and expertise who totally knows what they are doing and is so much more able to do it than you. Hiring to get the right person into a role just can't be underestimated.

Conversely, if you get the hiring wrong, then the impact can be hideous. That draining feeling of hoping that your impressions are incorrect and this person will prove themselves. The toxic depression as those around him/her realize that this person is a drain, not a radiator. The sinking feeling that your 'gut instinct' was wrong or that the investment of money and time in this exciting new person has been wasted and will be further compounded as you seek to undo what's been done. The tortuous wrangling with your conscience and HR lawyers to find ways to extricate yourself from the situation.

One of the most important things you can do to lead at speed is: find the right people (and keep them).

Of course, finding the right people is far, far easier said than done. Every single one of my interviewees for this book touched on the challenging nature of recruitment; it is universally acknowledged to be one of the hardest things to get right in business. Many of the interviewees and clients and friends have talked to me about how long it takes to find the right person (and to get rid of the wrong one). It takes time and a lot of effort.

So this is a tricky area. This is an important area. This is also part of leadership which can end up being a 'time vampire' and a speedbump. It can take up your energy and attention and it can slow down the organization's ability to move fast. In this chapter we offer some ideas and inspiration on how to get it right and – of course – how to get it done faster. Let's work out how to short cut the pain and get to success more quickly.

Why you should do it: the power of hiring and firing

We'll start with the three key principles in hiring and firing that show just how important these processes (and their results) are.

The power of a great hire: accelerators can come in human form

Few would argue that one of the biggest competitive advantages you can give yourself is bringing on board the best people. Of the 100 people I have interviewed for the book, well over 90 per cent spontaneously referred to this as highly correlated to the ability to lead at speed.

Steve Jobs claimed that 'The secret of my success is that we have gone to exceptional lengths to hire the best people in the world.' He went on to analyse why:

> I noticed that the dynamic range between what an average person could accomplish and what the best person could accomplish was 50 or 100 to 1. Given that, you're well advised to go after the cream of the cream. A small team of A+ players can run circles around a giant team of B and C players.

Getting the right people and putting them in the right roles has to be a top priority for those with ambition. It requires thought and it requires time. It is a priority for those leaders who know they want their organization to scale and grow. They need to spend time on this. But how much time? Sam Altman, the man behind Y Combinator, the accelerator behind tech success stories like Airbnb and Dropbox, advises company founders: 'Hiring is the most important thing you do; spend at least a third of your time on it.' Mark Zuckerberg has said: 'I spend probably 25 per cent of my time recruiting, finding good people, both outside the company and inside the company, to put them in more impactful roles.' Hiring well is hard whether you are a small or large organization but it is always absolutely fundamental. If you are a leader shaping a growing company, your role must include leading people by finding people.

Great hires can energize and accelerate a team. They can also provide essential balance for the team. We have all seen the effect of those who provide robust ballast and rigour to balance the impetuousness of a team. Many of the leaders I've interviewed for the book are fast pace-setters, and many are smart enough to have hired so as to surround themselves with pragmatic pessimists to provide a balance to their ambitious optimism, or to provide methodical analysis to help debate.

A great hire can bring new skills and experience or a fresh perspective to shake up and stimulate an organization. But how about a poor one? One tech COO I know talked about the impact of a negative hire on their executive team: 'We only realized what a terribly toxic impact he had once he'd gone; all of a sudden we felt like a team.' The continued presence of a 'dud' casts doubt on the judgement of a leader. The impact of a good hire is significant and the impact of a poor choice is equally dramatic.

Expect to be judged on how you do it (and how fast you do it)

The vast majority of Superfast leaders I spoke to for this book insisted that their motto is 'Hire slow, fire fast'. Probed on what they meant by this, they explained (in various formulations): 'Get the hiring right – and move decisively when you know you haven't.'

One interviewee who took this point of view was Simon Rogerson, founder of the Octopus Group. Any of Octopus's websites show you in seconds its people-centred approach and how critical the people it hires are to the business. For a long time, Simon Rogerson insisted on interviewing every-one who joined the organization; that's no longer possible in a company of 800 people but he still has a strong opinion on the importance of hiring:

> Choose the people you hire like you choose your partner. When you marry someone you don't go, 'Yeah, she'll do' ... It's an absolute bar, not a relative bar. You don't see ten candidates and say that was the best of them. ... Don't compromise. If it takes you 12 months to fill a post because you just can't find the right person, so be it.

Similarly, Greg Jackson, the CEO of Octopus Energy, knew he needed a certain type of person as his CMO, so he waited months until the right person turned up. When they did, within 24 hours he'd conducted the interviews and made the offer. Waiting until the right person turns up may seem 'slow' overall but it can be a quality check. In Jackson's case, he hired fast once he knew it was the right choice. This both flattered and impressed the candidate and meant that he secured the right person.

> Take time to find the right fit, the right person. But when you have identified the right person, get them in fast. Like everything else in this book, the speed of decision-making and action can drive an impressive pace. A flaccid hiring process can lead to you missing out on the candidates you want.

I've heard many people sharing stories recently where they have not accepted a role because it 'arrived too late'; people hiring miss out as their candidates have moved faster than them. How can organizations who can move hyper-fast to deal with new product launches and press issues be so slow to deal with hiring people to join them? It's tough because there are many people involved in hiring, because it's not always their priority and because checks and balances have to be conducted. It's a great opportunity to get a competitive advantage, though.

The 'millennial' tag is a rather worn-out cliché but the truth is that the data shows clearly that there is a generation (or two) for whom job-hopping is now more normal and desirable. They make their minds up quickly and have a poor opinion of slow, dull processes. Everything you do as an organization has an impact on your 'organization brand', including your hiring process. The recruitment process and how candidates are dealt with can be detrimental if you are slow or unresponsive, and make you an unattractive brand to those who are interested in moving fast.

The effectiveness and speed of a company's hiring process also have an impact on the perceptions of its employees. I'm conscious that whenever I meet someone from Google I am predisposed to think of them as smart, based on my knowledge of Google's intense hiring process. That's also true for Procter & Gamble. Wherever I go in the world, I notice that those in the know use the fact that I was once a 'Proctoid' as a short cut to judging that I'm likely to be good.

My colleague Andy Milligan was talking to a large group of high potentials about the recruitment process for Geek Squad (the distinctive computer company founded by Robert Stephens which was sold to Carphone Warehouse). One member of the audience piped up to let everyone know that he'd been rejected by this process but that its thoroughness and cleverness in approach left him feeling un-resentful and full of respect for the organization even so. I'll talk more about Geek Squad's recruitment process later but the key point to note here is that if you get your recruitment process right, you'll not only hire better but you will attract better people (and contribute positively to the overall impression of your company brand). It is well worth the investment of up-front time to set up a smart – and, ideally, distinctive – process for hiring with style.

A few of my interviewees were inspired by Jim Collins's *From Good to Great*, where he talks about getting the right people on the bus (and then finding them the right seats). The reality is that, in today's fast-moving world, often the job descriptions change fast anyhow. Karen Bowes, HR Director from Capital One, says that, when she brings in someone to start in the organization, within 12 months their role is different and requires different skills. So hiring for adaptability and aptitude remains essential. For the scale-ups and high-growth companies out there, the best people are making up their job responsibilities as they go. Act fast and get 'the good ones' on the bus.

Fire fast: when you know, let them go

'I'm a very strong believer that, when something isn't working out, then it should be handled at speed,' says Giles Andrews, co-founder of Zopa (and now Chairman). There was not one person I spoke to for this book who did not firmly agree with the importance of this: if there is one thing as a leader you absolutely must do, it is 'fire fast'.

In business, you'll know of many painful examples of those who made the error of waiting (the CEO who brought down a previously successful company while the founder, chair and investors couldn't quite bring themselves to admit they'd made a mistake with her; the company leader who couldn't understand why he got on well with an individual when all his direct reports and peers didn't). 'If someone's not working out, act fast. I've never ever seen someone fired too soon or too fast,' says Scott Button, co-founder and chief strategy officer of Unruly.

This is, of course, easier said than done. You need to check that you've given the person a chance. You want to behave justly and fairly. You need to be certain that there are no diversity or cultural issues. You need to check that they have been supported. Perhaps you want to be 'careful of blaming the lettuce for not growing when the soil is poor', as mindfulness guru Thich Nhât Hanh put it. Check those things quickly and then act. Follow the three-step process: Listen. Decide. Act. *Listen* to those with a perspective on this (their direct reports, those who have observed them) and look at the results. *Decide* quickly. Then *act* decisively and with clarity.

Rear Admiral Neil Morisetti gives a perspective from an organization – the Royal Navy – where the choice of the right person can be quite literally a matter of life or death. He shares the fact that a belief in the value of 'extreme delegation' is an important tool in the Navy's leadership. He believes in giving people a chance, letting them fail, letting them succeed. But even in that situation, if it's repeatedly proven that they can't do it (the 'three strikes' rule), it's smarter and better to 'call it' and let them go.

Firing fast is also fairer on the person being fired. If they are not the right fit, it's worse to keep them there, doing half a job, half happy. If your culture requires speed and they love to linger, don't make them and yourself unhappy. If their values aren't aligned with those of the company, they will feel out of place and out of sorts. Let them find somewhere that suits them.

It's also fairer on the team. Keeping on a poor performer or a bad fit has an insidious effect on those around them, especially if they are leaders or managers of others. Leaders reflect the organization to their teams. Not only will they not be effective in what they do but their continued sub-par presence will whittle away faith in the 'them' of senior management. 'Do not tolerate brilliant jerks – the cost to teamwork is too high,' says Reed Hastings, CEO of Netflix.

This is overtly a short-term issue but it's also a long-term one. The other truth is that 'B types' will hire 'C types'. Only hire A types and you keep the standard up. As the political scientist Leo Rosten explained in what has become known as 'Rosten's Law': 'First-rate people hire first-rate people; second-rate people hire third-rate people.' Knowing there is a 'poor fit' in a situation can be a time and energy drain as well; it can end up taking a disproportionate amount of time, management time and discussion. Move them on. Move on.

> Don't be afraid of the gap the wrong hire will leave. The work they did will not compensate for the negative ripples on everything else.

Adam Balon, one of the founders of Innocent, told me how he and his co-founders were deeply influenced by Dan Jacobs, Head of Talent at Apple, who talked about the worry people have in having a 'gap' in the business by letting someone go and why it should not detract you from firing. He memorably phrased his belief as: 'I'd rather have a hole than an arsehole.' Adam agrees:

> If someone's not performing, you're not doing the rest of the people in the business a service, and you're not doing yourself a service by not getting rid of people. It's so easy when you're busy to [put it off by telling yourself:] 'It's an awkward conversation. I'm not going to have it with that person. They might improve next year.' You tell yourself all sorts of lies and they stay in the business. Absolutely the wrong thing to do and you've got to move them out, for their own sake. It's not fair on them.

Of course, we are all haunted by the spectre of the angry white businessman with a hiring and firing trigger finger, and, for some, firing will always be an expression of power. We, however, must hire and fire sensitively, smartly and speedily. This is the subject of the next section.

Fire in person

I have always been fascinated by the reign of the English king Henry VIII and his evolution from love-struck boy to murdering monster. I find it fascinating to consider how someone could court, woo, sleep with, impregnate, and then divorce or, in some cases, behead a succession of wives. And, of course, one of the reasons why it was so possible for Henry to do this was that he never actually had to do the deeds himself. He didn't communicate to his wives the fact that they had fallen from grace; he did not take them to the Tower of London; he did not behead them. He got someone else to do all this for him – Thomas Cromwell and the other people he kept to do this kind of thing.

Contrast this with one of the most memorable scenes in *Game of Thrones* (yes, I see that I'm mixing real history with the dragon-laden bonkers-ness of one of the most fantastically popular epics of our time). But Rob Stark, the most moral of all the highly fallible monarchs featured in the series, is a leader who is insistent on the need to punish (aka execute) the failures himself.

In business, the direct link between decision and outcome is one that many leaders try to avoid when it comes to 'letting people go'. But you are not killing someone by firing them. Often, it is the kinder thing to do. Certainly, it's a tough task and oh, how we admire those who can do this themselves. Courageous leaders face up to the consequences of their mistakes. Akio Morita, the co-founder of Sony, recognized the importance of this: 'When I find an employee who turns out to be wrong for a job, I feel it is my fault because I made the decision to hire them.'

If it is someone you hired and who works directly for you, then fire them yourselves. This is partly for speed's sake. Someone who feels they have not been fairly treated or not fired by the right person will invariably try to speak to you anyhow. So, it all becomes messier and more time-consuming. And what's more, firing people personally sends a message to your team that you aren't afraid to do it, and to the person concerned that you really believe it's necessary.

Plan carefully before you do it. Work out clearly what you will say and why you believe it's necessary. Then carry out the firing as quickly as possible but also with as much compassion and sensitivity as possible. Wim Dejonghe, the Global Senior Partner at Allen & Overy, says it all:

> Fire fast. If the decision needs to be made, see it like a plaster. There's less pain if it's pulled off quickly – you know it has to be done so just do it. But do it with sensitivity as well as speed. It's the right thing to do.

How to do it: approaching hiring and firing with speed, skill and style

If we look at the maths, the wastefulness around the hiring process in many organizations will make investors and finance directors shiver with horror. A little rigour and vigour and you can hire fast and smartly. Believe in the importance of this and believe in your ability to improve this area of your business. You can filter better, process applications more quickly, and carry out interviews more efficiently. You can avoid losing the good ones and avoid hiring the duds.

All this does require some thought and time up front, however. Like the other areas covered in this book, this is an area where slowing down to think and plan can dramatically accelerate your execution. There are three areas to look at:

1 The fit
2 The filters
3 The fast-track process.

The fit

Do you know what type of person you want in your company? Think about your culture, your brand and your industry. Your brand is built in people's minds by communications, actions, products and people, so getting the right people on board, whether consumer-/client-facing or not, is an important factor. You can encourage self-selection in being clear about your requirements up front. For example, at Caffeine we have recruitment criteria which provide us with a checklist when we meet people, but we also publish some of this on our website so that people can work out whether our culture is right for them. We recruit 'people who take business very seriously but don't take themselves too seriously'. This is a surprisingly effective test of fit. If people are cynical, dismissive or flippant about business, they will not be able to help our highly driven clients. If they are pompous and humourless, they will not enjoy our sense of fun, our banter or team spirit. Simples, as they say.

There are some particularly strong examples of 'fit tests' for employees. No discussion of hiring could fail to mention Zappos, the billion-dollar online shoe retailer that is even more famous worldwide for its distinctive culture (and customer-centric focus) than it is for its phenomenal Superfast success. Zappos celebrate 'weirdness', so it will not be for all – and that's a distinct filter for the type of people that will fit. It also has a genius 'money back guarantee' for new employees which is so effective that I remain staggered that more companies don't adopt it. If you join Zappos and don't like it within a week, you can take a $4,000 bonus and leave.

It works both ways. You normally know, within the first hundred days, if someone is right for a place or will struggle – and the employee knows Superfast whether they will be happy or not. But how can you make the test period as flexible as possible? You do need to have sensible probation periods and rigorous assessments in place. Sara Tate, CEO of TBWA, talks openly about the challenge of recruiting in a creative, fast-moving advertising environment. 'You don't really know how they're going to work as part of a functioning dynamic … or maybe someone is great but just in the wrong position, at the wrong place and in the wrong team.' As with any business initiative (where you can't judge its success unless it's in front of the consumer/client), you can't assess someone's fit with the team, role, culture and company until they are in place. As Sara puts it, 'You need to manage quickly and see what's going on … so I like to think, to some extent, hire fast and part ways fast. In such a people-based business this is what you have to do.'

It's amazing how few people check references. It's even easier now, what with the glorious advent of LinkedIn and the nature of our tiny world. Chances are someone you know is 'six degrees' from the candidate. I met someone who on paper was a total success and quite dazzling. As I often do out of habit, I asked a friend if he'd come across this person. The tales he told and the previous boss he introduced me to saved me time, embarrassment and looking foolish. Take time to ask around – either formally by taking up references or by having a quiet word. You may still choose to give the person a chance or the benefit of the doubt but you'll have a wider perspective.

Or you can set up a situation to help you judge. Zappos famously sends a van to pick you up for your interview and then checks out how you treat the driver on the way. Alexei Orlov, the ex-Worldwide CEO of Rapp (one of the world's fastest-growing agencies), uses a meal as the final test:

> If I am hiring someone at a senior level, it's critically important they are decent people. So I always take them out for lunch – not a long one but enough so they relax, we talk, we get to know one another. But what I always do is notice how they treat the waiting staff; you can tell a lot about a person about how they do that.

It works the other way as well. Giles Andrews, the founder of Zopa, tells how he was hired by someone to set up a business for him who was charm personified in meetings but over supper behaved appallingly to the waitress. It didn't entirely put him off but it was helpful in letting him know that the persona was inauthentic; it was a warning sign.

It all depends, of course, on what the culture is and what will be required of employees. In an agency world, as in most companies, the ability to get on with others is essential. John Murphy, the serial entrepreneur known as 'The Brandfather', founded the branding giant Interbrand and went on to buy and sell Plymouth Gin and to run St Peter's Brewery. A firebrand with a fabulous sense of humour, he knew that much of Interbrand's business involved employees spending intense time working together and travelling together. So, he knew that one of his most important 'fit' questions was always about whether he would want to travel with this person – partly for selfish reasons (he believes that work should be enjoyable) and partly for pragmatic reasons (if he wouldn't enjoy this person's company, then the client wouldn't and the team wouldn't, and without that relationship glue the advice given would be less appreciated and less likely to be implemented). 'Could I bear to be on a long-haul flight with this person?' he asks himself.

Dan Warne, the UK MD of fast-growth tech company Deliveroo, follows the inspiration of the All Blacks recruitment policy who believe that you can develop skills but not character. When looking for people to join his hyper-fast scale-up, he applies the 'no dickheads' filter. Perhaps this is a little too subjective a criterion, but it makes me smile and it's a pretty interesting filter to be aware of. Its recruitment criteria: when looking for people to join this hyper-fast scale-up, it specifies 'No dickheads'. Perhaps this is a little too subjective a criterion, but it makes me smile and it's a pretty interesting filter to be aware of.

Many of the pace-setters I talked to for this book mentioned the danger of the one-on-one interview. Partly this is because we use our experience of other people to judge those in front of us in interviews. It can be a sensible short cut but sometimes it's fatally flawed. Agatha Christie's Miss Marple would always be suspicious of certain types of people because they reminded her of someone in her village. It's a smart short cut in many ways as there are often types of people who, as we get older, we learn to identify and work with. However, these same short cuts can sometimes cloud our judgement. I mentioned earlier the prejudices people have about former Proctor & Gamble and Google employees: 'If those great companies thought he or she was good, then they must be.' Or when the savvy interviewee finds common ground to make you feel like you and they are similar people ('I see you know so-and-so – she's a friend of mine'; 'Are you from West London? Don't you love it?'). This is all smart (and you will often want people who can do this), but, of course, the danger is that you miss what's behind it all or you end up hiring in your own image. In addition, many a psychopath or useless businessperson has perfected the art of the interview.

You can avoid these pitfalls by making interviewing a group activity. Even the notorious control freak Steve Jobs agreed: 'You need to have a collaborative hiring process.' When interviewing, therefore, bear in mind the following:

1 Make sure that a variety of people give perspectives (to guard against individual biases).
2 Be conscious of the phenomenon of hiring in your own image.
3 Make sure that the interview is only part of the process – test for teamwork and skills other than interview professionalism.

> 'Fit' means fit with the overall company culture; it should not just mean a reflection of those who are already there.

There are other smart ways in which fit can be identified. How do people manage in teams? Southwest Airlines uses a hiring process where they bring people in as a group and ask them to tell a joke. Naturally, it's not their stand-up potential that's being judged … it's actually the responses of those around them. Are they bored and thinking 'What next?' How do they work together?

Company values should be your first point of checking fit. Get them right. Make them distinctive (avoid the 'passionate' and 'trusted' clichés or define what they mean). At Unruly, the high-growth ad tech company, Sarah Wood and her team believe in being super clear on the guiding principles and cultural behaviour that the company is looking for. They've simplified it by talking about looking for 'PANDAS'. Here's how they describe the criteria:

Positive and passionate. When the going gets tough, Unrulies get going. We come to the table with suggestions and solutions rather than problems and complaints.

Agile. Communication, Simplicity, Feedback, Courage, Respect. These principles from 'Extreme Programming' methodology infuse our whole business.

No ego and nurturing. There's no I in team and there's no I in PANDA. There's a reason for that.

Determined to deliver. We believe anything is possible and we'll do whatever it takes to get there.

Action-oriented A+ players. We deliver nothing less than A+ results for our clients; we expect nothing less of ourselves. We keep our promises and measure ourselves and each other by performance.

Social DNA and sense of humour. We're hard-wired to seek out competitor intel, swap product ideas, disseminate industry news and share the love with clients, publishers and our fellow Unrulies. But we'll always find time for a bad joke or a funny video.

During recruitment they mine for these 'PANDA qualities', digging beyond the standard interview patter to see whether people have what it takes.

'Fit' can also mean recruiting someone to complement others; to fill a gap in the team or to fit a piece in the overall jigsaw. Smart leaders deliberately recruit to complement their weaknesses. Mark Zuckerberg from Facebook is a highly visible example of this: his hiring of Sheryl Sandberg is consistently cited as key to the fast acceleration of the business.

Consider the mix of the team to get the right jigsaw. Diversity is, of course, seen as desirable but it is a complex issue for many. My favourite point of view was that of a serial successful investor who said: 'It's smart to look for diversity and a diversified portfolio in investments and I look for the same in senior teams.' This goes beyond the obvious gender and racial or ethnic mix, though. Alexis Maybank, founding CEO of members-only flash sale site Gilt Groupe, says that 'a common start-up pitfall – which we fell prey to at Gilt – is to hire people with the same mindset and temperament as the founders'. When the Gilt team realized that the entire company was made up of big-picture thinkers, they knew they had a problem. A great team also needs people who are more cautious, who want to know all the details, she said. One of the growing pains of a start-up is making sure you have 'a balanced team that could tackle a concept, challenge and opportunity in a different way'. (Maybank co-founded Gilt Groupe in 2007, and while she is no longer the company's CEO, she still serves as a strategic advisor.)

'Diversity' matters. And it doesn't just start with the interview process. Martha Lane Fox's organization Doteveryone has developed a clever tool to assess the gender bias of the language used in recruitment ads: http://gender-decoder.katmatfield.com/ The smartest leaders recognize that diversity is not a decision you make because you want to be 'good' but because it makes good business sense. José Neves, the founder of Farfetch, the online fashion retail platform, says:

> Diversity isn't a moral choice – it's essential for survival. You need different points of view and different cultures, left brain and right brain, passion and technology. If everyone is looking in one direction, you'll never see what's coming up behind.

The filters

Here come the short cuts. Here's where you save time. Filter out the 'nos' with your rules and the experience you have had. Caution: here's also where you risk filtering out diversity, so you have to be careful.

Apply filters to your applicants so you don't waste time. If you are a fairly successful company, you are likely to receive a significant number of candidates. Actually, even if you're a start-up, that could happen. I set up a business and recruited on one website for customer service people. Because it was a well-written ad and because I was offering flexible work from home for an exciting and interesting company, I'd receive a thousand high-quality applications. It was for a job which paid the minimum wage and I had people applying who had been on salaries of over £60,000 previously. I needed to get to my shortlist quickly, so my general manager at the time filtered the applications out using the following criteria:

- All those who hadn't included a cover letter
- Any with typos (the job specified someone with a real attention to detail)
- Anyone who hadn't answered the questions in the ad (asking the applicants to tell us about themselves and why this job appealed).

Voilà. Filters applied, numbers reduced.

Filters can be your personal recruitment tool or they can be the company's. John Croft, President of the hyper-growth law company Elevate, which is being used by all the big names in global law, has had to hire well and quickly to meet the growth of the organization. He's keen to hire people who are going somewhere fast, with a sense of drive and a sense of pace. His specific recruitment mantra for the type of person he wants in his Superfast organization is: 'Hire fast walkers.'

Of course, all big companies will have their own filters. Procter & Gamble's graduate recruitment policy was, as you'd expect from the type of company it is, based on data. It had learned that those people who got involved with societies in university were more likely to be the proactive, creative leaders it wanted in the organization. So it systematically targeted the presidents and secretaries of university societies which gave it an automatic 'filter'.

Filters can date quickly and they need to be regularly reviewed. The Foreign Office has had to update its vetting process as societal norms change, and to reflect the differing experiences of a more diverse organization. Stephen Thorn, President of EY Foundation (a not-for-profit charity connecting disadvantaged young people with opportunities to work in business), tells a fascinating tale about filters holding back success. Thanks to the pioneering work his team had done, EY removed the 'must have university degree' filter to allow a more diverse set of recruitees. The result? EY dramatically improved its digital skills base.

Thoughtful filters

Make sure that your filter is a thoughtful one. Martin Lewis's book *Moneyball* is a fascinating study in how a poor baseball team, Oakland, ended up an incredible success. His research showed clearly the power of the recruitment process for the players. When he first met the team in the locker room, he was amazed at how little they all looked like his idea of athletes. But that was the secret – the team management knew that other talent scouts would be biased in favour of those who looked the part; they could pick up good players for a better price if they were not so obviously the right 'fit' or 'fitness'. Instead, the talent scouts used data, not just the short-cut heuristics and biases that skewed observation.

Heidrick & Struggles is one of the world's oldest and most prestigious senior placement companies. Despite its 'age', it is acutely conscious of the need for speed, so much so that it has developed a management consulting arm whose proposition is based on accelerating individuals', teams' and organizations' performance. A senior leadership hire is, of course, also a great catalyst to accelerate organizational success. If you are wanting to recruit someone who 'fits' an organization but who is still able to innovate, change and accelerate success, that's a real challenge.

Heidrick & Struggles calls this type of person a 'positive agitator': someone with enough people and political skills to be able to work effectively with the system to get things done, but with enough boldness and bravery to drive through change where needed and manage risk taking where required.

Exec search organizations support the appointment of senior leaders, typically in C-Suite roles; those hires can make or break success. Heidrick & Struggles has therefore developed its own 'filter' for this and can assess people based on their ability to be positive, to 'fit' enough with the culture to win friends and trust, but also with the courage and conviction to not always 'go native' and end up doing things as they have been done before.

> Filters can be effective short cuts to get you to the
> most likely people to succeed.

So filter, but filter fairly. You need people to fit, but you need people who'll fight for what is right and who'll bring stimulation, not just some more of the same.

Many leaders feel strongly that hiring for character is important. Ursula Burns, the erstwhile CEO of Xerox and new Uber board member, says that for her 'Character is a huge piece of the fit and fitness test.' She looks for a 'strong moral compass, humility, self-awareness, authenticity'. Warren Buffett has a great trio of hiring criteria, again focusing on character. He says: 'In looking for people to hire, you look for three qualities: integrity, intelligence, and energy. And if they don't have the first, the other two will kill you.' Peter Shutz, whose five years driving the Porsche brand as global CEO was marked by an acceleration of the company's success. His simple iconic mantra echoes Burns's criteria: 'Hire character. Train skill.' Many leaders to whom I spoke for this book had learned that hiring for attitude and aptitude are more important than hiring for skill. Sam Altman from Y Combinator advises entrepreneurs to look for alignment behind the vision: 'Hire smart and effective people that are committed to what you're doing. The last five words there are important. Hire people that you could describe as animals. Generally, value aptitude over experience.'

The right hire, the right people 'on the bus', will save you so much more time and effort throughout their career with you, says Jim Collins, who has studied the secrets of companies that have outperformed their competitors in his *Good to Great* canon of books. His perspective is: 'Expending energy trying to motivate people is largely a waste of time ... If you have the right people on the bus, they will be self-motivated.'

The fast-track process

Once you've thought about who fits and once you've looked at the filters, how do you then get good people tested, hired and fired up? Here's where a bit of Superfast thinking could dramatically increase your speed and success.

Having a clear plan at the start leads to speed in any process. Like any other part of business, a communications plan helps manage expectations and drives belief that people know what they are doing. So why not communicate with candidates clearly what the process is (how many interviews and tests, what the timing is, where and when)? Ask the interviewers to help by prioritizing the interviews and committing to the time slots.

One of the biggest insights for personal productivity is around 'batching'. If you put together the same types of tasks, you can dramatically increase their effectiveness. Answering emails all together in batches, making a series of phone calls together, doing chores together, spending a day just writing. A number of the Superfast interviewees have used this 'single-tasking and batching' technique. The same insight applies to many other parts of managing a business.

Take, for example, managing senior leaders' diaries to get a series of interviews with a senior candidate scheduled in. It can take weeks for a candidate to be assessed. If there are many candidates being run, there are endless diary management, travel, set-up and logistics to plan. Contrast, then, the pure productive joy when a candidate spends one or two days being tested, interviewed and reviewed. Yes, the back-to-back pressure can be hard for them but it's done and dusted with ease and effectiveness.

To get it right, many organizations rely on tests as well as interviews. These could be psychometric tests, but the most effective way to test someone in a role is to have them do that role. For Pret A Manger, the international sandwich shop chain, that's easy because candidates can serve in a branch for a week. For a customer service role, you can test them on how they respond to difficult customers or compose their responses to emails. For senior roles, of course, it's infinitely harder but many people will ask for candidates to present ideas, strategies or approaches to a challenging audience to test their thinking and their grace under pressure.

Where more than one candidate is being reviewed, it makes absolute sense to 'batch' the interviews and to test them together. This often happens to graduates. Both Unilever and Procter & Gamble have run tester weeks for graduates. The Marketing Vocation Course at Procter & Gamble allowed managers a whole week to judge people's creativity, communication skills and ability to work as a team.

In the recruitment process, the questions are all. If you are aiming for fair, consistent success in recruitment, there is a strong argument for standardizing the questions across interviewers and interviewees. At Procter & Gamble there was a consistent number of questions focused on what had been done in the past as an indicator of what would be done in the future. Questions included things like 'Give me an example of where you have changed someone's mind'. Including consistent questions allowed you to judge people on their answers and not get distracted by thinking up new questions; it allowed consistent judgement of results – and, of course, it drove faith in the fairness of the process. A template for recruitment can drive speed and consistency.

There's no getting round the fact that recruitment is an important part of your business, and getting decisions right must be given priority. Scott Button, co-founder of Unruly, comments:

> Your bad hires are the most expensive mistakes you ever make. Your best hires, your biggest contribution. So, take your time. Easy to say and hard to do, so enforce it through process. At Unruly, our second interview lasts between three and five hours: it acts like a truth drug and leaves nowhere to hide.

So, if you are fast-tracking an effective process, use the fit criteria, the filters you have and make sure you factor in understanding how the individual will manage those he or she works with to get the best out of them as well as achieve the best themselves – be thorough. And, above all, ask yourself or ask your head of recruitment/HR/People: 'How can we get there more quickly?'

The last word goes to Ursula Burns from Xerox, who leads us on to the next chapter neatly with her smart approach:

> I cannot hire people who have to be perfect. I want quick learners. Fast failers. I want the failure number to be small, but, when they do fail, I want them to do it fast and to learn how to do it the next time. I look for flexibility, agility for how quickly and smoothly you can make transitions. How fast are you? I look for fearlessness. I look for people who can decide things. Even if you decide the wrong thing, you can change really fast.

> Hire people who can decide, then you can delegate and then you can deliver.

Espresso takeaways

Hiring and firing checklist

HIRE SMART

- **Use your brand as a lighthouse and as a filter for recruitment.** Make sure that you are communicating the right messages to encourage the best people to come to you and that you are recruiting in a way which will build the culture and kind of company you really want.
- **Give new recruits every chance to succeed but give them a test period on both sides.** Smart induction and support from day one will make their success more likely, so it is the company's responsibility to do that well.
- **'Better a hole than an arsehole.'** Remember the strategic importance of the right hire. It is worth the time to get the process robust. Never ever hire to fit a gap unless that person feels right. Your gut instinct shouldn't be the only factor (and you need more than one gut involved in a decision) but it should not be ignored.
- **Take it slow so you know …** Make sure recruitment can be rapid but not rushed. Be smart about a clear process that manages biases, allows tests and different perspectives. Dig deep. Keep the data, learn and evolve your hiring skills and success.

FIRE FAST

- **Who remains is as important a message about the type of organization you want as who is recruited.** Damage will be done to teams if people are not performing to the 'same high bar'. Damage will be done to your culture if people (especially at a senior level) are not in line with your stated values.
- **When you know, let them go ...** Always. Do it fast. It's fairer and it's infinitely less damaging. We talk about the importance of editing, curating and eliminating elsewhere – that is particularly true when it comes to who you choose to be part of your company.
- **See above:** Allow me to repeat this one more time for emphasis: better a hole than an arsehole. The toxicity of the wrong person, and their impact on others, means that often it's better to be without a person than with the wrong one. (And remember that interims or consultants can be a helpful sticking plaster if you're stuck.)

10

Decide, delegate and deliver

Think slowly – act fast

'Leadership is coming up with an idea and executing it. Ideas are a dime a dozen – it is how it is carried out.'

*Anna Wintour, Editor-in-Chief
of* Vogue

In this chapter, I bring together the core message of this book: Decide. Delegate. Deliver. This is a simple three-step way to lead in a world of speed.

Apply it to life, apply it to your inbox, apply it to your work-load. When something comes in, you should 'triage' (like an emergency surgeon who assesses the relative urgency of their patients' needs) and then you can work out how you will make a decision on it (as quickly as possible) and who is best to do it. Once you've done that ... let them do it. Often, this is the hardest part, but if you've given people frameworks you then need to give them freedom.

Decision-making must be fast. Even if you decide not to act, it should be a conscious choice to pause or delay the decision. If you need more time to think, decide how you will do that and when. If you need to listen to people more or if you need more data, then that's fine but the discipline of making decisions sharply can lead to phenomenal 'unblocking' of energy and velocity. 'All business activity', says Dave Girouard, former President of Google Apps and now CEO of personal finance start-up Upstart2, 'really comes down to two simple things: making decisions and execut-ing decisions. Your success depends on your ability to develop speed as a habit in both.'

Once you have made a choice to do something, this should go hand in hand with choosing the right people. You need to assign responsibilities to the right people, making responsibil-ity and accountability clear. And you need to have clarity over what you will be delivering and make sure that there is tangi-ble, visible progress to make sure that there is focus and it gets finished. Fast.

> The three Ds – Decide, Delegate, Deliver – are the core message of this book.

The three Ds

Let's start with a quick overview of the three stages that are at the heart of the Superfast philosophy.

Decide

Clarity (about who makes the decision and when) provides focus and energy. Liv Garfield, CEO of Severn Trent and the youngest female CEO in the FTSE 100, comments: 'The first and most important thing in leading successfully at speed is being decisive. I think doing things once and doing it right the first time I'd say helps you be pacier.' In any organization, clarity over who will make decisions and when they will be made is key. Time is wasted if this isn't set up clearly.

Make sure that the decision is done once only, and make sure that it's clearly communicated. Sometimes the pain of making a decision is compounded by a team or organization not realizing that it's been done. Agile thinking should include working out how decisions are communicated fast to the right people.

Delegate

'The who' needs to have as much thought given to it as 'the what'.

'Delegation' is one of those words that everyone uses but which in practice can so often be overcomplicated or weakly handled. Understanding it and consistently delivering it is one of the hardest things for an impatient or a brilliant leader – putting the right people against the most relevant tasks and doing it quickly and in a way which motivates and energizes.

Consider the casting – who will work together well on this, complementing each other; who will make this happen. Think about who has the right skills and attitude, who wants to, who has time. Make that decision. Then give it to them to run with it and make it happen.

Deliver

Moving from debate to getting something 'out there' – the delivery – is so often surprisingly challenging for teams run by an impatient leader. But making things happen makes more things happen. Scott Button, co-founder of Unruly, has this advice:

> Adopt an action bias. You will never have perfect information. In a rapidly changing, uncertain and unpredictable world you may never even get to particularly good information! So act. Do something. Know what you're doing and why you're doing it. If it works, do more of it. If it really works, turn the dial to 11. Until it stops working, then do something else. Fear, uncertainty and doubt are paralysing. You have to overcome them. Failing is fine … as long as you do it fast.

Facebook was set up in 2004. Since then it has grown to a size where there are more users of Facebook than all the citizens in China. In fact, quite staggeringly there are more Facebook users than all the people who lived on the entire planet 100 years ago. Their teams have long lived with the 'Done is better than perfect' philosophy (which fills many a cautious plodder with terror but generates a culture where they can 'move fast and break things' with energy and positivity).

Digital entrepreneur legend Martha Lane Fox talks about what is needed to galvanize and coalesce teams, investors, audiences … : 'You need to find "A Thing",' she says, 'Something visible, tangible and a sign of progress that helps everyone believe something is happening.' Action generates acceleration. Progress drives pace. Delivery delivers the momentum for more.

Get started on delivering, and momentum will follow. Get to a point where your customer/client/consumer starts to see something. Internal debate may be marvellous but, all too often, people enjoy the 'strategic discussion' more than the delivery. Here's one of the world's great disruptors, Leonardo da Vinci, on the action imperative: 'I have been impressed with the urgency of doing. Knowing is not enough; we must apply. Being willing is not enough; we must do.'

> How confident do you feel about the decisions you make? How effectively can you delegate? And what does delivery really look like? There are approaches and frameworks which can help provoke your thinking and provide a structure for success in all these three areas.

Decision-making – fast and slow

Making a decision needs to be done with a clear understanding of the implications but also without analysis paralysis.

Too slow is stupid: make a decision

The interviewees for this book were all in agreement over the tremendous frustration and obfuscation that occur with a lack of decision-making. Conversely, there is a confidence in leadership when it is perceived to be brave enough to make/take decisions and to do it in a timely manner. Jeff Bezos, in his 2017 'playbook' to investors, reflects on the importance of this:

> You have to somehow make high-quality, high-velocity decisions. Easy for start-ups and very challenging for large organizations. The senior team at Amazon is determined to keep our decision-making velocity high. Speed matters in business.

This is about business success but it's also about your business being a good place to do work. As Bezos goes on to say, 'a high-velocity decision-making environment is more fun, too.'

Let's pause briefly to reflect on that last point. Business can be hard. Leadership can be a slog. But it can also be an exhilarating, exciting ride where you try things and some work and some don't. As with so much in life, the main thing you control is your mindset. Make some decisions, make some things happen, enjoy discovering. Do not go slow through fear and trepidation and bore yourself and your team who wait and wait and wait for decisions …

ANALYSIS PARALYSIS

Beware this omnipresent danger. There is no certainty. Nervous, fearful managers can try to find the answer in the data and it may not be there (and it may take time to keep looking for answers). Smart, curious, considered leaders may also pose the question: 'What more could we think about?' Data and insights matter in helping decision-making. But there has to be a point where a decision is made. The more senior you are in an organization, the more likely it is that you will have to make a decision that isn't clear or obvious, that the data doesn't have an answer to it – you will have to make a judgement call and often do it fast.

The creative strategist Pete Martin spent time in the 1990s with the legendary fund manager Mark Mobius of Franklin Templeton, who inspired Martin with his practical approach. His basic view was that those who were able to make decisions based on imperfect information and that frequently went against the established view were the most likely to be successful (if you follow the crowd or wait for the perfect information, the moment is gone and the opportunity is lost). But that takes discipline and courage. In the words of Google's Matt Brittin (talking about the essential Google hiring criteria), 'being comfortable with ambiguity' is essential for the world in which we operate now.

Ex-US President Barack Obama has also reflected often on the challenge of not knowing when decisions are right: 'Any given decision you make you'll wind up with a 30 to 40 per cent chance that it isn't going to work. You have to own that and feel comfortable with the way you made the decision. You can't be paralyzed by the fact that it might not work out.' Jeff Bezos agrees: 'Most decisions should probably be made with somewhere around 70 per cent of the information you wish you had. If you wait for 90 per cent, in most cases, you're probably being slow.'

Amee Chande, the UK MD of Alibaba, explains why this is particularly important in a digital world:

> The leadership structure has changed in today's world. In traditional companies there is scarcity of resource and so control, approval and precision are needed. In the digital age, the world is changing so quickly (it's like the Wild West) it's primarily speed that allows you to seize the market opportunity. It's not so much resource that's limited but management attention and focus. Precision is less important than moving fast with the minimum checks and balances with company values as the guide rails.

This issue of speed feels highly relevant now but 'twas ever thus for strategic leaders facing challenging times. General Patton, a US military leader who played a seminal role in the Second World War, was a controversial figure. His choice of language and his hard-driving personality, together with his strong emphasis on rapid action, proved sensationally effective in the course of the war. His simple philosophy was reputedly: 'A good plan violently executed now is better than a perfect plan next week.' Hubert Humphrey was a progressive, if complex, Democrat whose speech to end racial segregation in 1948 encouraged the Democratic Party as they 'walked into the sunshine of human rights'. He is reported to have built on Patton's aphorism with this one: 'More progress results from the violent execution of an imperfect plan than the perfection of a plan to violently execute.'

A more contemporary leader, Sir Martin Sorrell, who 'pivoted' a wire and plastic products business into one of the world's most successful agency groups, WPP plc, agrees with the need for speed in decision-making:

I used to say, perhaps unwisely, that a bad decision on Monday is better than a good decision on Friday. With the benefit of hindsight I might have modified that to 'an imperfect decision on Monday is better than the 100 per cent perfect decision on Friday.' Either way, you get the point. Strategy is critical, but without implementation it's nothing. While you strategize and over-intellectualize, others are getting on with things and building a lead.

Of course, this is one of those things that are easy to say and infinitely harder to do. When does the action imperative count as recklessness? How do you judge the right time to move? How do you lead in a decisive way in a world lacking in certainty? Can you have insight and foresight? Or do you just have to move and connect later, like Steve Jobs, who pointed out that:

> You can't connect the dots looking forward; you can only connect them looking backwards. So you have to trust that the dots will somehow connect in your future. You have to trust in something – your gut, destiny, life, karma, whatever.

Ripple intelligence

One of my senior interviewees for this book talked about a leadership paradox so many face:

> On the one hand, leaders must appear decisive to give people, to give the City, to give investors, to give their people, the confidence that they do have some semblance of knowing what they are doing. Equally, because things are moving so fast, they have to make a decision so they can't spend all their time weighing up whether they understand enough about what's going on. However, they can't possibly know and they have to be comfortable with the doubt that they face.

Having reviewed the experience of 150 CEOs, with 880 years' combined experience between them and $14 billion in revenues, executive recruitment and strategy consultants Heidrick & Struggles published a report looking at the need to be aware of (and comfortable with) 'The Power of

'Doubt'. This report outlines the recognition that you, as an individual C-Suite leader, do not need to know everything and that you *can't* know everything. However, you do have to make decisions in an environment where that will always be true.

You as a leader are captain of a ship. You are scanning the horizon for perils and pirates but also assessing where there is land to conquer. You will also be watching around for waves that will have an impact on your voyage. The Heidrick & Struggles report talks about strong leaders being able to read the 'ripple intelligence' – whether those little ripples are just that or warnings of more seismic waves. You don't want to be a leader who jumps every time a trend or prediction lands on their desk. Decision-making requires judgement as to the nature of the challenge and opportunity you see. 'The Power of Doubt' recommends that 'to prioritize, delegate, and manage their energy effectively, CEOs need to be able to understand the scope, speed, and significance (S3) of each challenge they face':

- **Scope:** How wide is the implication of what we see? Is this trend/this change purely enterprise-specific, industry-specific or more broadly macro-economic?
- **Speed:** This is about being less concerned with micro-managing pace and more about what uncertainties will dramatically affect us in a systematic and structural way.
- **Significance:** Is it noise and chatter or a genuine shift in the way the world works?

This is a measured and smart way to sense-check your decision-making. What is the challenge we're responding to? Are we jumping on a bandwagon or a fad? What impact will we face and when will that impact hit us?

Too fast is foolhardy: make the decision when you have the right input (but get that input fast)

'Know what you need to know before you believe what you want to believe.' This is reportedly a CIA mantra which is a sense-check to make sure that you are listening to the 'intelligence' properly before you jump too soon to conclusions. Sir Alex Ferguson, in his book *Leading*, grumbles that the impetuousness of youth can be a real danger as it leads to too fast decision-making. And, of course, in a world peppered by concerns about attention deficit, people get nervous about speed. So, judging how to be quick and decisive at the right speed is something leaders need to consider carefully.

Leadership in a Superfast team should never be about rushing. As already mentioned, Amee Chande is UK Managing Director of Alibaba, the world's largest retailer. Inevitably, because it is a tech company, it is very fast-paced but what really drives speed for her there is the fact that the culture is so customer-focused. And she cautions against rushing unnecessarily:

> On the battlefield and if you are a surgeon, then there probably are decisions that require split-second leadership but building businesses is not quite the same. The reality is that things that are important are often the things that require a little more time and consideration.

Like many, however, she speeds up decision-making with a simple framework: 'To make a decision, remind yourself – what are our priorities? What impact will this have on people?' This is a great check-step:

1 How does the decision I'm making fit with the priorities we've agreed?
2 What impact will it have on people inside and outside the organization?

The greater neuroscientific understanding of the way the brain works, which has been pioneered by the legendary

Daniel Kahneman, shows the danger in reactive, 'gut' decision-making being applied to complex questions. Perhaps we should take business inspiration from the ancient Greek proverb: 'Act quickly. Think slowly.' When we say 'slowly' in this context, of course, we mean it in the sense of 'deeply and considering the data'.

SOME HELPFUL MODELS

It's important to be conscious that there are ways to make decisions considered and thoughtful without losing the ability to carry them out in time. Giles Andrews, founder of Zopa, says in this regard:

> I think if you look at successful investment businesses, for example, they have really put time and effort in to formalizing how they make a decision, because they recognize that, 'Do I invest in this company or not?' is the most important decision that they make. Therefore, they set up a process which everyone understands: what reports have to be written, who does them, what research has to be written, what presentation has to be written, who gives it and when a committee is expected to make a decision, it's all understood. And some of that discipline is kind of helpful.

This type of structure and discipline can help. It removes the brainpower taken up by 'what next and why' and allows the brainpower to focus instead on the *content* going into the model. So question your decision-making structure. Does it encourage enough rigour without losing vigour? Does it give people a quick checklist to give them the confidence to be 80 per cent certain? It may help your board, your team or you to use a model which helps make sure you are getting the timing of decision-making right. And then you can speed that decision-making up ...

Accountability, responsibility and decision-making can be tremendously muddled. Every time you start a project, make sure that you have the discipline of asking 'Who is the ultimate decision-maker?' You often have to be diplomatic about it but never make the mistake of thinking that the noisiest and most opinionated person is definitely the one whose decision matters most. If you're putting together something you want to deliver at pace, always work out *when* the decision-makers can be involved. GV (Google's venture capital arm) runs a week-long 'sprint' to accelerate the evolution of ideas, and Jake Knapp, one of the inventors of this process, is clear that one golden unbreakable rule is always to make sure that the decision-makers are in the room.

Lessons from the battlefield

Moving from being a military commander to a tech start-up CEO might seem like an unlikely transition but, for James Meeks, the lessons he learned as a combat veteran and Purple Heart awardee served him well as SVP of Swissport Americas, a 10,000-person global aviation logistics company, and then as co-founder and chair of an international non-profit company 2Seeds and CEO of MOVE Systems. The military world is frequently one of action, but Meeks took a military tool which slowed down the process of thinking and applied it to the business world as well. He used the OODA loop – Observe–Orient–Decide–Act – to help him in the battlefield and then reapplied it to business.

The OODA loop has become popular in both commercial and military organizations and provides a framework loop which ensures that you are observing carefully and then orienting yourself before making a decision and then acting. Military strategist and US Air Force Commander John Boyd applied this as an agility model in combat operations. He also thinks that decision-making occurs in a recurring cycle of Observe–Orient–Decide–Act.

In military terms, this loop makes sense as observation is key. Observation is also a powerful tool in consumer innovation. Procter & Gamble created Swiffer from watching women 'hack' their mops with paper towels. Steve Jobs would hide in the bushes outside Apple stores to watch staff and customers.

In other situations, when making decisions personally as a leader in business, you might also want to consider a simpler loop. Andrew St George and Sharon Curry are coaches and consultants who use naval leadership examples and their Navy experience to help inspire businesses and they recommend to them the straightforward process of 'Listen, Decide, Act'. Listen first, get the perspectives you need, and then act. Microsoft CEO Satya Nadella gives gloriously simple, highly effective advice on how to run a meeting which echoes this approach: 'Listen more, talk less and be decisive when the time comes.'

Using a simple process will help keep decision-making moving at pace. That's why the Innocent founders introduced the Bain RAPID® model to identify who inputs and who decides. Adam Balon, one of the founders of Innocent, says that, for them, adopting the Bain RAPID® tool across their organization was a highly effective process to drive progress. Broadly speaking, it is a tool to clarify decision-making (I prefer it to the sometimes-used RACI model). It assigns owners to the five key roles in decision-making: recommending, agreeing, performing, inputting and deciding.

Some kind of framework is often useful to help provide a process which can be worked through (hopefully quickly). At the Caffeine Partnership, we helped one hyper-fast global tech company develop a highly effective decision-making tool at board level – this was PAARTY (Propose, Argue, Agree, Responsibility, Timing – Yes/No). PAARTY allows

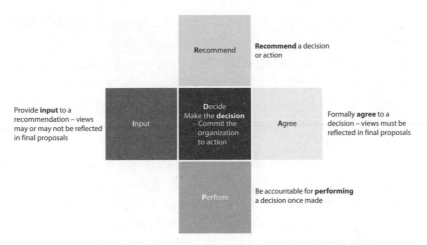

FIGURE 10.1 The Bain RAPID tool

time for constructive debate and input from the team but drives towards progress. Board meetings were precious time for the smart minds on this executive team of ten people and they wanted to make sure that they debated and discussed important issues but also to get to decisions.

They now use the simple PAARTY acronym to help the process:

1 A member of the team **proposes** something – 'I think we should/we need to …' – based on a problem or an opportunity.
2 The rest of the board then **argue** to make sure they consider different points of view and weigh up the issues until …
3 They get to some **agreement** on a way forward (the decision). They can then agree …
4 Who is **responsible**
5 What the **timing** is
6 And finally make absolutely sure everyone is happy with the recommendation with a simple **yes/no**.

This discipline helps the chair and the team to try and move forward from the argument towards a conclusion but not to do that too precipitously and thereby avoid the importance of 'creative abrasion' and debate to make sure the quality of the decision is the best possible. Like Amazon, they make high-velocity decisions because it's smart and because it's fun. It's great to PAARTY!

Whatever tools you use, be utterly ruthless about making them as simple and memorable as possible – this is always the advantage of an acronym. These tools should instil the discipline of clarity when making important decisions. They should be used to help get the pace right – fast enough to be effective without missing crucial thinking. Most people will agree that it's not the thinking about making a decision that takes up the time in an organization; it's about working out who decides and making sure they do it at the right time. Agreeing *who* and *when* at the start saves infinite time later.

Speeding up the structure

A decision-making model may be a helpful check-step to ensure smart input has been considered. Once you have one set up, then explore whether you can speed it up.

Speed can deliver a competitive advantage. If you can get through this process quickly, you can spot and react to events more speedily than your opponents. John Boyd, the military strategist and originator of the OODA loop outlined above, explains:

> In order to win, we should operate at a faster tempo or rhythm than our adversaries – or, better yet, get inside [the] adversary's Observation–Orientation–Decision–Action time cycle or loop … Such activity will make us appear ambiguous (unpredictable) and thereby generate confusion and disorder among our adversaries – since our adversaries will be unable to generate mental images or pictures that agree with the menacing, as well as faster, transient rhythm or patterns they are competing against.

Your ability to increase pace may be as simple as affecting how frequently you make sure that decisions are being made. Here's Liv Garfield, CEO of Severn Trent, explaining a key change she made relatively early on her role as Chief Executive:

> Accelerate it. Companies often run where the next decision-making committee for that thing is in a month. We used to run it that way. We used to have a policy meeting once a month. We had to wait for the next month for a policy meeting. That just didn't make sense. Instead, we now just have a weekly team meeting and the agenda is only set the week before. So anything goes into the agenda, so that means that you're always doing the right things for the moment and dealing quickly with stuff that comes up. I think it's looking at how decisions are made in your company and working out how you increase the frequency of where decisions can be taken.

Amee Chande, MD of Alibaba in the UK, spent time with Tesco and Walmart before her current role, so she is used to companies who want to move fast. Retail is an industry where speed is critical, and she points out that 'they're called fast-moving consumer goods for a reason'. Walmart used an awareness of time to get one step ahead by simply changing the timing of its decision-making. Traditionally, the key review meetings were on a Monday; by moving them to a Friday instead it had two extra days, because decisions made on a Friday were executed on a Saturday to capture the entire week.

How often are the important decisions being made? What proportion of working time is spent researching, exploring or delivering versus questioning and making decisions? You can make a significant difference to speed just by looking at the 'frequency' of decision-making. Are the debate and discussion and decision-making sessions being held at the right time?

Separating these out, or labelling the point where the decision needs to be made (and being clear on who makes it), helps save time and repetition.

Label the decisions. Minute them. Shout about them.

When we work with executive teams and with boards, one of the frustrations that frequently occurs is when the same topics come up again and again. In a busy week, in our busy brains, people forget that a decision has been made or that new people joining don't appreciate what's happened. Sometimes in meetings people may find themselves in a discussion but no one articulates when a decision has been reached (or asks for a decision). Avoid these situations by adopting the following procedure:

1 **Focus the debate.** Asking the question 'What decision needs to be made here?' clearly in a given situation helps those around you to articulate more plainly what needs to happen in a meeting or in the project.

2 **Label the decision clearly.** Meeting chairs or project leads are responsible for labelling, confirming and calling it. It's interesting how infrequently someone clarifies the fact that an agreement has been reached by saying 'Are we all agreed?' or 'So, we have decided that …' A good chair or meeting facilitator is one who calls and confirms what progress is being made. The more consultative a process is the more important this is.

3 **Record it and circulate it.** If a decision has been made, it should be clearly communicated.* Remember that 'the person who has the pen wields the power' (I've heard a few tales of where the minute taker or the flipchart owner in a meeting has somewhat steered the conclusion in writing it up). Make sure you share the decision with those people who need to know. Speed is screwed up when communication slows down. Ask: 'Who needs to know we've decided this?' If it's an important decision, you might want to think about ways of articulating

it that will be memorable, using language or memorable visual tropes to help. Leadership guru Tom Peters puts it like this: 'Don't say "I want to increase net promoter score."Winners say,"We're gonna make this place so cool customers pee their pants with joy."' Labelling the decision as a decision and clarifying your understanding is a critical, simple practice that anyone can do and which can reduce confusion and repetition and help increase your ability to move forward faster. Say it. Write it. Then it's done and you can move on.

*Bear in mind that people's memories of meetings and discussions are shockingly inaccurate. Scientific studies on the reliability of eyewitness testimonies are worth reading. People may hear and remember different conversations and conclusions. Clearly articulating your understanding is incredibly important, to avoid having to get to a decision over and over again.

Whenever you make a decision or take a key decision, write down what you expect will happen. Nine or twelve months later, compare the results with what you expected. Management guru Peter Drucker called this self-reflection process 'feedback analysis' and credited it to a fourteenth-century German theologian. He said it was the 'only way to discover your strengths'. Warren Buffett has made it a habit for years to write down the reasons why he is making an investment decision and later looks back to see what went right or wrong. Record it, review it, and learn, learn, learn.

When do you debate and when do you move to action?

Patrick Lencioni, in his writing on how to work as a functional board, first introduced me to the concept of 'disagree and commit'. Lencioni talks about how often teams become paralysed by their need for complete agreement and their inability to move beyond debate. The structure of people being allowed and indeed encouraged to say 'I disagree but I agree to commit' is a strategy adopted at Intel and Amazon and is an incredible tool for making meetings and teams more productive. According to one of Amazon's leadership principles, it works if: 'Once a decision is determined, leaders commit wholly.'

We should support decisions when they've been made (particularly when made by our vertical team, our board or our 'tribe' at work). We've talked elsewhere in this book about the importance of candour and disagreement but a call needs to be made, a decision needs to be taken, and teams and organizations need to work to deliver once that's happened. This helps your stress levels as well:

> Amazon's Jeff Bezos says: Stress primarily comes from not taking action over something that you can have some control over. 'I find as soon as I identify it, and make the first phone call, or send off the first email message, or whatever it is that we're going to do to start to address that situation – even if it's not solved – the mere fact that we're addressing it dramatically reduces any stress that might come from it.

Make a move and decrease that feeling of overwhelm or worry.

Sara Tate, the creative and charming advertising CEO at TBWA and formerly Managing Director at Mother, talks about the debate that inevitably happens at Mother where each team is headed up by a triumvirate of leaders. They get to a point where they can say they are 80 per cent agreed and then they move. This mantra of '80 per cent Agreement, 100 per cent Alignment' means that their teams are not divided by their disagreements or discussions. The focus is on moving forward.

Delegation: casting, supporting and letting go

Put A-list people on A-list priorities

Some leaders spread their best people 'democratically' around, hoping that talent will infect more people. The choice of where you put your people in the structure is important. The correlation between company success and the distribution of star talent has been tracked by Michael Mankins and Eric Garton in their book *Time, Talent, Energy*. They have found that companies like Apple, Netflix, Google and Dell are 40 per cent more productive than the average company, not because they start with more star players but because they distribute their star players more wisely:

> The average company follows a method of unintentional egalitarianism, spreading star talent across all of the roles. Companies like Google and Apple, however, follow an intentionally non-egalitarian method. They select a handful of roles that are business critical, affecting the success of the company's strategy and execution, and they fill 95 per cent of these roles with A-level quality ... The rest of the roles have fewer star players.

> Look at Apple and Microsoft in the early 2000s as an example. It took 600 Apple engineers less than two years to develop, debug and deploy iOS 10. Contrast that with 10,000 engineers at Microsoft that took more than five years to develop, debut and ultimately retract Vista. The difference was in the way these companies chose to construct their teams.

In a fast-moving world, you need your fastest people to be in the most important parts of the business. Every single organization will talk about the need to innovate, the worry about being the latest 'Kodak' and missing the big developments, the pressure of consumer and shareholder expectation on innovation. But if you put your best people only into the day-to-day business (the 'jam today') or you ask them to 'innovate on the side', then the likelihood that there will be 'jam tomorrow' will be reduced.

Watch out for the trap of 'flogging the willing horse'. In organizations those people who are good and hard-working get loaded and loaded and loaded with initiatives that are in addition to their day job. That will make them learn and grow, but watch out – they will sometimes need support and short cuts to make sure they can continue to achieve.

> Choose the whos. Pause to get the casting right at the start – it's about pausing to make the right choices.

GIVE THE FRAMEWORK AND THEN THE FREEDOM

We mentioned willing horses. Let's stay in the equine arena. Think about the reins you use when riding. They exist so you can correct your course, but, if your horse is moving forward, you shouldn't hold them too tight as that causes upset or the horse to stop. Take heed of the ex-Mayor of New York City Rudi Giuliani, who said: 'When I delegate, I delegate.'

If you have set up a good framework (the purpose and the values of your organization or team plus a structure which encourages fast feedback), you'll be more comfortable letting go. Senior leaders have 'control' in their nature; they've often succeeded by focusing on detail and controlling what they personally do. I've spoken to many brilliant managers and leaders for whom this balance has been the challenge: they know that a command-and-control approach does not work in a world of speed, uncertainty and human business … but they also want things to be 'done right'. Anna Wintour, doyenne of *Vogue*, is an ardent believer in the value of strong delegation but is a classic example of someone who wants to make sure she's kept in the loop:

> People work better when they have responsibility. We talk about what needs to be done, and then I assume it is done. I like to know what's going on, but I'm not double-checking and triple-checking. But at the same time, I don't like surprises. I like to be aware at all times of what's going on.

How you delegate and what the expectations are will need to be consistent with the organization's culture or you will need to communicate your way very clearly. If you don't want to be surprised with bad news, what's your check-in mechanism? Many an organization's speed is constantly torpedoed as people wait to get time with a senior leader.

Be realistic. If you have expectations or you want people to keep you posted, be clear with them on that. Delegation is a communication challenge: you need to be crystal clear on the expectations and the person you delegate to has to understand what level of communication and check-in suits you.

The more of a leadership role you have, the more you need to work out what you control and what you absolutely mustn't. Give people clear parameters around where they need to go with their work and, if they operate in a culture where the values and principles of the organization are clear, you can let go (or at least hold the reins a little less nervously).

This is because people need autonomy. (Dan Pink's famous trio of motivations on what drives people at work – autonomy, mastery and purpose – needs to be tattooed on your brain.) And it's because *you* don't have enough time. Giles Andrews gives the classic advice (which supports the advice given about 'strategic laziness' mentioned in Chapter 5):

> Don't interfere, if you've defined their role and ownership, don't interfere directly. You have to respect their territory, because if you start interfering in every decision they make it will always come back to you. You have to respect their authority because, if you don't, then every question or if anyone disagrees with anything it will end up on your desk.

Often this is about avoiding wasting time, energy and resources on managing things that don't matter. At Netflix, this is partly why there is a 'no expense' policy within the organization – a radical approach that shocked and surprised many when it was first introduced. The only policy is 'Act in the best interests of Netflix.'

By doing this, the company is telling employees that it trusts them not 'to rip off the company' and is not willing 'to put in place processes that consume human capital, waste time, and zap energy'. It's also about accepting that, if you have chosen the right people to work on this, they will know better than you how to respond. Your control and influence and help come from the framework and from assigning the right people to the right roles.

Empowering customer-facing employees to make the right decision has saved companies millions in wasted administration and the negative impact of inhuman, slow decision-making on customer relationships. The Timpson chain of key-cutters (often to be seen at underground and train stations or in high streets across the UK) is famed for adopting 'upside-down management', which means their customer-facing staff are the ones empowered to make decisions about how to deal with customers – they are well trained and then given up to £500 each to make the right call about any customer issues.

Rear Admiral Neil Morisetti, now an advisor to the UK government and business, believes that the very best leaders practise what he calls 'extreme delegation'. This often surprises those who think of naval and military leaders as the archetypes of 'command and control', but he explains that in the Royal Navy those on the frontline are the ones who can judge the situation best and they should be the ones who do so. Delays in getting approval can be a life-or-death situation. In our fast-moving world, businesses stymied by over-controlling bosses will rapidly become snail-like in execution.

The other way in which you can adopt a 'tight and loose' approach is to be crystal clear on 'the brief'. This obviously applies particularly to those in the creative industries, but thinking about 'the brief' for any project is a great discipline. Taking the time up front to clarify expectations, goals and measures as well as including any insights or parameters that are in the mind of the ultimate decision-maker means that you can save endless wasted work and development.

ROWE to make the boat go faster

A 'results-only work environment' (ROWE) is a clear way to increase the speed and focus on delivery. Delegation and trust for your people is a radical and complex issue for some. Many leaders I spoke to told me that thinking smarter about how people work is a key way in which to move faster.

Wim Dejonghe, Senior Partner of law firm Allen & Overy, talks about remote working as a useful tool for speed in his organization. The UK communications giant BT has also led a movement where flexible working is used as a way to save the company millions in terms of increased productivity and reduced costs as well as to motivate people – seven out of ten of their people work flexibly.

In an analysis BT conducted as far back as 2007, it demonstrated that flexible working led to the following benefits:

- **Greater productivity:** for example, home-working call-centre operators handle up to 20 per cent more calls than their office-based colleagues
- **Improved employee satisfaction, motivation and retention:**
  - BT home workers take 63 per cent less sick leave than their office-based counterparts
  - the retention rate following maternity leave is 99 per cent
  - the absentee rate among flexible workers is down 63 per cent and is now 20 per cent below the UK average

- Cost savings:
  - over €725 million a year through reduced office estate
  - €104 million a year through reduction in accommodation costs associated with home working
  - €7.4 million a year in recruitment and induction costs through improved retention following maternity leave.

A results-only focus for an organization is a great filter for success. Having worked in two businesses that operated a ROWE policy, I've seen the way that this focuses people on delivery and the burden and time it takes away from others.

> Set the brief, set the framework, be clear on expectations, and you can judge people not on late nights and jackets left on chairs (that trick where people pretend they are still in the office) but on actual, tangible results.

Delivery

There's a lot to review on the 'getting it right' side of things but here we're looking at the 'getting it done' challenge (or the 'getting it done at speed' challenge). When it comes to delivery, here are three ways to help make sure you drive with rapidity and momentum:

- Deadlines deliver.
- Measure what matters.
- Progress drives pace.

Deadlines deliver

In planning what you want to do, take control of the expectations. Lead expectations clearly. Change the timelines to what you believe are right.

With teams, deadlines focus work, galvanize action and get things done. However, managing the expectations of stakeholders and shareholders, allies and investors, partners and customers is the delicate balancing act of a leader working in a Superfast world where expectations increase daily.

In the same way as you sometimes need to increase the frequency of things (like decision-making opportunities), sometimes you need to slow down the frequency of reporting or the expectations of those around you. Otherwise deadlines set and not delivered on will destroy your reputation, your share price and your peace of mind.

The most audacious – and effective – example of this is Paul Polman, Global CEO of Unilever, whose dramatic transformation of the way the company reported to shareholders completely altered the shape of its future. He joined the organization (the world's largest consumer goods company) in 2009, slap bang in the middle of a global financial crisis. On the first day at the helm he let shareholders know that they would no longer receive quarterly annual reports from the company or earnings guidance for the stock market. He declared firmly that the organization was now taking a longer-term view and invited shareholders to take their money elsewhere if they didn't want to 'buy into this long-term value-creation model, which is equitable, which is shared, which is sustainable'. Even more sensationally, this was his first day in the job: 'I figured I couldn't be fired on my first day.'

This is a great example of a leader acting decisively, acting fast. It's also a courageous and smart example of slowing something down to get a better result. And, finally, it's a perfect story illustrating the firm management of people's expectations.

A serious leader has to work with multiple 'pressure points' – regulators, shareholders, investors, teams, bosses, leaders and employees – as well as the expectations of increasingly intolerant and impatient consumers. Keeping your head and keeping people clear on what to expect is a task that takes skill. It doesn't surprise me that so many CEOs and entrepreneurs have worked in communications, with a natural ability to tell a compelling story, and, equally, have the brain that's needed to deal with multiple timelines and timings (or a very good right-hand chief of staff to help).

We often need the ability to punch fast and hit quickly. And, here, deadlines deliver. There's nothing like a set deadline for making sure that things really do happen. Those who've worked in managing sporting events will testify to that. Alan Gilpin, the CEO of Rugby World Cup, talks about the power of a deadline in the sporting world: 'It's not like a brand launch; it can't be moved back. The Olympics, the World Cup, they're happening on a certain day and you've just got to be ready for it.' Those who work in organizing sporting events can testify to how much can be achieved in a focused period of time.

A deadline can help you make things faster and drive progress through: you need to set expectations as well as manage them. Paul Polman may have changed expectations and deadlines with a reporting structure to slow down the pressure. He knows, though, that a deadline can help you make things faster and drive progress. He works solidly for the long term but is the type of leader with a natural bias towards action. He manages time and expectations in another way by setting a clear '30-day plan' deadline for his leaders. This means that, when there is a problem in the business, he asks people to return in no more than 30 days with a plan. He does not rush a response ('Tell me now what you will do to sort this'). He does not rush to his solution ('What we need to do is …'). Instead, he gives them time to collate data and insights and empowers them to lead the solution themselves, all while insisting on a very focused deadline to make sure that progress happens.

'Never waste a good crisis.' Winston Churchill's adage about a crisis is sage advice for leaders operating at velocity. Crises will hit. They will galvanize and energize and can be used productively. They also often deliver a drop-dead urgency and a deadline which helps focus the team like nothing else. They instil drama and excitement and a reason to move fast. Paul Willcox, Chair of Nissan Europe, talks about the power of a crisis, citing the 2008 economic crisis (which triggered a stagnation of the European new-car-buying market) as an example:

> Crisis is a great opportunity to drive change and we did so many different things and it was fantastic. Some people enjoy crisis because they can clamp down and stop things. For us we saw it as a great opportunity to make a change because to get people to move, you need to set their hair on fire, set their tails on fire, give them a real reason to move. Crisis is a great stimulus for that and you can use it to move a whole organization dramatically.

The story behind Pixar's *Toy Story* contains drama and crisis. In November 1993 Pixar was in the process of producing their first full-length feature film. Pixar had been pioneering computer animation for decades (and losing money for as long). This movie was a pivotal opportunity for the company, and it had been greenlighted the year before. The 26 November is a day the makers of *Toy Story* refer to as 'Black Friday'.

There was a screening of the first half of the film, from which both the Pixar and Disney teams emerged in shocked consensus over their verdict – the film was terrible. Production was shut down. This was a crisis like no other for the Pixar team, representing the nadir of decades of work. The team talked the Walt Disney head of animation out of his desire to close everything down and asked for a fortnight. They had two weeks to save the film ... and the entire company. Khoi Toi, teamwork specialist, shares what happened: 'They launched themselves into a fortnight of hyper-intense activity, of physical and mental stress, all barriers down, dealing with the issues with brutal honesty.'

This crisis solidified the team and forced them to address some personality differences and work as a team together and the imposed deadline delivered. *Toy Story* went on to score 100 per cent on the Rotten Tomatoes review aggregation site and generate $361 million at the box office worldwide.

If you can take a call about where crises are real (looking at the 'ripple intelligence' and making a judgement call about timing), if you can instil a sense of pace without panic, if you can set deadlines which allow the right amount of focus but don't create a short-term blinkered view that loses the ability to win the war as well as the battles, then you can allow your teams to deliver successfully.

Success is, of course, relative and subjective. That's where choosing the right measures helps.

Measure what matters

Habits can be changed through recording and measuring progress. It's true in your personal life, with eating, exercising and learning new things. Author and habits researcher Gretchen Rubin calls this 'the strategy of monitoring': 'The fact is, if you want more or less of something in your life, it's very helpful to measure it, because you manage what you measure.' Choosing what you decide to measure in your organization, team and projects is one of the most important decisions you make.

> What gets measured gets done. We treasure what we measure.

Measurements help us focus and help give us a sense of progress. As I write this I'm tracking wordcount and chapter writing each day - the glorious feeling of ticking a goal gives me a satisfying feeling of achievement. It's on an Excel spreadsheet and visually shown on a Trello board and I announce to whoever is interested enough to listen at the end of the day: 'I did 3,000 words today and my target is 2,000 a day.' Admittedly 2,750 of them may be rubbish words but the very act of writing builds momentum, progress and energy and hitting a goal gives me a hit of pleasure.

It's the 'dopamine drug' – something it's worth being aware of if you're interested in leadership and speed. It's not a performance-enhancing steroid that will get you disqualified from the race but instead an entirely natural brain chemical which is something that can be triggered to encourage action or positivity – in yourself or in others. Dopamine motivates you to take action towards your goals and gives you a surge of reinforcing pleasure when achieving them. In the brain, dopamine functions as a neurotransmitter – a chemical released by neurons (nerve cells) to send signals to other nerve cells; it's linked in popular science to being the 'pleasure transmitter'. It certainly helps give you a hit if you are meeting goals. Setting measures matters. Achieving them feels good.

Anne Boden, founder of Starling Bank (an innovative fintech mobile-first bank), keeps a highly visual track of progress and does it in a very agile way. Some of the tools are 'old-school': the office is covered in whiteboards and there's a stand-up meeting every day. But there's also Jira software, which is probably the industry-leading tool in managing big projects. Tools that highlight visibly people's progress give a real-time motivation for accountability which she says helps drive the 'rhythm' of progress: 'Everything we do is about visibility and seeing the process and having a common visual objective of what we're going to do and having very clear schedules of what we're going to do today.'

Another entrepreneur, Benji Wakeham, who had founded four tech start-ups before he was 26 uses the project management tool Asana to help manage his double pace of short- and long-term objectives. The sense of progress tracking tools give is powerful as it helps set the pace. Simon Devonshire talks about fintech Zopa's early days when getting traction to grow was hard but measuring growth times and beating it helped galvanize the team:

> Getting that first bit of momentum was the hardest ... And once we got it rolling, we rolled, and we turned over a million, and then I said, 'How many days did it take to do that?' They said 190 or something. The next one we did in 90, and the next one we did in 60; then we did it in 30 – you see the momentum?'

Progress drives pace

A sense of build for employees is one of the biggest drivers in making things happen – the feeling of mastering stuff and improving. We've already seen how Dan Pink, one of the world's leading business thinkers, sees 'mastery' as one of his holy trinity of things which motivate people at work ('autonomy, mastery and purpose'). His research shows that money is not the key motivator for people in general. To deliver the motivation and momentum you need sounds simple when Pink talks about it but in reality it's complex to deliver.

Mastery is a sense of progress from a personal point of view, and it's highly motivating to feel that sense of progress on projects, aspirations, dreams and ambitions within your organization, within your team. Belief gives people energy and speed. Belief comes from a sense of the vision, the mission and the purpose involved in a business. Belief also then comes from seeing the miracles and sharing the wins.

Marketing itself is often about communicating stories of progress to consumers, giving them reasons to be interested in you, and finding excuses to talk to them. Simon Devonshire used the approach of using 'six-week shouts' when he worked with O2, helping double their customer base in five years:

A 'shout' can be whatever you want it to be. It can be as profound as the incarnation of an entirely new product, like the launch of the new iPhone, or it can be as flippant and trivial as getting the Prime Minister to visit your factory. A shout is simply something that is remarkable. I don't mean remarkable as in 'good'. I mean remarkable as in 'to be remarked upon'. We live in a world of social media, so what you want is for people to be your mouthpiece and be compelled to promote, elevate and circulate your message. You've got to give them the messages.

So, why six weeks? Why that pace? More frequently than that is hard. It's hard for the team to deliver. Even just doing the marketing admin, it's hard to deliver more frequently than that. It's hard on the engineers and on the actual coders. Less frequently than that … is an age in the life of a consumer. If I were to ask what you were doing three weeks ago, most people struggle to answer. Six weeks [works] actually, if you've got the permission to email somebody, one email every six weeks. That's not unreasonable. Six weeks and you're building the pace and the repetition.

Sam Altman, serial investor behind successes like Airbnb, gives this as one of his key tips for start-ups: 'Momentum is critical. Don't lose it.' Start with something. Start with something that will lead to something else. Think about what 'visible wins' you can aim for, get and share. As fintech Zopa grew, its leaders used the doubling of customer wins as proof that it was a great idea and that progress had been achieved once and could be done again. Calling out progress helps build believers, and this is particularly critical when you are pioneering or doing something differently. It could be as simple as getting a website up in 24 hours. It could be about focusing on the 'halo effect' of an action. Serial entrepreneurs Douglas and Estelle Lloyd generated significant momentum when setting up their venture Azoomee (an innovative 'safe place' to play for kids on the Internet) by achieving two great partnerships in the early days of the business with O2 and with the NSPCC. That encouraged others, who saw that successful organizations were backing them and wanted to be associated with them.

This example also is evidence of the power of 'social proof' when you are trying to get people to believe in something.

This means the proof that other people who are like you (or other companies or people you want to be like) have invested in you or partnered with you or used something you've produced – it gives reassurance. 'Social proof' is a persuasive tool in getting people to agree to, or buy, something. It is about showing people that people like them have bought something or bought into something. It is a short cut that drives pace: if other people have bought into something, you are more likely to get your advocates or investors on board. VC investment is a great example of this: it's a club where people judge the investment opportunity mainly on who else has invested. Find progress, find social proof, and delivery will continue at pace. Visible tangible 'wins' create their own momentum.

Espresso takeaways

Decide. Delegate. Deliver.

- **Decisions:** Clarity (about who makes the decision and when) provides focus and energy.
- **Delegation:** 'The who' needs to have as much thought given to it as 'the what'.
- **Delivery:** Get moving, get motivating, get momentum.

Decide. sharply, smartly.

- Too slow is stupid: make a decision.
- Avoid analysis paralysis.
- Speed up decision-making with a structure.
- Increase the frequency of opportunities to make a decision.
- Too fast is foolhardy: make a decision when you have the right input (and get it fast).
- Check you've listened. Who can give you a perspective to help? Who will ask the right questions?
- 'Argue like you know you're right, listen like you know you're wrong.'
- Embrace the paradox of doubt.

THEN ...

- Label the decisions clearly, and articulate, record and share them
- 'If it's inevitable, get enthusiastic.' – 'Shut up and row.'

Delegate. Sharply, smartly, clearly and making a careful choice.

- Put A-listers on A-priorities.
- Provide a firm framework and then give them freedom.

Happy deliveries. Sharp and smart, too.

- Move from debate to action without too much delay – 'A little less conversation, a little more action, please.'
- Deadlines deliver (and destroy). Manage expectations and timings firmly – what can you push and what can you push back?
- Progress Drives Pace. Find wins, share and amplify belief.

Be impatient: don't tolerate the superfluous, the unnecessary, prevarications and complications, and lack of ambition. Be patient and persistent, knowing that the bigger goals will take more time than you think.

Epilogue: a happy ending

I want to finish with some personal reflections.

Whether it's a question of effective communications, clarity of business plans, creating pieces of music, or the construction of stories (fictional or business), it's worth starting with the ending first.

Endings are important. No matter how fast things are, keep the end in sight.

Your role as a leader should include thinking about stories and thinking about how they are constructed. If you want to increase the performance of your organization and your own pace, working out the stories will help you. Stories have power: not just the stories you tell and convey to others but also the stories you tell yourself. And stories are defined by how they finish.

> That's about the ending. But will you get there fast enough? Are you feeling impatient about getting moving?

Patience and impatience

Throughout this book, I've been thinking about the question of patience and impatience and the role they play for those leading in a high-velocity context. These are the two things you need to have to lead in a world of speed.

Is patience a virtue in a fast-moving world? Is there a role for impatience, which as children we are taught is a less-than-desirable attribute? In adults, impatience is often portrayed as morally wrong, as a sign that we are a culture addicted to instant gratification and a fix.

The answer to this is complex but important. It's a question I've looked at with all the leaders I interviewed for this book and which I have considered carefully. Some things can be simplified to a guideline; this certainly can't. Even in a world moving with the power and speed of a jaguar, things will take time.

Changing an organization, changing people's minds, building brands, building a team, building a culture … these will not be delivered overnight. As in the rest of life, some things need to be carried out at a slower pace.

A predilection for impatience is important in a leader, an awareness that the world is moving faster and that competitors are forever hungrily snapping away at your heels. Impatience is a driver, impatience makes things happen, a sense of urgency about getting started is absolutely, critically essential if you want to have a hope of moving as fast as technological advances and your competitors will do.

Jeff Bezos, one of the world's most impatient entrepreneurs, is a lover of 'velocity' and is a man who has, arguably more than anyone in the last three decades, fuelled the world's desire for speed of delivery. However, he has also demonstrated a determined patience as he's built new and innovative ideas which have changed markets. 'We've had three big ideas at Amazon that we've stuck with for 18 years, and they're the reason we're successful: Put the customer first. Invent. And be patient.'

Every single person I interviewed who was asked 'Do you consider yourself an impatient person?' answered 'Yes' – amusingly, most without a pause. Paul Willcox, the Chair of Nissan Europe, expresses what many interviewees acknowledged about themselves: 'I am where I am because of my impatience. Not accepting mistakes, not accepting excuses – people are driven by different things but I think if you don't push you don't succeed. That's basic.'

Most interviewees quantified their admission with a caveat, with a significant number using this phrase, like Wilcox: 'I'm impatient with some things and patient with others.' There's an impatience with wasting time – especially in light of a sense of urgency with most leaders who passionately want their company to move fast.

There is, however, the need for tenacious, conscious, considered patience as well – the understanding that transformations take time (changing people's minds particularly is a slower process than people want). The patience to persist and an understanding that to get real change you need to repeat, repeat, repeat – what you are communicating, what you are testing, what you are doing.

There's also a realism that needs to be built in. Alexei Orlov, the former Global Chief Executive of Rapp, talks about 'the magic of the twos' that he learned early on:

> Years and years ago, it must have been 15 years ago, I was impatient to be out there conquering the world. An inspiring older gentleman I knew called Sully told me something that I thought was genius. 'I'm going to tell you, old boy,' he said to me, 'about the magic of the twos.' I said, 'OK.' He said to me – and I'll never forget it – 'Always remember that whatever they tell you is going to take twice as long.' Then he added, 'Whatever they tell you, it's going to take twice the cost.' So, I've never forgotten this and I use this religiously now. It's a phenomenally useful sense-check: whatever time period people give, whatever cost they give, ask yourself, 'Could I survive if this turned out to be twice as long or twice as expensive?'

Adam Balon, co-founder of Innocent, has an even more extreme approach when it comes to setting up a business – showing, yet again, the challenging nature of start-ups:

> Whatever length of time you think it is going to take, triple it and then add some more. Everything takes longer than you think. We gave ourselves one month and it took us nine. As a result, we financially ruined ourselves.

Be prepared to work out where you will have to be patient. A number of interviewees were clearly impatient and intolerant about many things. These could include impatience with unnecessarily cumbersome processes, with bad behaviour in their team and toxic hires, with slow decision-making. Many stressed, however, the importance of being patient with people.

Timing

Judging whether your patient or impatient side should be let loose is a question of working out 'when'. In business, timing – when a few things come together at the right time – is critical. Idealab founder Bill Gross was involved in starting over a hundred companies and he wanted to understand what drove success versus failure. Was it the originality of the idea? Was it the skill and delivery of the team? Was it about the money – the access to funding? These are all the elements one would expect and ones we know are important. But the number-one factor according to Gross's analysis?

Timing.

In his analysis, 'Timing accounted for 42 per cent of the difference between success and failure.'

The analysis of the companies that outperformed their rivals by more than ten times covered in the *Good to Great* books and studies also looked at timing. It wasn't just about speed but about getting the timing right. Business analyst and author Jim Collins explained that the leaders of the companies he studied in *Good to Great* which were ten times more successful than a similar competitor were able to

recognize changes and threats early … but then take the time available –
whether that be short or long – to make rigorous decisions and take
disciplined action. The key question is not 'Should we go fast or slow?'
but 'How much time do we have before the risk profile changes?' They
go slow when they can, fast when they must. If they have time, they're
comfortable letting events unfold, while preparing to act decisively
when the time comes.

Timing is particularly challenging for business leaders in
today's rapidly accelerating world. Many focus internally and
on the numbers rather than taking the broader view. 'So many
CEOs, CFOs and others spend time staring at the spreadsheet
but that's not how you make the numbers change. You've got to
look up and out for that to happen,' says Simon Bailey, ex-CEO
of Interbrand Europe. It is hard to predict the future from a tech
point of view, from an economic point of view, from a political point of view, but you do need to keep a weather eye on all
that. You need a clear perspective and you need to be ready to
act. The ability to move fast when it's needed helps many to be
ready to grab the opportune moment.

In an entrepreneurial environment, the ability to get stuff done
matters. In a big organization, the ability to cut through and
unblock gets momentum going. Once you get started on something, you know it has more of a chance of reaching a glorious end.

The urgency of doing

It isn't what you know, it isn't who you know, it isn't what
you want, it isn't what you'd like. It's about you getting on and
doing it. It's about getting started and getting moving.

Keith Yamashita, founder of San Francisco design and leadership firm SY Partners, has worked with leaders from Oprah
Winfrey to Howard Schultz. He reflects on the challenge of
leading through uncertain times, 'in a world with monumental
forces at play', and goes back to the wisdom of the visionary

designer Buckminster Fuller, 'who reflected on what one person can do':

> Something hit me very hard once [Fuller writes], thinking about what one little man could do. Think of the *Queen Elizabeth* – the whole ship goes by and then comes the rudder. And there's a tiny thing at the edge of the rudder called a trim tab. It's a miniature rudder. Just moving the little trim tab builds a low pressure that pulls the rudder around. Takes almost no effort at all. So I said that the little individual can be a trim tab. Society thinks it's going right by you, that it's left you altogether. But if you're doing dynamic things mentally, the fact is that you can just put your foot out like that and the whole big ship of state is going to go. So I said, 'Call me Trim Tab.'

Can you be that Trim Tab for your organization? So many of us think of our organization as a big amorphous blob, a supertanker. Each person can play a role – if you are, as Buckminster Fuller put it, 'doing dynamic things mentally'. There's an interesting challenge.

The need for motion? The need for action? We think it's a contemporary issue and it is, but it was ever thus (and smart people have always seen it).

Here's someone who thought about *her* ending. The inspiring widowed wine-maker Barbe-Nicole Clicquot Ponsardin (the 'Veuve Clicquot') wrote to her great-grandchild towards the end of her life, urging a sense of urgency: 'The world is in perpetual motion, and we must invent the things of tomorrow. One must go before others, be determined and exacting and let your intelligence direct your life. Act with audacity.'

It's a message from the 1860s which feels as relevant today. What a great call to action! This woman was a success long before anyone had even defined the glass ceiling, someone with an obsession about her product and craft as well as a commercial genius who found creative ways round blockers to her business during wartime. Audacity is defined by the dictionary as 'impudence' or 'a willingness to take bold risks' – and Mme Clicquot had it in spades. There is a real thrill and drama in her call to 'act with audacity'.

Skipping forward a century and you find one of the most interesting British businessmen of the twentieth century, Joseph Cyril Bamford, who founded the JCB company. A hard-working teetotaller, Bamford was famously careful with his own money but consistently paid more than fair wages to his workforce. In 1967 he stood on a farm cart and handed out personal cheques totalling a quarter of a million pounds. His focus on employees led to unprecedented levels of workplace flexibility, with the average JCB employee being seven times more productive, through the strike-dominated 1970s and early 1980s, than the average British manufacturing worker.

Bamford reflected on a common attribute that he saw across 'the people who make things move in this world' – of which he was certainly one (when Bamford's life reached its end in 2001, JCB was the largest privately owned engineering company in Britain):

> The people who make things move in this world share this same sense of URGENCY. No matter how intelligent or able you may be, if you don't have this sense of URGENCY now is the time to start developing it.

> The world is full of very competent people who honestly intend to do things tomorrow or as soon as they can get around to it. Their accomplishments, however, seldom match those of the less talented who are blessed with a sense of the importance of GETTING STARTED NOW.

The end of the story

This is the end of this story. Through it we have explored other stories, from leaders who have operated at high velocity and who have worked out, sometimes through hard experimentation, how to understand their own pace and how to help others move at the right speed.

I want this end to be a beginning. The start of some sparks that ignite your personal ambition. The inspiration that sets alight your confidence to move through this volatile world with grace, pace and certainty. Start with a sense of purpose. Be patient and persistent with building the long term but keep an awareness of the right pace. Be intolerant of unnecessarily tardiness, plodding and protracted processes.

I want to end this with a request to you:

> Stay curious and stay positive.

Your desire to learn, to think, to move forward that led you to read this book is one of your strongest weapons against the ambiguity of an accelerated, AI-driven, constantly changing world. Surround yourself with stimulation and ideas. Find fast ways to keep understanding the magnitude of our positively accelerating world: ideas can be accessed in a bite-sized way so you are adopting the micro-learning approach but make time every day to listen, read and learn.

Help us all learn. We can go further and faster together. Join our Superfast community for more and read more of our 'Pace-setter Profiles' online at superfastthebook.com or talk to @caffeinepartner or @s_devonshire on Twitter.

Think slow but move fast. *Citius est melius* (quicker is better). Let's keep discovering stories, secrets and stimulating ideas together.

Make it fun, make it fast.

Superfast.

Pace-setter profiles

The research for *Superfast* has been a joy, from start to end.

I've been lucky enough to speak to a diaspora of highly intelligent leaders to help pull together stories, evidence and examples to form the content of this book. It was a deliberate choice to interview people from different types of organizations and to try to find different personality styles and approaches to give as diverse and rich a range of experience as possible.

The interviewees included those heading up enormous global conglomerates and those who had just founded start-ups. There were leaders working in organizations which are hugely technology driven and those who were much more traditional in style. I spoke to people who had had decades of experience and those who were younger when they reached success. They include those who are the face of big public conglomerates as well as the leaders driving growth in private companies or family-owned organizations. They may have managed businesses with huge investment behind their growth, but there have also been those who have funded themselves all the way through.

All interviewees had one thing in common: their generosity of time and insight and their desire to share what they'd experienced and learned in order to help others.

I am phenomenally grateful to all those who agreed to be part of the research for this book and to all the friends who suggested and introduced people who they believed were great 'pace-setters'. I would also like to thank the diary organizers who helped make time for interviews and follow-ups to happen – particularly Natalie and Tanja who helped me enormously playing endless games of diary Tetris. Thank you so much to everyone for all their help.

Here are 'espresso' profiles of the key interviewees who helped shape the thinking of this book. Discover fuller profiles and more stories at www.superfast.com and follow me on LinkedIn and Twitter (@s_devonshire) for up-to-date stories.

Aaron Simpson	*Adam Balon*
Group Executive Chairman and co-founder of global luxury group **Quintessentially** (founded in 2000), which includes the world's most successful concierge business, 'fixing' the lives of the wealthy and time-pressed in 65 countries worldwide. The ex-film producer divides his time between London and Ibiza and, as part of the growth of the group, also supports the charity Quintessentially Foundation which has raised over 10 million in ten years.	**Founder JamJar Investments (and founder of Innocent Drinks).** The insouciant and ridiculously likeable Oxbridge and McKinsey graduate Adam Balon is sharp-brained and sharp-witted, and has a strong interest in businesses with principles and purpose. Adam co-founded Innocent drinks in 1999; the company was sold to Coca-Cola in 2013. Following on from helping create a standout brand and 'unpolitical' culture at Innocent, he'd like to see other food and drink brands develop with the help of JamJar's investment.

Professor Alan Barrell

Chair of a $3 billion RMB Chinese Venture Tech Fund, author and 'meta-connector'. Professor Alan Barrell DBA, FRSA is a live-wire of initiative and energy, fascinated by business, funding for entrepreneurs and the growth of Chinese business. Honoured for his services to UK and Finnish enterprise and education, he has had wide experience as chair and chief executive of different businesses, as well as teaching posts and angel investments. He believes in a vision of 'A World without Borders'. He co-authored *Show Me the Money: How to Raise the Cash and Get Your Business Off the Ground* (also available in Chinese).

@alanbarrell

Alan Gilpin

COO and Head of Rugby World Cup at World Rugby and one of the true gentlemen of the business world. Alan's sharp mind and immense drive never get in the way of manners and principles. Like all great rugby players he understands focus and the need to perform while being able to play 'the long game' for the good of the team. He has had a long successful career in the world of sports, including rights management at IMG and overseeing the award-winning hospitality programme for the 2012 Olympic Games.

@alangilpin2

Alexei Orlov

Founder and Global CEO of mtm choice worldwide. Experienced marketer, business leader and a self-styled philosopher of 'the business of life'. After a career in various senior roles in marketing including becoming global CEO of the agency RAPP, he now heads up mtm, the boutique media and brand activation agency (mtm stands for 'moments that matter)'.

@alexeiorlov

Amee Chande

Managing Director of Alibaba UK. Amee is a successful senior leader in one of the world's fastest-moving organizations, Alibaba. She is also passionate about the need to schedule time off from work and to give the brain a break by developing other pursuits. With McKinsey, Tesco and Walmart on her CV as well as the world's largest retailer, Alibaba, she understands how to operate in organizations which want to move at warp speed.

@AmeeChande

Andy Milligan

Founder, The Caffeine Partnership and a leading international brand and business consultant who is acknowledged as an expert on all areas of brand development. Andy is the co-founder of the Caffeine Partnership and one of my best friends. He advises CEOs and senior management teams on strategies for developing and exploiting brands and growing their business, and is the co-author of several prestigious books on branding including the award-winning *Bold: How to be Brave in Business and Win*.

@AndrewMilliga14

Anne Boden

CEO and co-founder of Starling Bank. The determined dynamo that is Anne Boden has founded a pioneering new bank with a clear purpose and an awe-inspiring sense of pace. After 30 successful years in the traditional banking world, she has launched her lean start-up as a truly digital current account. Fintech is a classic test of leadership and speed: keeping regulators happy, getting the rigour of the finances right while achieving the vigour of moving fast vs. the other 'neobanks' snapping at your heels.

@AnneBoden

Anthony Wreford

President of the MCC (the cricket club based at Lord's) and former CEO of Omnicom's marketing services division (DAS). Anthony is an advisor, non-executive director and investor in people businesses. He is a veteran of the advertising world and a super-connector with charm and ambition. He finds time for his passion for music in addition to golf and cricket.

Antony Jenkins

Co-founder and CEO of digital fintech 10x Future Technologies. Moving to a start-up was a surprising move from the former CEO of banking behemoth Barclays, but follows on from his prediction that traditional banking is facing a 'Kodak' moment. After 30 years in traditional banking, he co-founded 10x Future Technologies, which launched in 2016 and grew rapidly behind its vision of a core digital banking platform, based on advanced data modelling and database design.

Benji Wakeham

Founder and CEO of Pollen, an open banking platform for businesses regulated by the FCA, and helping SMEs scale efficiently via its market leading technology. A serial entrepreneur, packed full of drive, determination and charm, Benji started five businesses while still in his twenties and is fascinated by learning how to manage himself and his businesses at speed.

@BenjiWakeham

Brad Goodall

CEO and Founder of Spunge. Brad is a seasoned tech entrepreneur obsessed with the power of data to enrich human lives, having spent over 17 years building disruptive teams and businesses that challenge the status quo. As co-founder of the fast-growth fintech 10x Future Technologies, he helped design and define a visionary new company. Currently accelerating an innovative new initiative, he is a man to watch.

@bradgoods81

Carl Honoré

Award-winning writer, broadcaster and speaker. Carl is also, in the words of *The Sunday Edition* (CBC), 'the world's leading evangelist for what has become known as the Slow Movement'. Author of *In Praise of Slow, The Slow Fix and Under Pressure*, he is a charming, insightful man who is convinced of the need to slow down to go faster and has helped millions of people understand how to do that.

@carlhonore

Charlotte Vicary

Co-founder of The Customer Closeness Company. Charlotte is a charismatic and energetic evangelist of bringing the customer voice into businesses for the benefit of customers, companies and their shareholders. She has spent her career working with a variety of businesses as a brand consultant and is now helping organizations see the importance of customer-centricity in helping them stay one step ahead. Her company is unique in its ability to stage global customer-centric events for leaders and has worked with companies such as BT, Sky, Nissan, Sainsburys and eBay.

@CustomerClose

Chris Britton

Co-founder & Chair of Green Park Brands, a food/drink portfolio company. Chris is also an investor in consumer brands including Bounce and Plenish, a non-executive director of DS Smith, the FTSE 100 packaging company, and Chair of Graze and Dr Gerard, both private equity-backed food companies. An investor/entrepreneur who has accelerated brands to success fast, this straight-talking, fast-thinking Yorkshireman has been the energy, inspiration and guidance behind a number of significant investments across the years.

Christopher Fielding

Senior partner at Charme Capital in the UK, a European mid-market private equity fund, supporting management teams and shareholders to achieve transformational change, growth and internationalization – fast. Chris is a quick-thinking businessman whose background in Classics and the Grenadier Guards helps him bring a creative clarity and discipline to his work, matched with an insatiable interest in the world and in people.

Craig Kreeger

CEO of Virgin Atlantic, one of the world's most interesting businesses. Craig is also one of the world's most interesting CEOs. His pragmatism and principles have combined with his ability to inspire to take Virgin Atlantic to new heights under his stewardship, accelerating the process of returning Virgin Atlantic to profitability and growth. Craig's love for his role, the people and the brand is infectious but do not act in conflict with his sense of financial discipline and courageous leadership with a customer and people focus.

Dan Warne

Managing Director, Deliveroo UK. Dan is a relentless achiever with a great sense of pace and great sense of humour who heads up the most successful and largest part of the fast-growth fast-food empire which has been delivering meals across the world since 2013. His career includes working on strategic partnerships at mobile giant Orange and setting up e-commerce launches for Travelzoo in the USA at a time when the business was scaling rapidly. After he joined Deliveroo, the business scaled to 100 markets in the UK and 11 internationally in the first three years.

Darren Childs

CEO of multi-award-winning media company UKTV (one of Britain's largest TV companies). Darren has spearheaded a seven-year period of growth and success, doubling revenue and the number of people in his business. Energetic, creative and strategically determined, he's built change through a dynamic culture.

@DarrenMChilds

Dave Ridley

Leadership Speaker and former CMO of Southwest Airlines. With a 25-year career spanning several C-Suite roles at Southwest Airlines (the renowned low-fare airline success story), Dave has had immense experience navigating the hyper-successful business through changing and challenging times.
Southwest Airlines is the only US airline to have consistently made money across 46 years in arguably the most difficult business there is. Dave now is a highly sought-after speaker for business conferences and events, telling the story of how the power of a people-centred business has been the long-term driver of Southwest's success.

David Giampaolo

CEO of Pi Capital, the London-based investor club. David is an experienced and successful entrepreneur in the global health and fitness sector with an insatiable interest in business, leadership and people. He is a great connector and enjoys bringing different perspectives together. This Florida-born business brain was described memorably by *The Times* as 'London's most networked' man.

@dg_pi

Deborah Hale MBE

Founder, Brightpath Communications. Awarded an MBE for her incredible work on the London Olympics in 2012, Deborah was the producer of the London 2012 Olympic and Paralympic Torch Relays with overall responsibility for vision, programme development and delivery for the iconic odyssey that symbolized the unity of the UK. Her career has also included a number of marketing communication roles, helping support Brand London, Project Everyone and Facebook, among others.

Douglas Lloyd

CEO and co-founder of Azoomee.
Douglas is a serial entrepreneur,
founding and funding four start-
ups including the latest which he
co-founded with his wife – Azoomee,
an award-winning digital playground
for children, which has partnered
with the NSPCC, Vodaphone and O2
among others. With an investment
finance background and an insatiable
interest in business, Douglas became a
friend when we bonded over the pain
of writing investment decks If you
have kids aged four to ten, download
Azoomee today.

Eddie Selover

**Founder, PechaKucha Nights in
Orlando, Writer and Consultant.**
Eddie is a talented coach, writer
and thinker who has successfully
championed the 'PechaKucha' style
of presenting in the USA and works
as a communications consultant. His
story is beautifully told in a TED talk
which you can see here: https://bit.
ly/1KHPEOd

@EddieSelover

Emily Evans

**CEO and Founder of the
Economist Educational Foundation.**
This purpose-driven Chief Executive
determinedly steers the success of this
independent charity from inside *The
Economist* magazine. The Foundation
aims to tackle inequality by giving
disadvantaged young people the skills
to think about current affairs for
themselves.

Baroness Gail Rebuck

**Chair and former Chief Executive
Officer of Random House UK.**
For over 20 years, Baroness Rebuck
has headed up of one of the world's
largest publishers, leading it through
a complete metamorphosis of the
industry. She's also Chair of the Royal
College of Art, has four non-executive
directorships, is the founder of World
Book Day and Quick Reads, and, last
but not least, is (since 2014) a Labour
peer attending the House of Lords.
Passionate, disciplined, committed and
gloriously sharp, she is the paradigm
of a dynamic role model.

@gailrebuck

Gary Coombe

Global President of Procter & Gamble's Grooming Business. This position follows on from a role as President of P&G EMEA. Gary was also named as one of the 'Agents of Change' by *Management Today* in 2018 for his work on diversity. I have known Gary for many years and he has always been an inspiration – authentic, human, humble and thoughtful, he is also decisive and clear-thinking. His consciousness of the need for speed, managing a 'supertanker' company which could have been criticized for its slowness has helped his career accelerate. He is a leader for our times.

@Zardy

Giles Andrews OBE

Co-founder of Zopa, the innovative peer-to-peer lending platform, Chair of MarketInvoice and Chair of Kreditech, the fintech lender serving consumers with less access to credit in multiple geographies (most recently launched in India). Giles is also Chair of Bethnal Green Ventures, the accelerator for businesses using technology to make social or environmental impacts. He is a calm-speaking, sharp-thinking visionary fintech hero.

@zopagiles

Greg Jackson

Founder and Chief Executive of Octopus Energy. Greg is a serial entrepreneur and investor with the capacity to understand technology, customer communications and investment and to make things happen fast. He launched the hyper-successful Octopus Energy in 2015 with a clear purpose and customer-focus, but its success has not stopped his interest in and investment in other areas, such as being co-Chair of the Hammersmith and Fulham Business Commission and a new (and old) father. The energy industry is an appropriate place for this dynamo.

@g__j

Greg Reed

CEO of Homeserve UK Membership. A fascinating man, Greg is a supremely talented communicator and a man with a heart and a passion for his work. An inspirational leader who has played a foundational role in making the culture of Homeserve UK incredibly attractive for all who work there and who has helped position the organization as one with a clear purpose and focus on results. The level to which this purpose and focus are shared by the people who work for and with him is singularly impressive, as are his energy and ability to squeeze so much out of every day.

@MGregoryReed

Guy North

Managing Director of Freeview (Britain's biggest TV platform). Following a career in media, the charity sector and Bass Brewers, sports fanatic Guy North today oversees a fast-changing commercial and consumer challenging category. He has led a rebrand and the launch of Freeview Play, the biggest development in the company's history which brings both catch-up TV and live television to the mass market. A charming man and a reflective thinker, he's had to balance the impatience to innovate with the need to move at the right pace in an organization which is owned by a variety of shareholders.

@GuyNorth1

Howard Ting

Founder and Managing Partner of Considea Consulting, based in San Francisco. Howard is a thoughtful and measured consultant and coach who helps CEO-level clients and their teams thrive by creating high-performing teams and culture for organizations ranging from Fortune 500 businesses to late-stage start-ups to NPOs.

@howardting

Jackie Lee-Joe

CMO of BBC Studios. Jackie brings experience from disruptive organizations like Skype and Virgin to the BBC Studios commercial and creative challenge to grow the BBC's iconic brands across the globe, in the face of a fast-changing media landscape. She is a delightful whirlwind of ideas and action, moving Superfast with flair.

Jane Marriott OBE

Head of the Joint International Counter Terrorism Unit (JICTU) and one of the most senior and high-profile women in the FCO, Jane was awarded an OBE in 2004 for services in Iraq. The challenge of changing the world for the good and for the long term, while facing urgent imperatives every day, keeps her very busy and her sharp brain very engaged.

@JaneMarriottFCO

John Blakey

CEO of the Trusted Executive Foundation, former FTSE 100 international managing director, highly successful entrepreneur and executive coach to over 120 CEOs from 22 different countries. Author of *The Trusted Executive* and *Challenging Coaching,* John is committed to helping CEOs and organizations achieve their goals by relying upon the power of trust rather than trusting in power.

John Murphy

The Brandfather! John is a serial entrepreneur, maverick and a highly successful business brain. He was the founder of the global success story that was Interbrand, the first and the largest brand consultancy (acquired by Omnicom) and the first person to value and talk about 'branding'. He went on to buy and build Plymouth Gin before selling it successfully to Absolut, and is now Chair of St Peter's Brewery and Ruffians the barbers. He is the author of *Brandfather*, the fascinating story of his entrepreneurial life.

José Neves

The founder, Co-Chairman and CEO of Farfetch. This charismatic leader created and has grown the revolutionary e-commerce company from scratch to a 'unicorn' and now a global powerhouse which connects the world with the best in luxury and partners with other game-changing leadership brands. José has presided over the vertiginous growth of this fascinating company, and has done so with incredible judgement, humanity and flair. An entrepreneurial icon who is changing the world fast.

Justine Roberts CBE

The founder and CEO of Mumsnet, a unique organization with great purpose which has forged its way in a rapidly changing world to become a positive political force. She was given a CBE in 2017 for her services to the economy. Considered by Richtopia as one of the most powerful CEOs in the world, Justine is an authentic and thoughtful leader of resilience and strength. Fearlessness is one of the company's values and one which she embodies.

Kamal Dimachkie

Executive Regional Managing Director for Leo Burnett – UAE, Kuwait and Lower Gulf. Kamal's experience of leading this global advertising agency has involved him being at the vanguard of a world increasing in speed. This rapid-growing and changing region requires those who help support the businesses in the area to have nerves of steel and patience and impatience in equal measure. Kamal is financially astute and emotionally stable in a creative and combustive environment.

Karen Blackett OBE

WPP's first ever UK Country Manager and Chairwoman of MediaCom UK and Ireland. It's not hard to see why *Campaign* readers voted her the 'most admired leader in adland'. Fast, fabulous and a force for positivity in the media world, Karen was awarded an OBE for services to the media industry and has championed diversity, apprenticeships and incredible business growth in the businesses she has led. Her energy and stylish determination make it impossible not to like or admire her.

@Blackett_kt

Kate Wylie

Global VP of Sustainability at Mars Incorporated. This smart leader has helped shape environmental and social strategy for the likes of eBay and Barclays, has worked at smaller social enterprises, and is now driving forward an innovative corporate sustainability strategy for Mars. Kate is a visiting Business Fellow at the Smith School of Enterprise and the Environment at Oxford University, holds a first-class honours degree in economics from Manchester University, sits on the advisory boards for the Sustainable Food Lab and DEFRA's Advisory Council for Sustainable Business.

@katewylie

Katherine Bennett OBE

Senior Vice President of Airbus, leading the company's external engagement and strategy in the UK. Katherine was awarded an OBE for services to industry and charity. She is also Chair of the Engagement Group of the Aerospace Growth Partnership and a smart, strategic leader, committed to supporting the businesses and women in her sector.

@Westminstrwings

Lee Hodgkinson

Chief Executive Officer of OTSC, a leading global proprietary trading company. With over 25 years' experience in financial markets, Lee has held a wide range of senior executive positions at global trading exchanges including CEO of Euronext London. Lee has a proven track record in driving profitable growth in a broad range of asset classes across Europe, America and Asia, and is passionate about creating an innovative, purposeful global business with OTSC.

Lindsay Pattison

Chief Transformation Officer at the advertising holding giant WPP. Lindsay is responsible for looking at capabilities and talent across the group, looking to accelerate the potential to help clients move in a fast-changing advertising and media world. She is also a vocal supporter of female leaders in the communications world and is an inspiration because she has achieved success in traditionally male roles at a young age. She also continues to hold the same CTO role for GroupM, the media arm of WPP.

@lindsaypattison

Liv Garfield

Chief Executive Officer of Severn Trent and the youngest female CEO in the FTSE 100. Straight-talking, fast-talking and Superfast at getting results, Liv is an incredibly engaging leader who made history in taking up her role heading up the water company which serves 4.5 million households. In 2018 this high-energy leader won the prestigious Veuve Clicquot award for Businesswoman of the Year, a public recognition of the inspirational leader that she is for so many people.

Maggie Philbin OBE

CEO of TeenTech. An ardent supporter of diversity in the science, technology and engineering world, Maggie set up TeenTech in 2008 to help young people understand the real opportunities in a fast-changing world. An in-demand speaker and media presenter on digital and tech subjects, she is known by many as the erstwhile presenter of the iconic BBC technology programme *Tomorrow's World* and she now helps shape tomorrow's world with passion and purpose. She was awarded an OBE in 2016 for her services to the science, technology and engineering communities.

@maggiephilbin

Martha Lane Fox CBE

Founder and Chair of Doteveryone.
org.uk and co-founder of Lastminute.
com and Lucky Voice. A crossbench peer
in the UK House of Lords, Baroness
Lane-Fox of Soho is an energizing force
for digital progress, starting with her
co-founding of LastMinute.com, one
of the original digital dotcom success
stories. From 2009 to 2013 Martha
was Digital Champion for the UK
and helped to create the Government
Digital Service, launching gov.uk, which
transformed government service delivery.
In 2017 she was appointed a member
of the Joint Committee on National
Security Strategy. Martha is Chancellor
of the Open University, Director of
Twitter and a non-executive director
of Chanel. She is also a non-executive
director of the Donmar Warehouse and
the Queens Commonwealth Trust as
well as a Patron of AbilityNet, Reprieve,
Camfed and Just for Kids Law.

@marthalanefox

Matt Brittin

**President of Google across Europe,
Middle East and Africa.** Matt started
out his career in a chartered surveyors
firm and then McKinsey and the
Mirror Group before joining Google
where he quickly shot up the ranks
to become UK MD before taking on
his current role overseeing operations
across EMEA. A medal-winning
rower who represented Britain at the
Olympics, he has become the face of
Google in the European press through
exciting, if challenging, times for the
organization.

@MattBrittin

Michael Birkin

Chief Executive of kyu, the strategic operating unit of Hakuhodo DY Holdings (HDY). Michael is widely credited with being one of the first to pioneer the concept of brand valuation as Group Chief Executive of Interbrand. When Interbrand was acquired by Omnicom, he was promoted fast through various roles to become worldwide president of DAS, the fastest-growing part of the group. He subsequently became Vice-Chairman of Omnicom Group and CEO of Omnicom Asia-Pacific. He left Omnicom to found Red Peak Branding and became (at the same time) the CMO of Acer – one of Red Peak's clients. Red Peak was acquired by HDY in 2014 to help form kyu, which was created at that time with Michael as CEO.

@MBRKN

Michael Greenlees

Former Chief Executive and Chair of Ebiquity. As a leader of the fast-growth AIM-listed media and marketing specialist, Michael presided over phenomenal growth and success before stepping down recently to develop a new direction. That business highlight built on a long career including roles as EVP of Omnicom, President and CEO of TBWA Worldwide as well as CEO of Gold Greenlees Trott, the iconic, witty and well-known agency which was bought by Omnicom. Charming, clever and focused, Michael moves Superfast and super-strategically in business and in life.

Miles Young

Warden of New College in Oxford, former Worldwide Chief Executive and Chair of Ogilvy & Mather. Miles Young has now swapped advertising for academia, but for a number of years, he was the successful head of international advertising, marketing and public relations agency Ogilvy & Mather (he remains a non-executive director there). A charming and erudite communicator, he has built his career on understanding people and how to drive the right pace.

Maureen Taylor

Chief Executive Officer and co-founder of SNP Communications, a global communication coaching consultancy that has worked with leaders at places like Google, Airbnb, Facebook for over 20 years. Maureen is, in the words of one media profile, a 'C-Suite Groomer for Silicon Valley' – an executive coach and communications trainer with a get-it-done style and a fast-talking, fast-focused approach.

Rear Admiral Neil Morrisetti CB

Vice Dean (Public Policy), Faculty Engineering Sciences at University College London. This inspiring leader is an ex-senior British Royal Navy officer who has regularly advised governments and business on geopolitical issues, including transnational and non-traditional threats. During his naval career he commanded ships including the destroyer *Cardiff* and the aircraft carrier *Invincible*. He also served as NATO High Readiness Force Maritime Commander. Following his retirement from the Royal Navy, in January 2014 he was appointed an Honorary Professor and Director of Strategy at UCL's Science, Technology, Engineering and Public Policy Department. He was made a Companion of the Order of the Bath in the 2009 Birthday Honours.

Olaf Swantee

Chief Executive Officer of Sunrise (the Swiss telecoms giant). Olaf was the CEO and founder of EE in the UK, creating the country's most advanced digital communications company incredibly fast before preparing it for sale to BT for £12.5 billion, less than five years after launch. This followed a 20-year career in the IT and technology industries, first at Compaq and Hewlett-Packard, and latterly with Orange. His vigorous approach to the launch of EE is told in his book (co-authored with Nissan's Stuart Jackson) *The 4G Mobile Revolution: Creation, Innovation and Transformation at EE.*

Oliver Tress

Chief Executive and founder of Oliver Bonas. The creator of the group of iconic high-street stores Oliver Bonas, Oliver Tress has built the business over time, learning and honing his skills and the company's approach with resilience, resourcefulness and thoughtfulness. Through challenging economic times the business – one of the UK high street's consistently winning brands – has flourished, run with style by Oliver and with a positive working culture for all involved.

Paul Polman

Chief Executive Officer of Unilever Worldwide. Paul has, without doubt, been one of the most influential business leaders of our times. He joined Unilever after a successful career with arch-rival Procter & Gamble and has systematically transformed the business into a purpose-driven and profitable giant which tops the 'places people want to work' lists globally and which proves that scale does not have to sacrifice speed. Razor-sharp when it comes to business, highly principled when it comes to people, Paul is a phenomenon.

@PaulPolman

Paul Willcox

Former Chairman of Nissan Europe. In his role as leader of the car giant in this important area, Paul Willcox dramatically transformed the region's success for Nissan, building the business to become the number-one Asian car manufacturer in Europe. An automotive veteran, Paul is a self-confessed 'impatient leader' working determinedly to build brand growth and a customer-centric culture across the European region.

Peter Williams

Chief Executive Officer & Co-Founder of Jack Wills. Peter launched the business at just 24. In the retail world of bland brands, the polarizing brilliance of Jack Wills and its 'Fabulously British' approach catapulted the business to international success. Peter, the astute and principled co-founder of the business, has steered it from launch to global expansion and through the rollercoaster ride that has affected many global retail brands across the last two decades. Taking a brief break from the CEO role, he returned to re-energize the multimillion-pound-revenue business, which now ships to 79 countries.

Renn Vara

Co-founder of SNP Communications, the San Francisco, NY and Dublin - based consultancy. Renn is a business coach, mentor, facilitator and provocateur. His irrepressible energy, sense of humour and straight-talking have made him an inspiration to significant numbers of entrepreneur-founders over the years. He has seen what helps businesses grow Superfast and has helped their leaders grow, too.

@rennvara

Rosie Millard OBE

Chair of Children in Need. This articulate and energetic woman has run nine marathons and is a prolific presenter, writer, 'doer' and leader. She was the BBC's art correspondent for ten years as well writing and editing for numerous publications including *The New Statesman* and *The Sunday Times*. She is also the author of four books including *Bonnes Vacances* a humorous travel memoir that was made into a TV series, and was the Chair of Hull City of Culture 2017, for which she was awarded an OBE.

@Rosiemillard

Sara Bennison

Chief Marketing Officer of Nationwide Building Society, where she is rapidly transforming the purpose and the brand story inside the organization to connect more with communities and individuals via a Superfast/responsive communications campaign co-created with real customers. She joined Nationwide after a seven-year stint at Barclays, where she made marketing central to the bank's business to drive its brand recovery. A meticulously organized woman who knows how to get the most out of every moment of the day, she has a busy personal and professional life. She is a fundamentally strategic thinker, and her love of words and ability to synthesize words and ideas fast have helped her gain rapid success and friends and followers in all her roles.

Sara Tate

Chief Executive Officer of TBWA London. Previously the UK Managing Director of Mother and a Lucky Generals Partner, she describes herself as 'tall, clumsy, good at strategy'. The last is certainly true, and she is proving very good at running, inspiring and exciting agencies as well, building strategically rigorous, ground-breaking cultures. Very clever, very creative, very charming, she is also a founder member of the London Two Percent Club, which works to solve the issue of the underrepresentation of women in senior UK corporate positions.

@saraktate

Sarah Wood OBE

Co-founder, Chair (and former CEO) of the media phenomenon which is Unruly, a viral video ad tech company that sold to New International for £114 million ten years after launch. Fast-talking, incredibly energetic and a clear-thinking, outspoken advocate for a purpose-driven approach to business, she admits that one of the benefits of her role was 'having a business where no one tells me to walk or talk slower'. Sarah was awarded her OBE for services to innovation and technology. She is also the author of *Stepping Up: How to Accelerate Your Leadership Potential*, a practical, energetic leadership guide and a highly recommended read.

Shamus Rae

Head of Digital Disruption, KPMG UK. This innocuous title belies this innovator's ambition to positively disrupt the industry he is in. Shamus leads Intelligent Automation (transformation/automation through the use of AI) for clients of KPMG and for the company itself. He has spent the last 20 years delivering major transformation programmes and was one of the founders of the Offshoring Industry in the late 1980s. Shamus also founded WNS, now one of the largest offshore BPO providers.

@RaeShamus

Simon Calver

Head of Investments Ventures and a founding partner at BGF Ventures (the UK and Ireland's most active investor in growing businesses). An incredibly smart person who is also exceptionally good company and generous in helping friends and people he admires, Simon is best known for his seven-year tenure as CEO at LoveFilm, one of the successes of the UK venture industry – leading the eventual exit to Amazon in 2011. He went on to become CEO of Mothercare plc, kick-starting its turnaround plan and accelerating international expansion in over 30 countries.

@SimonJCalver

Simon Devonshire OBE

Entrepreneur, non-executive director and investor, Simon was previously Entrepreneur in Residence – Scale-up for the UK Government, reporting to the Department for Business Innovation and Skills as well as being a director at Wayra, Telefonica's accelerator business. This follows a career in telecoms (O2 and Virgin Mobile). He also founded One Water, a bottled water which donates all of its profits to building wells across Africa. He also has a great surname (no relation).

@tallmanbusiness

Simon Calver

Head of Investments Ventures and a founding partner at BGF Ventures (the UK and Ireland's most active investor in growing businesses). An incredibly smart person who is also exceptionally good company and generous in helping friends and people he admires, Simon is best known for his seven-year tenure as CEO at LoveFilm, one of the successes of the UK venture industry – leading the eventual exit to Amazon in 2011. He went on to become CEO of Mothercare plc, kick-starting its turnaround plan and accelerating international expansion in over 30 countries.

@SimonJCalver

Simon Hay

Chief Executive Officer of Outra, a data company that helps brands harness the full power of connected data, insight and opinions. Simon has spent 30 years at data giant dunnhumby, leading change through data, analytics and customer focus for many of the world's leading retailers and brands, helping them put the customer at the centre of every decision. He is also a trustee of the Brain Tumour organization. Outra is his third start-up.

@simon_hay

Simon Rogerson

Founder and Chief Executive of the Octopus Group. Octopus disrupts complacent industries by bringing the needs of the customer back into focus and reminding the corporate world of its responsibilities to society. So far Octopus has entered and disrupted two of the least trusted industries in the world – fund management and energy supply. Octopus employs more than 800 people and has more than 300,000 customers across the group. Simon Rogerson is a competitive clear thinker who believes in the power of a culture where the customer comes first. He dislikes rudeness, dithering and time-wasting, and has a long-term vision of building a group of companies that make a difference and that people are really proud of. In 2017 he and his co-founder were named 'UK Entrepreneurs of the Year' by EY with Octopus named as a 'role model business for our time'.

Tamara Lohan

Chief Technology Officer and Co-founder of the boutique hotel online travel specialist Mr & Mrs Smith. The global 'travel club for hotel lovers', founded in 2003, now operates from offices in London, New York, Los Angeles, Ibiza and Singapore, with 1.5 million like-minded members in more than 100 countries. Starting as a self-published guidebook, it is now an award-winning global website which continues to grow year on year. Awarded an MBE for services to the British travel industry, Tamara brings empathy, energy, vision and resilience to an innovative and successful global business.

@TamaraLohan

Tim Leberecht

Founder of The Business Romantic Society, a global collective of strategists, advertisers, curators, artists, developers, designers, researchers and data scientists with the shared mission to bring beauty and enchantment to business, and the author of the international bestseller *The Business Romantic: Give Everything, Quantify Nothing, and Create Something Greater Than Yourself*, which has been translated into nine languages. A three-time TED speaker, prolific writer and speaker, Tim also organizes the House of Beautiful Business, a pop-up community that aims to humanize business in the age of machines.

@timleberecht

Toby Roberts

Vice-President of Technology at Zillow Group, the US-based online real-estate database company, Toby is an innovative global technology executive with 20 years' experience delivering competitive advantages for Fortune 500 organizations and developing and executing transformative business strategies in fast-paced, dynamic, highly matrixed corporate environments.

Will King

Co-founder of Savage & King and founder of the Entrepreneur in Residence company, King of Shaves and King of Shades. Will is a force of nature who is involved in many, many pies as an advisor and investor. He is best known as the successful entrepreneur who founded the category-changing King of Shaves product. When asked what he specializes in, he says: 'I make things happen.'

@iamwilliamking

Wim Dejonghe

Senior Partner of Allen and Overy LLP, the legal powerhouse that positions itself successfully as 'the world's most innovative law firm' and the fastest growing of the 'big four' Magic Circle firms (his role as Senior Partner follows two terms as Global Managing Partner of the firm). Wim heads up the firm, which now has 5,500 staff including over 500 partners in 44 offices worldwide. He is the personification of the organization's stated values – instinctively thoughtful, ambitious (but with a 'working together' approach), insightfully inventive and refreshingly open.

Additional sources

Arden, Paul, *It's Not How Good You Are, It's How Good You Want to Be* (Phaidon Press, 2003)

Bezos, Jeff, Letter to Shareholders 2017, available at http://phx.corporate-ir.net/External.File?item=UGFyZW50SUQ9N jkyMDIyfENoaWxkSUQ9NDAyOTk0fFR5cGU9MQ= =&t=1

Blakey, John and Ian Day, *Challenging Coaching: Going Beyond Traditional Coaching to Face the FACTS* (Nicholas Brealey International, 2012)

Collins, Jim, *Good to Great* (Random House Business, 2001)

Collins, Jim and Morten T. Hansen, *Great by Choice* (Random House Business, 2011)

Conner, Tamlin S. et al., 'On carrots and curiosity: eating fruit and vegetables is associated with greater flourishing in daily life', *British Journal of Health Psychology* 20:2 (May 2015): 413–27

Dillon, Jeremiah, 'Read this Google email about time management strategy', *Fast Company*, 14 December 2015, available at https://www.fastcompany.com/3054571/the-better-time-management-strategy-this-googler-taught-his-coworkers

Ferriss, Tim, *The 4-Hour Work Week: Escape the 9–5, Live Anywhere and Join the New Rich*, updated edition (Vermilion, 2011)

Friedman, Thomas, *Thank You for Being Late: An Optimist's Guide to Thriving in the Age of Accelerations* (Macmillan, 2016)

Gallwey, Timothy W., *The Inner Game of Tennis*, new edition (Pan, 2015)

Goleman, Daniel, *Emotional Intelligence: Why It Can Matter More Than IQ*, new edition (Bloomsbury, 1996)

Google re:Work, 'Project Aristotle', available at https://rework. withgoogle.com/print/guides/5721312655835136/

Grant, Adam and Sheryl Sandberg, *Originals: How Non-Conformists Change the World* (WH Allen, 2017)

Harvard Business Review, *On Leadership Lessons from Sports* (HBR, 2018)

Harvard Business Review, *The Business Case for Purpose* (HBR, 2015), https://www.ey.com/Publication/vwLUAssets/ey-the-business-case-for-purpose/$FILE/ey-the-business-case-for-purpose.pdf

Hirshberg, Jerry, *The Creative Priority: The Creative Priority: Driving Innovative Business in the Real World* (HarperBusiness, 2008)

Honoré, Carl, *In Praise of Slow: How a Worldwide Movement is Challenging the Cult of Speed,* new edition (Orion, 2015)

Huffington, Arianna, *The Sleep Revolution: Transforming Your Life, One Night at a Time* (WH Allen, 2017)

Isaacson, Walter, *Steve Jobs* (Little, Brown, 2011)

Kahneman, Daniel, *Thinking, Fast and Slow* (Farrar, Straus and Giroux, 2011)

Knapp, Jake, and John Zeratsky, *Sprint: How to Solve Big Problems and Test New Ideas in Just Five Days* (Bantam, 2016)

Lencioni, Patrick M., *Overcoming the Five Dysfunctions of a Team: A Field Guide for Leaders* (John Wiley & Sons, 2002)

Lewis, Martin, *Moneyball: The Art of Winning an Unfair Game* (W. W. Norton & Company, 2014)

Mankins, Michael C. and Eric Garton, *Time, Talent, Energy: Overcome Organizational Drag and Unleash Your Team's Productive Power* (Harvard Business Review Press, 2017)

O'Brien, John and Andrew Cave, *The Power of Purpose: Inspire Teams, Engage Customers, Transform Business* (Pearson Business, 2017)

O'Connell, Fergus, *Leadership Lessons from the Race to the South Pole: Why Amundsen Lived and Scott Died* (Praeger, 2015)

Pink, Daniel H., *Drive: The Surprising Truth about What Motivates Us* (Canongate, 2011)

Randall, David K., *Dreamland: Adventures in the Strange Science of Sleep* (W. W. Norton & Company, 2013)

Ressler, Cali, and Jody Thompson, *Why Work Sucks and How to Fix It: The Results-Only Revolution*, reprint edition (Portfolio, 2011)

Ries, Eric, The *Lean Startup: How Constant Innovation Creates Radically Successful Businesses* (Portfolio, 2011)

Ries, Eric, *The Startup Way: How Entrepreneurial Management Transforms Culture and Drives Growth* (Portfolio, 2017)

Robertson, David, with Bill Breen, *Brick by Brick: How LEGO Rewrote the Rules of Innovation and Conquered the Global Toy Industry* (Random House Business, 2014)

Rossman, John, *The Amazon Way: 14 Leadership Principles behind the World's Most Disruptive Company*, 2nd edition (CreateSpace, 2014)

Schwab, Kurt, Chairman's Briefing, Annual Meeting of the Wold Economic Forum, Davos, Switzerland, 10 January 2017, available at https://www.weforum.org/agenda/2017/01/a-call-for-responsive-and-responsible-leadership/

Scott, Kim, *Radical Candor: How to Get What You Want by Saying What You Mean* (Pan, 2018)

Smith, Shaun and Andy Milligan, *On Purpose: Delivering a Branded Customer Experience People Love* (Kogan Page, 2015)

Unerman, Sue, and Kathryn Jacob, *The Glass Wall: Success Strategies for Women at Work – and Businesses That Mean Business* (Profile Books, 2016)

Webb, Caroline, *How to Have a Good Day: Harness the Power of Behavioral Science to Transform Your Working Life* (Penguin Random House, 2016)

Wujek, Tom, 'Marshmellow Challenge', https://www.tomwujec.com/design-projects/marshmallow-challenge/

Index

Acknowledgements

I would like to thank the following people for their help and support during the research, writing and preparation of this book:

Graham Allcott, Author of *The Productivity Ninja*

Simon Allen, Non-Executive Director, Wonga

John Allert, CMO, McLaren

Jenny Ashmore, Portfolio NED

Simon Bailey, Partner, The Caffeine Partnership

Alex Bazin, VP Advanced Technology, Fujitsu

Laszlo Bock, CEO and Co-Founder, HUMU

Karen Bowes, Head of HR, International & Small Business, Capital One

Will Bowler, CEO, Popchips

Paula Bernasconi, Regional Director BD, Ogilvy & Mather

Liv Brafman, Head of Business, Ministry Does Fitness

Nic Brisbourne, Managing Partner, Forward Partners

Peter Callender, Executive Coach

Jane Capper, Executive Coach

Jon Card, Journalist and Consultant, Full Story Media

Louisa Clarke, Partner, The Caffeine Partnership

Fiona Clutterbuck, Chair, Paragon Bank

John Croft, President and Co-founder, Elevate Services

Jack Diggle, Global Head, Consulting, Elevate Services,

David Dutton, Business angel

Alex Davison, Managing Director, L'Oréal

Ged Equi, Creative Director, The Caffeine Partnership (who also designed the front cover of the book)

Peter Fisk, Strategic Advisor and author (Gamechangers)

Amy Fowler, Head of External Relations, ADA Digital College

Dan Godsell, Executive Coach

Graham Hodgkins, Organization Development & Communication, SMBC

Prema Gurunathan, MD, Partnership for Growth & Innovation (Imperial College & Hammersmith and Fulham)

Alex Haitogolu, CCO, Utility Warehouse

Stephen Harris, Creative Director

Zoe Howarth, Board Director, Hofmeister

Carola Hoyos, Writer and Consultant

Vicky Keith-Roach, Consultant

Jo Liddell, Operations Director, The Caffeine Partnership

Jill Marshall, Edit Producer

Pete Martin, Content Strategist, AlwaysBeContent

Simon Michelides, COO, UKTV

James Meeks, CEO, Move Systems

Nella McNabb, Executive Coach

Cresta Norris, Owner, Premium Publishing Audio

Kate Nightingale, Founder, Style Psychology Ltd

Tyson Niemeyer, Global Operations Leader, Gett

Gavin Patterson, former CEO of British Telecom UK

Roger Perowne, CEO, MIG Global

Annabel Purves, Executive Coach

Emma Roberts, Founding Partner, Pea Consulting

Karen Rivoire, Chief People Officer and Mentor, Microsoft Reactor

Rose Sandy, Author and Affiliate Publisher, HarperCollins

Michael Saunders, CEO Bibendum PLB

Rory Singleton, Korn Ferry

Sir Tim Smit, Founder, The Eden Project

Shaun Smith, Smith & Co.

Andrew St George & Sharon Curry, Fathomicity and Curry St George

Simon Thomas, former MD and Global Head of Marketing, VW Group

Stephen Thorn, Managing Consultant, Hodwell Associates

Dan Todaro, Group Managing Director, Gekko Field Marketing

Robert Tuesley Anderson, Editor

Kirsty Walker-Niemeyer, Operations Manager, Talent & Development, Group M

Clare Weatherill, Social Media and Marketing Specialist

Tim West, Partner, Head of Wealth Management & Asset Management Consulting, KPMG

Tim Wigham, Author, !nspired

Rob Wylie, Co-founder and Chair, WHEB

Image credits

p21 Figure 1.2 © Dave Walker www.DaveWalker.com

p10 Figure 4.1 © Kevin M. McCarthy / Shutterstock.com

p137 Figure 5.1 From the Churchill Archives Centre

p171 Figure 6.2 © Roger Sedres / Shutterstock.com

p199 Figure 7.1 © Radical Candor

p287 Figure 10.1 © Bain & Company

Used with permission from Bain & Company

www.bain.com/publications/articles/RAPID-tool-to-clarify-decision-accountability.aspx